Achieving

QTS

meeting the professional standards framework

Teaching Primary Geography

Achieving
QTS

meeting the **professional standards framework**

Teaching
Primary
Geography

Simon Catling and Tessa Willy

LearningMatters

First published in 2009 by Learning Matters Ltd.

British Library Cataloguing in Publication Data
A CIP record for this book is available from the British Library.

ISBN 978 1 84445 192 0

Cover design by Topics – The Creative Partnership
Text design by Code 5 Design Associates Ltd
Project management by Deer Park Productions, Tavistock
Typeset by PDQ Typesetting Ltd, Newcastle-under-Lyme
Printed and bound in Great Britain by Bell & Bain Ltd, Glasgow

Learning Matters Ltd
33 Southernhay East
Exeter EX1 1NX
Tel: 01392 215560
info@learningmatters.co.uk
www.learningmatters.co.uk

Contents

The authors

Simon Catling taught in several primary schools in London before moving to Oxford Brookes University, where he is Professor of Education and tutor in primary geography in the Westminster Institute of Education. Widely experienced in primary initial teacher education, he has been Assistant Dean for programmes and research development. In 1992–3 he was President of the Geographical Association. With more than 200 publications, he has written for children, students, teachers and researchers on geographical education, presented at national and international conferences, and contributed to developments in primary geography and to teachers' continuing professional development programmes. His interests include children's geographies, sustainability education, and citizenship and social justice in primary geography. Currently, he is research leader in the Department of Early Childhood and Primary Education.

Tessa Willy is senior lecturer in primary geography initial teacher education at Roehampton University. Prior to this she was a primary teacher in a variety of different settings across the country and a secondary school geography teacher in the UK as well as in Africa. Her areas of particular interest are in issues around the ethics of geography, notably climate change, sustainability, social justice and global citizenship. Currently she is developing an outdoor environmental area at Roehampton University to be used as a model in initial teacher education and continuing professional development for teachers.

Acknowledgements

The authors and publisher wish to acknowledge the sources of illustrations used in the book.

Wendy North for the original of the diagram in Figure 2.1 on page 12.

Paula Richardson and the Geographical Association for the idea for the fieldwork sites diagram in Figure 7.1 on page 75.

QCA for the global dimension teaching opportunities in Figure 11.2 on page 129.

Daphne Gunn, St Paul's Church of England Primary School, Winchmore Hill, London for the example of children's writing in Figure 13.1 on page 162.

Diane Ramsey, National Junior School, Grantham for the peer-assessment example in Figure 13.2 on page 163.

Paula Owens and the Geographical Association for the self-assessment chart in Table 13.1 on page 163.

Sam Woodhouse and QCA for the level descriptions chart in Table 13.3 on pages 167.

Other photographs were taken by the authors.

The authors acknowledge the support of and offer our thanks to the children, teachers, students, teacher educators and others who have inspired our views on primary geography. There are too many to name individually, but we must mention the stimulation and debate provided by members of the Geographical Association's Early Years and Primary Committee and all those who have attended the Charney Manor Primary Geography Conferences over the years.

List of figures and tables

Figures

Tables

Dedication

We wish to dedicate this book to our patient and long-suffering partners, Lesley and Terry, and especially to Tessa's mum, Gilly, for her support and encouragement, who sadly died during the writing of the book.

Simon Catling and Tessa Willy

Introduction

Teaching Primary Geography is part of the Achieving QTS series. It has been written to support the needs of Early Years and Primary initial trainee and newly qualified teachers, to help you meet the Professional Standards for Teachers (TDA, 2007a, 2007b). These are noted at the start of each chapter. It provides a secure base for understanding and teaching geography to younger children, as part of your preparation to achieve Qualified Teacher Status (QTS).

Teaching Primary Geography covers the development of geography subject understanding and of geography teaching capability, with attention given to how these two key aspects of subject understanding and teaching support children's progress in learning geography. To provide the best teaching for learning for children, you need a secure understanding of the nature of geography, its curriculum requirements, how its teaching may be planned and undertaken, a variety of the ways in which children's geographical learning can be addressed and assessed, and the variety of resources that can be used. This book explores these aspects of geography teaching.

Teaching Primary Geography is organised in 14 chapters. The first half of the book explores what geography is and children's geographical experience. In the second half the focus is on approaches to geography teaching, planning and assessment. Chapter 1 outlines the state of primary geography and notes some of the current influences on its future for children and schools. Chapter 2 examines geography as a subject and considers its role and value for us all. Understanding and appreciating its centrality to our lives is vital for our futures. Chapter 3 examines the variety of children's geographical experience, emphasising that children bring geographical awareness and engagement into the classroom throughout their schooling. Chapters 4 and 5 look in greater detail at the ideas of place and environmental impact and sustainability. These are considered separately here but are brought together in later chapters. Chapter 6 explores geographical enquiry, while Chapter 7 considers fieldwork, photographs and mapwork as key to geographical learning.

Chapter 8 introduces the teaching and learning of geography in the Early Years Foundation Stage key area 'knowledge and understanding of the world'. Chapters 9, 10 and 11 look at contexts for geographical learning and teaching to connect studies of place and sustainability. Chapters 12 and 13 provide advice about the planning and assessment of geography teaching and learning. Chapter 14 draws together aspects of children's geographical learning, offers a basis for constructing the primary geography curriculum, and concludes on matters related to researching primary geography.

Throughout the book you will find, at different points, examples of geography teaching and learning from across the primary age range, references to relevant research and guidance and suggestions for geography topics. Other elements include practical and reflective tasks and examples of classroom practice.

A key element of the Standards for QTS and the Core Standards is for you to keep up to date with developments in the subjects you teach. Geography sessions in your ITT course will help you become aware of the subject in primary education. For the sake of the children's learning and development, you are responsible for developing your practice in teaching geography, just as in your other subject and cross-subject teaching. *Teaching Primary Geography* can be used to help meet your early development needs for teaching geography, supporting you in the early years of your teaching career, as will the Geographical Association's Early Years and Primary website and the Geography Teaching Today website (see the ends of the chapters and book).

Whether you already enjoy geography and have studied it in some depth or you come to it needing to be convinced of its relevance for primary children, we hope that you will find this book opens your eyes to a wider sense of what geography is about, how it can deepen children's inherent geographical awareness and understanding, and how you can contribute confidently, effectively and excitedly, to their learning.

Simon Catling
Tessa Willy

1
Geography in primary schools

Chapter objectives

By the end of this chapter you should:

- **have developed an understanding of the situation of geography in primary schools;**
- **be aware how geography's teaching and learning can be enjoyed;**
- **have reflected on your own experiences in learning geography;**
- **be aware of various initiatives supporting primary geography's future.**

This chapter addresses the following Professional Standards for QTS:

Q7(a), Q14, Q15.

Introduction

Geography is a fascinating, invigorating and exciting subject. It is fundamental to our understanding and appreciation of the world in which we live, through our daily interactions and through the ways it impacts on us, though the causes may be far away. This chapter begins by considering the state of geography in our primary schools and what makes for stimulating and enjoyable teaching and learning. It concludes by noting that various government initiatives provide opportunities for geography's role and development. A variety of sources for you to use to follow up and develop your understanding are given at the end of this chapter.

Geography in the primary curriculum

Following the introduction of the National Curriculum in 1989 (HMG, 1988) and geography's first programmes of study in 1991 (DES, 1990, 1991), geography teaching was developed or reintroduced in primary schools. Though primary teachers did not necessarily feel very confident about teaching geography at this time, considerable efforts were made by schools to introduce and develop geography teaching. While in the 1980s it had been a 'Cinderella' subject (DES, 1989), by the mid-1990s geography was a secure subject in the primary curriculum and teachers had made considerable progress from a very low base. Real improvements in the quality of geography teaching and in children's learning then levelled off towards the end of the 1990s (Ofsted, 1999) and remained static until the latter part of the first decade of the twenty-first century (Ofsted, 2008a).

Characteristics of good quality geography teaching

Well-taught geography is exciting and enjoyable, uses a variety of approaches to teaching, engages the children through topical matters and issues of interest which often relate to their experience, challenges their thinking, introduces them to new themes and ideas, and has high expectations of them. A vital motivating factor for primary children is gathering material at first hand, through learning outside the classroom. This means undertaking fieldwork in the school grounds, in the local area and further afield. The first quotation in Figure 1.1 reinforces this. This practical approach is emphasised in the second quotation, where the children's knowledge of their area is drawn out and enhanced through the use of the

photographs and the floor map. The third quotation, from the Ofsted lead geography inspec-
tor, reinforces these points and notes the value of examining topical issues with primary
children, such as concern about climate change and its possible impact. Ofsted has noted
various positive attitudes to the learning of geography that emerge from such studies.

- Children examine local planning issues and put forward development plans of their own.
- The initiation and use of links with schools elsewhere in the UK and in other countries involves children in
  exchanging local information and gaining insight into each other's lives and communities.
- The investigation of topical events, as and when they occur (perhaps suspending the planned topic of
  study) – Hurricane Katrina in 2006, the various floods in the UK, Bangladesh and elsewhere in 2007, and
  the earthquake in China in 2008 – enables children to explore the natural processes involved, their
  impacts on people, and how people locally and elsewhere responded to and dealt with them.

In successful schools, fieldwork, both local and beyond the locality, is an integral part of
the teaching programme and so adds a practical element to the development of pupils'
geographical skills, knowledge and understanding. Pupils are very enthusiastic about
fieldwork. (Ofsted, 2005, p 5).

... in (a) Reception class pupils sat around a floor map of the locality around the school:
*Initially, the teacher used photographs she had taken to enable the pupils to recognise
buildings they were familiar with, such as the doctor's surgery, the local church, the
pub and a range of different shops. The pupils began to build up a vocabulary and
were able to identify a range of buildings. The teachers then transferred to the floor
map, and pupils applied what they knew about the location of the buildings, recognising their position in the high street. Pupils identified the building, for example using
crosses for churches and books for the library. This proved to be a very effective
introduction to maps and plans which was further reinforced through independent
group work where pupils used a range of media including LEGO®, sand and building
bricks to produce imaginary places with a range of different buildings. Throughout the
activity, pupils were building up a sense of place and those specific features which
constitute that place.* (Ofsted, 2004, pp6–7)

I recently visited a school where Year 6 pupils were discussing the impact of climatic
factors on Britain in preparation for producing a weather report for their area. Their ability
to understand and articulate the effects of altitude, latitude, continentality and the Gulf
Stream was worthy of GCSE pupils. In an inner-city school, a charismatic young teacher
inspired her Reception class through song, rhyme and a floor map to identify locations
they had visited on holiday. These young pupils were able to identify and name the major
continents as well as specific countries visited.

Elsewhere teachers have made good use of topics and fieldwork to develop literacy. One
teacher used photographs taken during a fieldwalk to support a discussion on environmentalism in literacy. This was used to develop persuasive writing to influence the local
council to improve transport. More recently I watched a class role play at being trainee
travel agents. This involved passing an exam on their knowledge of places. Once 'qualified', the pupils used wireless-linked laptops to search websites for the best travel and
hotel alternatives for clients. This made excellent use of practical geography. These are
magic moments which make the subject come alive.

(Iwaskov, 2004)

Figure 1.1 Ofsted perspectives on stimulating primary geography

These, and many other examples, illustrate six characteristics of high quality geography teaching (Catling, 2004b), points reinforced by Bell (2005).

1. The geography teaching is *purposeful*; that is, the children recognise the point of what they are studying, see its relevance and value and have their curiosity whetted and engaged.
2. Their geographical studies are *problem oriented*, not limited to information gathering and description, requiring children to investigate, analyse, evaluate and propose possible, even most likely, solutions.
3. Their geographical learning is structured through an *enquiry-based* approach, involving the children in asking, selecting and structuring questions, working out how to investigate them, and in drawing conclusions based on evidence and rigorous thinking.
4. Geographical studies are undertaken *co-operatively*, probably drawing on independently pursued contributions to a problem or issue, where the focus is on learning with and through each other in paired and larger group project investigations.
5. Their geographical enquiries involve *active engagement with the world*, perhaps through fieldwork locally or further away, linked to topical issues, or by making contact with experts and inviting in visitors from whom to seek information, insight and understanding.
6. Children are stimulated by *engagement with good quality resources*, be these the stimulus of the outdoor environment or the use of photographs, maps, leaflets, postcards, rocks, newspapers, artefacts, websites, even some resource packs, and the many other types of resource that can be drawn upon. Along with high quality geography teaching, informative resources can be the catalyst that makes the difference between satisfactory learning and high achievement by children.

Concerns about primary geography

Recent analyses of the status, teaching and learning of geography in primary schools in England (Bell, 2005; Catling et al., 2007; Ofsted, 2008a) have noted that there are challenges alongside the achievements. A key challenge is that for some years geography has been identified, albeit narrowly, as the least effectively taught primary curriculum subject. It seems that geography is less well understood and not fully appreciated by too many primary teachers, who give it limited time in their curriculum. There remains continuing concern for the 'geographical' confidence of many primary teachers, who teach the subject satisfactorily enough but who find it hard to excite and stretch children. Hence, children also achieve least well in geography. Apparently linked to this lack of self-esteem in and motivation for geography, teachers have relied too heavily on the use of the units from the QCA Geography Scheme of Work (DfEE/QCA, 1998/2000), inhibiting their development of enquiry approach to teaching and learning, their focus on geography's key ideas and their adaption of these for their school's and children's context. There appears often to be over-reliance on prepared resources, like worksheets, unsupported by a wide range of books, materials and software. This seems to link to an unwillingness to draw more fully and effectively on children's personal geographies and the everyday geographies that affect them (see Chapters 2 to 5), and on using child-focused enquiry and fieldwork-based studies (see Chapters 6 and 7). As we saw, there is high quality geography teaching provided by many teachers in many classrooms, though consistently in and across too few schools.

Find reports on geography on the Ofsted website. Select the two most recent reports covering primary geography. (After 2005 Ofsted changed its procedure from a subject report each year to one every three to four years covering both primary and secondary geography.)

- Read through the reports and identify the three most important achievements or developments in learning and teaching in primary geography and the three most important concerns facing primary geography. List these under the headings: 'positive' and 'critical'. Note your reasons for selecting them.

- Consider how these positive and critical points might affect your teaching of geography – you may have observed or taken part in some geography teaching already. Under another heading, 'practical action', list three things you want to understand better that will develop your teaching of geography effectively.

Enjoying geography

Enjoyment is the birthright of every child, as the DfES pointed out in their major initiative for primary schools, *Excellence and enjoyment* (DfES, 2003b). This strategy has allowed teachers to develop their curriculum in creative, imaginative and stimulating ways, resulting in many classes in enriched learning experiences for children. Geography is very well placed to realise this aim, affording many opportunities for children to be active participants in their learning through its rich and diverse subject matter and engaging its enquiry-based approach. To enjoy their learning children must be excited and inspired by what they do, necessitating a creative and flexible approach to teaching. Geography offers all this and, to enable it, highly relevant and inspiring subject matter.

When asked what they remember about geography at primary school, people tend to recall a diverse set of experiences, ranging from colouring maps to eating sandwiches in the rain on a beach during a field trip. When asked what were the truly enjoyable and memorable learning experiences that they had, the response, if at all, is invariably to do with being outside and carrying out one form or another of experiential, interactive fieldwork, usually connected to an enquiry of some kind which had obvious purpose and relevance. People talk about how this stimulated their enjoyment of the countryside, generated an interest that led to a job in planning or just opened their eyes to how we pollute but can look after our streets and urban places.

Ofsted has made the point that geography teaching that informs, stimulates and motivates children, and which really involves them in their learning, is at the heart of enjoyable learning, as the examples in Figure 1.1 illustrate. What you need to do, as prospective and new teachers, is to make the geographical experiences you provide purposeful, meaningful and relevant to the children and, equally important, enjoyable. If the children enjoy the activities, they will be engaged and committed to them and effective geographical learning will take place as a matter of course.

Making geography learning and teaching enjoyable involves a range of skills and processes and a commitment to keeping an open and creative mind (Mackintosh, 2007). It necessitates flexibility and a willingness to make mistakes occasionally and to learn with the children. It is about giving children permission and creating opportunities for them to find their own enquiry path and to explore and discover issues and situations that are real and relevant for them. It involves, inevitably, using a range of appropriate resources from the sophisticated, such as geographic information systems (GIS), to the basic, for instance a piece of string and a story book, and developing stimulating and inspiring ideas in a creative and open-minded way. It involves understanding the geography you teach.

IN THE CLASSROOM

The classic and hugely popular picture story, *We're going on a bear hunt* (Rosen and Oxenbury, 1989), has been a stunning stimulus for geography teaching. Children in a Reception and Year 1 class were entranced with the *swishy, swoshy grass* and the *splashy, sploshy water*, subliminally learning about direction and developing their geographical vocabulary as they practised going *over*, *under*, *into* and *through* all sorts of exciting natural features: rivers, mud, caves, forests and snowstorms. Making a 3-D model map of the area travelled through in the story enhanced the learning opportunities for one group as the children navigated their way around the increasingly familiar land forms and natural features. For another group props, including a map, binoculars and a compass, provided the stimulus for planning a 'journey' in the playground using questions such as *Where are we going?*, *Which way do we go?*, and *How do we know it's the right way?*. To assess their understanding and recall of the story, as well as developing their spatial awareness, these children painted picture maps of the bear hunt, identifying and depicting individual features and their locations. Encouraging children to talk about their map as they created it, using prompt questions, such as *What is that feature?*, *Which way do you go?*, *What is it like there?*, and more openly *Tell me about your map*, involved them in describing and explaining what they knew and understood.

REFLECTIVE TASK

Think back to your geography teaching in secondary school. Did you enjoy it? What has stayed with you about the teaching and what you learned? Why is this? Would you have wanted it to be different or to be even better?

- Now recall your geographical learning and teaching from your primary school. What do you recall? Did you realise that you were taught geography? Why do you think this is so?
- As a primary teacher, you will teach geography. How do you feel about this, and why? What would help you to teach geography well? What would provide the children with memorable learning experiences? Make brief notes about your views.

Initiatives in education

You know that governments persistently take new initiatives that affect the organisation, curriculum and teaching in primary schools. Several recent initiatives have directly affected the teaching of subjects, including geography. Use the Teachernet website to keep up to date about such developments. Look at the government and agency websites of the Department for Children, Schools and Families (DCSF) and the Qualifications and Curriculum Authority (QCA). Website details are included at the end of the book. Following the Independent Review of the Primary Curriculum (DCSF, 2009), other initiatives will develop.

National Curriculum Geography

Geography is a legally required subject in the national curriculum and is taught throughout Key Stages 1 and 2. The National Curriculum for geography, introduced in England in 1991, was last revised in 1999 (DfEE/QCA, 1999a, 1999b). The programmes of study (PoS) state what to cover in a school's geography Scheme of Work (SoW). The attainment target describes what is expected of primary children through its first five levels.

Early Years Foundation Stage Guidance

In the Foundation Stage Guidance, revised in 2007 (DCSF, 2008a, 2008b, 2008c), one of the six areas of learning and development is 'Knowledge and understanding of the world'. Through it young children are introduced to aspects of geography which are later developed in National Curriculum geography.

The Independent Review of the Primary Curriculum

The Review's remit (DCSF, 2008d, 2009) considered, among other matters, how the primary curriculum can be less prescriptive and enable increased flexibility for organisation and planning through reduced content while supporting breadth, coherence and progression in learning from the Foundation Stage to entry to Key Stage 3. In promoting its six 'areas of learning' it retains a geographical focus in the 'Historical, geographical and social understanding' area, where the link is with history and citizenship. Views about geography's contribution are on the Geographical Association's website.

The Primary Review

The Primary Review's first report presented the perspectives of the people in communities about the lived and educational context of their lives. Children, teachers and other adults identified concerns that link directly with geographical interests and topics, e.g. concern for the local area, pollution, climate change and matters of topical importance in the news (Alexander and Hargreaves, 2007). Later reports covered other school and community aspects of direct relevance to geography (Mayall, 2008; Wall et al., 2008). This independently funded, national study of primary education, based at Cambridge University's Faculty of Education, noted how vital geography is in children's and adults' lives and how important it is that children's geographical experience and understanding is developed and harnessed in their wider learning, particularly to develop their sense of a positive future (Alexander and Hargreaves, 2007). The *Primary Review*'s analysis of the curriculum argued strongly that geography, through a focus on 'place', should form a key 'domain' linked with history and 'time' (Alexander, 2009; Alexander and Flutter, 2009).

Learning Outside the Classroom

In 2006 the government launched *The Manifesto for Learning Outside the Classroom* (DfES, 2006c) to promote and support increased learning for children in the school grounds, the local area, and on school visits to other places, e.g. museums, theatres, field centres, etc. A key feature is support for fieldwork, which is a required teaching approach in primary geography. Detailed information can be accessed on the *Learning Outside the Classroom* (LOtC) website.

Sustainable schools

The environmental sustainablity of schools is a key part of *The children's plan* (DCSF, 2007). Environmental sustainability and sustainable development are core aspects of primary geography (DfEE/QCA, 1999a, 1999b), and have clear links with subjects such as science. The Sustainable Schools approach (DfES, 2006a, 2006b) links education for sustainable development (ESD) ideas, values and approaches with key areas of environmental care and improvement in school localities, and connects this with the global dimension, all key elements in geography teaching and learning.

National Curriculum citizenship

Citizenship became an element of the Primary National Curriculum in 2000 (DfEE/QCA, 1999b, 1999c), incorporating aspects of environmental awareness, knowledge and understanding, linking well with geography's programmes of study and the Sustainable Schools initiative. Its scheme of work (DfEE/QCA, 2002) illustrates how primary schools can develop citizenship in local and global contexts through geographical units.

Every Child Matters

The Every Child Matters (DfES, 2003a, 2004a) agenda refers to increased children's participation in decisions that affect them and greater recognition of children's 'voice'. Examples include children having a stronger say in matters affecting them in their school, communities and neighbourhoods, for example by working on a local environmental project or through their school council to propose improvements to play spaces. Clear opportunities exist for geographical studies linking citizenship, environmental improvement and local place appreciation.

Excellence and Enjoyment

The government's proposals in *Excellence and Enjoyment* (DfES, 2003b) have encouraged primary schools to balance children's core learning needs with a broad and balanced curriculum, to develop motivating and stimulating, as well as rigorous and challenging teaching alongside personalised learning, and to make effective cross-subject connections reconstructing the subject-based curriculum by creating and using topics and projects to extend and deepen learning.

Geography teaching today

This web resource is a central strand in the Action Plan for Geography, led by the Geographical Association (GA) and the Royal Geographical Society to support the continuing development of primary and secondary school geography teaching. It is an invaluable resource for primary teacher trainees, alongside the GA's own Early Years/primary website.

A different view

The Geographical Association continues to promote geographical education at all levels and recognises the importance of primary geography, particularly through its CPD work in 'living geography' for 'young geographers' but also in its publications. Its manifesto, *A different view* (Geographical Association, 2009), enhances this process across the school sector and is supported by developments on the Association's website. *A different view* affirms geography's place in the curriculum, argues for its value, promotes the links with children's experience and of learning in the real world out of the classroom, focuses on the world today and about alternative futures, and is inspirational in illustrating the power of geography in our lives.

A SUMMARY OF **KEY POINTS**

This chapter has:

> **noted the opportunities and challenges for geographical learning and teaching in primary schools;**

> **illustrated the enjoyment that can come through and from geographical learning;**

> **identified several initiatives that already affect geography in primary schools.**

MOVING *ON* > > > **> > >** **MOVING** *ON* > > **> > >** **MOVING** *ON*

Keep abreast of the curriculum initiatives by government and other agencies and organisations concerning developments in primary geography. Look out for reports in the press, including the *Times Educational Supplement*. Make a note of geography curriculum developments and changes. Use the Geographical Association and Geography Teaching Today websites to help you.

FURTHER READING FURTHER READING **FURTHER READING** FURTHER READING

Many books, journal articles and websites will help you to develop your understanding and appreciation of primary geography and its teaching. The following debate, stimulate interest in and provide ideas for teaching and learning geography with younger children.

Cooper, H, Rowley, C and Asquith, S (eds) (2006) *Teaching geography 3-11*. London: David Fulton.

Geographical Association (2009) *A different view: A manifesto from the Geographical Association*. Sheffield: Geographical Association. www.geography.org.uk/adifferentview

Martin, F (2006c) *Teaching geography in primary schools: Learning how to live in the world*. Cambridge: Chris Kington.

Owen, D and Ryan, A (2001) *Teaching geography 3-11: The essential guide*. London: Continuum.

Palmer, J and Birch, J (2004) *Geography in the early years*. London: RoutledgeFalmer.

Scoffham, S (ed) (2004), *Primary geography handbook*. Sheffield: Geographical Association.

See the magazine:

Primary Geographer, published by the Geographical Association (GA) three times a year, available as a primary school member of the GA (see the GA website).

Useful websites

Geographical Association
www.geography.org.uk

Geography Teaching Today
www.geographyteachingtoday.org.uk

Ofsted geography reports and school reports
www.ofsted.gov.uk/geography

2
Valuing geography: the importance and nature of geography

Chapter objectives

By the end of this chapter you should:

- be able to say what geography is about and why it is relevant for all of us;
- be aware of some of the key ideas that are important for understanding geography and what it studies;
- be able to give examples of geography in everyday life from your own experience;
- know about the Foundation Stage and National Curriculum requirements in Key Stages 1 and 2 for geography.

This chapter addresses the following Professional Standards for QTS:

Q14, Q15.

Introduction

This chapter develops your understanding of geography. It shows how you are already involved in geography, explores geography and its 'big ideas', and considers geographical significance. It examines ways in which geography helps us understand topical events and issues in our world, outlines the contribution geography makes to children's learning about the world, and indicates what is currently required in Foundation Stage and Key Stages 1 and 2 geography. Whether we recognise it or not, geography is very much part of daily life.

Everyday geographical encounters

Geography is such a commonplace aspect of daily life that we overlook it, because our use of the environment, our connections with people and places, the goods that we consume, and the decisions we make about how we go about our daily business are so obvious and mundane that we scarcely notice them, until something untoward happens. Our 'routine' geography seems invisible, like much else we take for granted until brought to our attention (Moran, 2008). Yet, this *everyday geography* (Martin, 2006a) is not habitual for young children; it is novel, fascinating, wondrous and important. We need to be conscious of it. It is the 'stuff' of geography for younger children, easily dismissed as parochial – yet it is exactly the opposite. From our earliest years we are constantly interconnected with our local and wider world.

A bite to eat

Lunchtime in the refectory. You fancy a salad and tea. You add rice to your mixed salad. You collect a bottle of water from the cooler. You head to the fair trade drinks counter for your tea. You add a chocolate bar, and pay the Romanian cashier, find a seat and chat with friends, one of whom is French.

What is the everyday geography? – A commercial outlet; produce on sale, delivered by lorry from a wholesaler; you are unsure where the food originates, since there are few labels; some may be locally sourced, while other unseasonal ingredients must come from abroad; goods from fair trade with less economically developed countries; energy use to cool the salad bar and refrigerators; manufactured, recyclable, containers; waste; migrant workers; and friends. Just to have lunch you are linked to many other people and places.

News time

You get home and turn the television on: news time. Its lead is a hurricane hitting the Florida coast, the precautions taken by shopkeepers and the initial impact on the seafront and hotels. It turns to continuing peace negotiations in the Middle East and refers to the various factions' positions on territorial control and annexation, illustrated by maps. Local news covers the city council's decision about your local shopping centre redevelopment, which sounds good since it will increase your choices. You change channel to watch a daily soap opera set in northwest England.

What is the everyday geography? – Communicating global information into our living rooms; how a natural phenomenon looks and is responded to as a natural hazard; how political conflict in places relates to who 'owns' or wants territory; who decides about change at a local scale; what redevelopment is and what impact it might have on whom; the use of maps and other pictorial representations to communicate images of places and the lives and activities of people there, about which you have a view. Current and topical events affect us directly or indirectly whether locally or in a distant part of the world.

These scenes are commonplace geography, reflecting situations, events and activities that are part of people's everyday lives. Martin's notion of 'ethnogeography', or everyday geographies, describes them (Martin, 2006a, 2006b, 2008).

> *Ethnogeography reflects the view that all learners are geographers because they all live in the world. They all negotiate and interact with a variety of landscapes (human and natural) on a daily basis... They will have built up a knowledge base about the world, near and far, through a range of direct and indirect experiences. What they don't perhaps recognize is that this knowledge is useful geographical knowledge and a point from which deeper conceptual understanding can be developed.*
>
> (Martin, 2006b, p180)

Everyday geographies matter. They are the context and ingredients of our daily decisions about what we do, how and why we do it, our understandings of the world, and of our feelings and views. It is not just our own daily geographies that matter, but also those of people around the world. Hurricane damage to banana crops in the Caribbean not only cuts the income of the farmers, it raises the price in our supermarkets. We pay more or do not buy them, with consequences to the supplier and the supply chain.

PRACTICAL TASK PRACTICAL TASK PRACTICAL TASK PRACTICAL TASK PRACTICAL TASK

What is your everyday geography? Make some notes about two or three contexts in the style of the scenarios above. Try to identify as many everyday geography connections as you can. You might consider:

- your journeys to college, work or out for an evening;
- your mobile phone use;
- where you live and what that means to you;
- your uses of energy and water;
- travelling and visiting places nationally and abroad, across the world;
- how you treat places and the environment, e.g. through care and recycling.

What is geography?

Bonnett (2008, p121) describes geography as a *fundamental fascination*, as an *exploration* and about giving order and meaning to the world. Geography helps us make sense of the planet we live on and discover all we can to understand our 'home' (Matthews and Herbert, 2008; Martin, 2005). It is a wide-ranging discipline, providing structure to what we observe and find out, through investigation, organising information and the use of our imagination. We order the myriad information about the world to appreciate what is vital about the natural and human processes that create, modify, adapt and influence what goes on – whether earthquake occurrences and their impact; where and how our food is grown, manufactured and reaches us; or how and why various goods are made and what value they have for us and the people who made them. We use our imagination to decide how to organise the information so that we can explain it, so that we can make sense of what other places and environments are like, perhaps through pictures or words, and what it may be like to live in those places, so that we have some appreciation of how people live and what effects change may have on them.

Geography is a creative discipline (Catling, 2009c), not simply about the facts about the world. Without information there can be no creativity. It was information mapped about the location globally of volcanoes and earthquake events that led to the theory of plate tectonics, the notion that it is the interconnected movement of massive plates riding the crust of the Earth that causes volcanic eruptions and earthquakes. This explanation initiated the idea of continental drift to describe the movement of the continents across the globe over many million years. It helps to explain how the Earth is an active planet (Thomas and Goudie, 2000).

Research into how people use their local environment to go about their daily business provided the information to understand that we carry all sorts of knowledge about places mentally and that we make use of our mental maps to work creatively for us. The research has investigated how we find our way about, and how we use that information for shopping, leisure and other activities. This became encapsulated as a theory of mental mapping to explain our behaviour in familiar and novel environments, providing insight into how children and adults understand and make use of places. Without the information and the capacity to think innovatively there would not be such an interesting and insightful way to account for these phenomena (Downs and Stea, 1977; Kitchen and Freundschuh, 2000).

Central to understanding geography's way of thinking are a number of 'big ideas' or key concepts. While different geographers debate their importance or how they might best be described, they serve modern geography well in helping to understand how the world works, what we do in and to it, and what the effects of natural and human actions are and might be. Figure 2.1 shows these key concepts. These concepts, set out slightly differently, also underpin the developments in the Key Stage 3 geography requirements (QCA, 2007a).

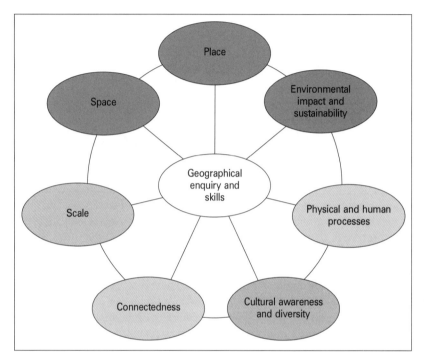

Source: This diagram is modified from North (2008) and Martin and Owens (2008)

Figure 2.1 Geography's 'big ideas' or key concepts

Geography's key concepts need some explanation. At one level they are all obvious ideas, concepts of which we have some everyday understanding. In geography that 'everyday' understanding is useful, but they have more particular meanings within geography.

The three core key concepts in geography

Place

Places are physical entities – the town or village where we live – and can be as small as a room in our home or as large as a nation or the Earth. They have physical and human characteristics we can represent in words, pictures and maps. We develop images of places from our direct and indirect encounters of them. From personal experience we develop our perceptions of and feelings and viewpoints about places. In this way we develop a sense of place, how we connect and identify with (or disconnect from) places familiar to us, such as home and our favourite places (or places avoided). Places are real and they exist in our images of them, arising from our experience. Different people hold very different ideas and have very different feelings about the same places.

Environmental impact and sustainability

Environmental impact examines the interactions within and between the natural and human environments, focused on people's effect on each other and the environment and the natural environment's impact on itself and people. This connects with human and physical processes but emphasises the effect rather than the processes of change. *Sustainability* concerns the sustainability of the natural environment and the development and sustainability of communities. It explores environmental quality, how and why places are managed and damaged or improved, the provision and distribution of goods and wealth and their effect, and issues of social justice concerning access to goods and services, where and why this is and with what effect. Environmental impact and sustainability considers the future, how things might change, what we would want such changes to be and what are the most probable outcomes.

Space

For geographers space concerns where features, sites and places are located. Studying spatial layout explores the interactions between features and places and how they affect each other. Geographers look for the distribution of features and at the patterns they show to see how and why they create networks and what the effect is. Geographers are particularly interested in the natural, social, economic and political processes that help to explain distributions and networks. Such processes may be fluid rather than fixed (Massey, 2005).

Four further key geography concepts support and enhance the first three

Scale

Geographers study features, places and environments at a range of scales from the immediate (a room or floor layout), to the local neighbourhood and community, to the regional, national, continental and global. Scale affects what happens in places, what we observe and the way we see things. Depending on who is looking, we may see scale differently; a large place to a young child may seem to be a small place to an adult very familiar with it.

Connectedness

Connectedness concerns the interrelationships we have at different scales. It includes the connections between people in their local community and its features and services, as well as the global trade links that encourage, for instance, coffee to be grown in various places and transported and traded for others to drink around the world. Connectedness shows our interdependence locally and globally.

Physical and human processes

These encompass the natural processes, such as our daily weather and climatic characteristics, the changes created by sea floods and the characteristics of volcanoes. Human processes cover such contexts and activities as the manufacture of goods, transport and travel, the development of settlements, our planning for and responses to natural hazards, and how we change our environments. They examine how decisions are made, how people respond and the consequences of change, socially, economically, politically and environmentally. Understanding such processes and the changes created helps explain the distributions and patterns we see in places and the environment and allows us to make predictions.

Cultural awareness and diversity

The world is diverse, with a wonderful range of environments and an exhilarating variety of peoples who have created their communities through, for instance, beliefs, social structures and norms, varied ways of living, relationships with those outside their culture ('others'), and how they see themselves. Cultural awareness is the starting point for intercultural under-standing and for appreciation of the diversity of people and their lives around the world. It concerns ourselves as much as anyone else and explores ideas such as identity, our sense of ourselves and our communities at various scales, and our appreciation and valuing of others elsewhere, never even known. Geographers consider how our communities and nations work and examine international relations and their impacts.

The key geographical concepts are developed through investigations enabled by skills

Geographical enquiry and skills

Geographers gather information through many and varied investigations, known as geogra-phical enquiries. Physical geographers almost always use scientific processes of investigation. Some human geographers use similar approaches when studying large-scale phenomena such as populations and gathering and analysing statistical data to look for explanations. Other human geographers, perhaps exploring aspects of neighbourhood geographies, may use more qualitative approaches where they are trying to find out what people think and feel, how people are affected by changes or what people might want undertaken to improve an area. Inevitably, geographers will engage in fieldwork, working in the real world to gather the data that they need, using a variety of techniques from land-use mapping and interviews to traffic counts and time-lapse photography to air pollution lichen studies, river flow measurement and chemical weathering studies. A wide variety of techniques and tools are used in geographical studies.

Geography uses a variety of skills or literacies. Graphicate literacies are as essential as textual literacies. The term 'graphicacy' encompasses the visual skills geographers and others use to gather, interpret and explain evidence (Balchin and Coleman, 1965). It includes using and making maps and photographs and visual observation, as well as skills in reading, understanding and making sketches, diagrams, charts and graphs, and in annotating maps, photographs and drawings. To facilitate these and to enhance numeracy skills and work with virtual and dynamic models are computer software and related technological skills that can aid weather recording, traffic counts, chemical analysis, and so forth. Geographers decide how best to gather and record relevant information, how to analyse and evaluate it, and how most effectively to communicate it through articles and books, the press and television, and in conference presentations. Such literacies are essential to investigate geography and to communicate its ideas to a wide variety of audiences.

PRACTICAL TASK PRACTICAL TASK PRACTICAL TASK PRACTICAL TASK PRACTICAL TASK

Use the scenarios at the start of the chapter and/or your own. Make a chart with two columns, listing the scenarios in the left-hand column. In the right-hand column note which of the key concepts are most appropriate to help understand the situation outlined in that scenario. Add a note about why you selected them.

- In 'A bite to eat' the refectory is a distinctive type of place with particular features and layout. Both the goods and the person serving at the till indicate local or wider world connections, and the products on sale are the result of the physical and human processes of farming, commerce and transport. Recycling and energy use link with sustainability and the environmental impact of people's actions.

The role of geography

Geography is a living and topical discipline. Its content is not just the stuff of the everyday, such as shop locations, the countryside and parking issues; it is also the things that have wider regional, national and global impacts, such as the changing prices of food and energy. It is important, therefore, to appreciate what makes something geographically significant. This is where the importance and value of geography lie.

Living geography

The essence of living geography extends the idea of everyday geographies noted earlier. Its characteristics draw on and focus geography's key concepts (Owens and North, 2008; Mitchell, 2009). These have developed in the context of enhancing children's geographical awareness and engagement. Living geography's characteristics include:

- focusing on people's everyday geographies – children's and adults';
- examining what is relevant to and affects people, daily and longer term, directly and indirectly;
- being locally interested but set in and connected to the wider world context at a range of scales (regional, national, international, global);
- investigating environmental processes, changing environments and the impacts of change on people, places and environments;
- developing critical awareness and understanding of sustainability;
- encouraging curiosity and enquiry in and about the world;
- exploring current times and being 'futures'-oriented, looking at what is and could, should and might occur;
- involving creative and critical responses to everyday matters and issues.

Living geography is active and pertinent. It focuses on what is topical and significant for us, and what has daily meaning and impact in our lives. It introduces us to geography's key concepts through this liveliness and immediacy.

Topicality

Geography examines topical matters and concerns to provide insight into our own and the wider world. Geographical topicality can be at the level of the personal and everyday, about the weather or travel to work; about local matters and concerns, such as street closures to create pedestrian areas in the city centre; or about national to global actions and events that affect us directly or indirectly, such as the effect of government decisions to increase airport facilities and the debate about carbon impacts on global climate change. The events, people and places reported and commented on in the local and national news provide us with our daily sense of the world. Using and understanding topical reports keeps us informed. However, important topical matters may pass all too quickly through the 'news', providing a superficial perspective. To that extent what we understand as topical is determined for us, at local, national and international scales.

Topicality cannot be considered uncritically. We must question the particular information, perceptions and understandings of the world we take from the news and why and how these topical events are put before us. While topical issues bring geography alive, we should be concerned about the images of places and peoples that are portrayed and wonder what is excluded or unconsidered. We should use topicality to evaluate our own perceptions and understanding of the world. For example, what do we really know and presume about people's lives in the countries south of the Sahara in Africa? How does the 'newsworthy' focus on deprivation and hardship create single rather than multiple perspectives on these millions of people? When we hear about a redevelopment in our neighbourhood, how do we react? Do we look for the range of arguments, hear the variety of points of view put forward, and consider what might be for the better beyond our own interests? We may support or challenge this change, but is it through emotional reaction or considered thought? Geography's interest in the topical provides opportunities to investigate the topic and the ways information is communicated, who makes the decisions, and how we think about and respond, or not – the 'stuff' of critically effective environmental citizenship (Dower and Williams, 2002; Hicks & Holden, 2007). Geography gives us clarity and keeps us informed. It alerts us to our preferences, biases and prejudices, providing opportunities to reconsider.

Geographical significance

To gain the most from geographical studies, we need to appreciate what is significant to study. Geographical significance concerns understanding what is most appropriate to focus on in geography and to whom and at what scale matters are significant. No geographical features, places or events are in themselves significant. Significance is an attribute that individuals or groups ascribe to such geographical phenomena. In terms of what is topical, it would seem that a particular event and place, such as Hurricane Katrina, which hit New Orleans in 2006, were given significance by the media which reported it; equally it was devastating for those who lived through it and was ascribed significance by the government of the USA because of the damage to a 'world' city. For geographers it is globally significant because it illustrates key geographical concepts, including place, environmental impact and sustainability, physical and human processes, scale, and cultural awareness and diversity. In a national park in England a planning application might generate local debate because it is about encroachment and the loss of farmland in a sensitive environment. Locally it may be considered of geographical significance because of its connections with the key concepts of place, scale, environmental impact and sustainability, and physical and human processes.

We must consider carefully what makes an aspect of the social or physical environment significant and worthy of geographical study. The questions in Table 2.1 below can be used to consider the geographical significance of a place or event.

Table 2.1 Questions to use in considering geographical significance

In relation to features, places, environments, and events and/or changes in them.
1. How and why are place and location significant? • Why is this location worth considering? What does it say about the role of location?
2. How, why and to what extent is the scale significant? • At what scale is it? Is it significant at local, national or global scales? What makes the scale important to note?
3. How and why does it have meaning for people? How might it be revealing through its representation of how individuals and groups of people think about a place or event? • How does it contribute to personal or collective perceptions, meanings, images and representations of places and environments? Is the meaning significant locally and/or more widely? What different meanings do different people (including from the past) attach to it?

4. How does it help understanding of the way natural environmental systems and places function and are created, shaped and change, and why this happens?
   - How do functions and change help us identify patterns in the world and the processes at work creating and changing them? Why do places and environments develop the characteristics they have?

5. What types and levels of impact does it have on people, places and environments, and why?
   - How does it change the physical and/or human environment? What effect is there on people's lives and activities, indeed, on their perceptions of places and environments? What actions and changes does it lead to?

Source: Modified from Catling and Taylor (2006, p37); Taylor and Catling (2006, p124)

We make daily decisions about where we will shop, meet friends or spend our holiday. Local and national politicians decide about housing developments, aid to support people caught up in disaster events and areas, and trade agreements and subsidies. These decisions may affect us as much as our own personal decisions. They interweave our everyday geographies, are our 'living geographies', and are matters of environmental topicality which we know are significant, though do not always recognise as aspects of geographical studies.

REFLECTIVE TASK

List examples of some ways in which geography plays an active role in your life. Describe what you consider geography to be about. Draw on what you have read above and state in a few sentences your idea of geography and its relevance to your life.

Now write down, similarly, in a few sentences how geography is relevant to children's lives and why it should be part of their primary education.

Geography in primary children's education

The six years of geography in Key Stages 1 and 2 provide a vital grounding for children's geographical understanding, as two-thirds of their compulsory geography education. The Early Years Foundation Stage curriculum initiates this period of geographical study, as part of 'Knowledge and understanding of the world', between the ages 3 and 5 (DCSF, 2008c). Effectively, children have spent eight years undertaking some level of geographical studies by the time they are 11 years old.

The original rationale of the geography national curriculum (DES, 1990, p6) stated that:

geographical education should:
a) stimulate pupils' interest in their surroundings and in the variety of physical and human conditions on the Earth's surface;
b) foster their sense of wonder at the beauty of the world around them;
c) help them to develop an informed concern about the quality of the environment and the future of the human habitat; and
d) thereby enhance their sense of responsibility for the care of the Earth and its peoples.

There are direct links to the key concepts in geography. The study of places, not least their own, is central, as is understanding physical and human processes, alongside environmental impact and sustainability. Fundamentally, these aims for geographical education are focused on values and attitudes, to be underpinned by knowledge about the world and understanding of the ways in which it works. The attitudes of *interest in their surroundings* and *a sense of wonder* are aligned with the values of *concern about the quality of the environment and the future* and *their sense of responsibility for care*. That these attitudes and values applied to all children from the youngest to the oldest children emphasised that geographical education intended to look to the present and the future and to their personal role and involvement. Geography is not described as a subject separate from children but as a perspective on the world in which they are integral players. These attitudes and values identify a sense of living geography in which children's everyday geographies play a central role but which also requires consideration about the significant geographies for study among their own and topical interests. This is reinforced in the statement on The Importance of Geography in the National Curriculum 2000 revision (DfEE/QCA, 1996, p108).

The aims for geography and the key concepts provide a basis, engaged with everyday and living geographies, for stating the main themes to be developed through primary geography. These must support children's everyday geographical learning. The purpose of primary geography is to:

- help children wonder at, make sense of, put into context and develop further their own experience in the world: their everyday geographies;
- introduce children to the excitement of and extend their awareness, knowledge and appreciation of peoples, cultures, places and environments in the wider world;
- develop their sense of wonder, their understanding and their critical questioning of what places and environments are like, why they are like they are, how and why they are changing, what processes and patterns shape them, and what impacts there are or might be and why;
- foster children's critical interest in and valuing of the environment and of the Earth as their home, and help them understand why a sustainable approach to the future is vital but contested;
- encourage children to be thoughtful as global citizens about the impression or 'footprint' they leave on places and the environment and about making decisions which affect their lives and the lives of others, including those they will never know;
- develop children's spatial awareness and understanding of distributions and networks and of the representations of places and the environment, through such skills as mapwork, using photographs and making sketches, and through their studies of places and environments;
- engage them in geographical enquiries about place and environmental matters and issues and about the wider world;
- foster their fascination with places through fieldwork and the use of new technologies in and beyond the school grounds and the local area;
- stimulate and develop their locational knowledge and understanding about the world.

Requirements for children's geographical learning

The focus of the Foundation Stage and primary geography programmes of study and attainment targets is on three of geography's key concepts. These are: places, environmental impact and sustainability, and space. The core elements of geographical enquiry and skills, including fieldwork and mapwork, are also essential (DfEE/QCA, 1999a). These aspects of geography are retained in the proposed revisions to the primary curriculum (DCSF, 2009) where geography is a component of the area of learning 'Historical, geographical and social understanding', though they are expressed with a little re-emphasis and linked with citizenship and history in the area of learning. This is taken into account in outlining the primary geography curriculum elements below.

Studying places emphasises developing children's initial understanding of the idea of place through the study of small-scale places such as their own locality and other similar sized localities, through setting these in their wider national context and learning where in the world they are, encouraging awareness of space. In this way ideas about scale are introduced, as is the notion of connectedness. Cultural awareness and diversity and the physical and human processes creating and changing places are considered. There are opportunities for children to develop a 'sense of place' and to explore their perceptions and images of places, as well as their identity with places and communities, and to consider environmental impact and sustainability.

Environmental impact and sustainability is focused on personal responses to the environment, the ways in which physical and human processes create and change the environment including how and why decisions are made that affect the environment and people's lives for better or worse. Older primary children are invited to consider how they might help to manage the environment sustainably, considering decision-making and their own engagement and participation. Again scale and connectedness can be used to help develop understanding, looking at local, regional, national and global examples.

Examining space is concerned with location and the distribution of features and events and with recognising and explaining patterns in places and the environment. The connectedness and scale of features and phenomena are an inevitable part of the understanding of spatial patterns in the environment. This helps to understand the interdependence of people, communities and places.

Geographical enquiry develops children's questioning and investigative skills and their capabilities in undertaking enquiries from inception to presentation. It involves children in recognising differing points of view about issues. Geographical skills emphasise the development of vocabulary, observational skills, using and understanding of globes and maps, undertaking fieldwork employing a variety of techniques and resources, and using a variety of other sources of primary and secondary evidence including new technologies. It introduces children to decision-making skills.

There is breadth to geography across the Foundation Stage and Key Stages 1 and 2. For the youngest children this begins with their immediate environment in the nursery school, its outdoor area and the streets beyond. For primary school children it covers the school grounds, the local area of the school and other localities in or beyond the United Kingdom, including in a less economically developed country in Key Stage 2, alongside some national and global locational knowledge. Several themes can be examined across the key stages, from local to global scales, including our communities, the use of resources, recycling, sustainability, weather, climate change, water's accessibility and its affect on the landscape and the impact of new technologies on communication. Places, environments and issues should be studied in a variety of contexts and at a range of scales. Fieldwork must be undertaken throughout the primary years.

These requirements in the breadth of learning again identify how several key geographical concepts are central to primary geography. Place and environmental impact and sustainability are required. Scale, connectedness and space are interwoven. Physical and human processes and cultural awareness and diversity are inextricably aspects of geographical studies.

These aspects of the geography curriculum are outlined further in Chapters 4 to 7. The details of the Early Years Foundation Stage and Key Stage 1 and 2 geography requirements are available on the relevant websites (DCSF, 2008c; DfEE/QCA, 1999a, 1999b).

A SUMMARY OF **KEY POINTS**

This chapter has:

> argued that geography is a core aspect of our lives;

> introduced the idea of 'everyday geographies';

> provided several illustrations of geographies in and impinging on our lives;

> introduced geography's key concepts;

> developed the ideas of 'living geographies', topical geography and geographical significance;

> considered the purpose of geography in the primary curriculum;

> made connections between geography's key concepts and the geography curriculum requirements for the Foundation Stage and Key Stages 1 and 2.

MOVING *ON* > > > > > > MOVING *ON* > > > > > > MOVING *ON*

Develop your understanding of everyday geography. Follow local, national and international news online or through television bulletins or the newspapers. Notice when and how news reports refer to or are provided from different places, the aspects of the places and the environmental impact and sustainability matters they refer to and the range of scales involved. Use these and the other geographical concepts to reflect on the ways in which you interact with the world and how it affects your day-to-day life.

FURTHER READING FURTHER READING **FURTHER READING** FURTHER READING

To discover more about geography, the following books are informative and accessible introductions.

Bonnett, A (2008) *What is geography?* London: Sage.

Holloway, L and Hubbard, P (2001) *People and place: The extraordinary geographies of everyday life*. Harlow: Prentice Hall.

Matthews, J and Herbert, D (2008) *Geography: A very short introduction*. Oxford: Oxford University Press.

These books provide valuable introductions to National Curriculum primary geography.

Halocha, J (2001) *Pocket guides to the primary curriculum: Geography*. Leamington Spa: Scholastic.

Martin, F (2006c) *Teaching geography in primary schools: Learning how to live in the world*. Cambridge: Chris Kington.

Useful websites

Foundation Stage Guidance
   www.everychildmatters.gov.uk
   www.standards.dcsf.gov.uk

Geographical Association
   www.geography.org.uk
Geography Teaching Today
   www.geographyteachingtoday.co.uk
National Curriculum Geography
   www.nc.uk.net
   www.standards.dcsf.gov.uk
Qualifications and Curriculum Authority (QCA)
   www.qca.org.uk

3
Children's geographies: experience, awareness and understanding

Chapter objectives

By the end of this chapter you should:

- be able to explain that children have a range of geographical experience that develops their awareness, knowledge and understanding of the world around them and more widely;
- appreciate that children's geographical experience is changing;
- recognise that children hold views, ideas and values in relation to the nearby and wider world, about places and the environment;
- realise that adult geographies affect them.

This chapter addresses the following Professional Standards for QTS:

Q10, Q14, Q18.

Introduction

This chapter focuses on children's place-based and environmental experiences, their awareness and understanding of the world through direct and indirect experience and sources, and their values and perspectives about their world. It develops your understanding of what are termed 'children's geographies'. This encompasses children's personal geographies and geographies not of children's making but those that affect their lives directly and indirectly. It concerns children's experience of their lived or everyday geographies, as well as their awareness of distant places encountered only through secondary sources and their virtual and imagined 'worlds'. It includes their environmental understanding, interests and concerns.

Current understanding of children's geographies has developed from observation-based studies in psychology 'laboratories' to real-world studies of children's activities and behaviours in and uses of real places and environments. Through their 'voices' it has sought their views and concerns, recognising their full membership of society (e.g. Ataöv and Haider, 2006; Cele, 2006; Christensen and James, 2000; Christensen and O'Brien, 2003; Fog Olwig and Gulløv, 2003; Fraser et al., 2004; Greene and Hogan, 2005; Hallett and Prout, 2003; Jones, 2009; Lewis et al., 2004; Lolichen, 2007; McLeod, 2008; Smith, 1995; Spencer and Blades, 2006; Waller, 2006). There is much research into children's environmental and place experience. A number of useful texts are listed at the end of the chapter.

The youngest children coming into school

Children enter school with an embryonic geographical background (Catling, 2006b; Cooper, 2004a; Matthews, 1992; Palmer and Birch, 2004; Stea et al., 2001). Within home and play centre environments children play inside and in the garden or the outdoor area, possibly 'explore' a little, watch television, and talk. Children are taken out and make journeys because parents or siblings go shopping, visit places and meet relatives and friends. Through such experiences the youngest children begin to develop a number of facets of their personal or everyday geographies (Catling, 2003, 2006a).

Children's awareness of the local and wider environment

Very young children learn the layout and location of features and items in their home. Children notice landmarks, routes and directions when out walking or in a bus or car. From as early as 2–3 years old they build a sense of the places they encounter and familiarity with those they are taken into often. Evidence suggests that while they find it hard to communicate their awareness, they can retrace some routes even after their first experience. Many 3–4 year olds can say what activities like shopping are about and know of places elsewhere. This awareness draws on their travel experience, what they have heard through the family, and from stories and television. Their experience and knowledge are partial and may at times be less than accurate.

RESEARCH SUMMARY RESEARCH SUMMARY **RESEARCH SUMMARY** RESEARCH SUMMARY

A cross-cultural and national study led by Palmer into 4-year-old children's 'emergent environmentalism' identified that young children construct conceptions about people, places and environments from an early age. Children could associate trees with forests, explain that melting snow makes water and talk about not throwing away items but recycling them. Within these embryonic environmental and scientific understandings young children clearly have considerable gaps in their knowledge and understanding and certainly have naïve ideas, though some might be the result of adult stories (Palmer and Birch, 2004; Palmer and Suggate, 2004; Palmer, et al., 1996).

Children's representations of places

From their first naming of objects, children build a vocabulary about various everyday features, e.g. home, street, tree. This enables them to talk about places and environments as well as about journeys and basic directions. Verbal representations are supplemented by the capacity to begin to use visual/graphic images. When children of 4–5 are introduced to large-scale aerial photographs and clear plans/maps of particular large-scale places, many can use them to identify and locate features in these places (Plester et al., 2006). Their doodles and drawings will need explanation but young children depict features and where they are in 'pictures' of places, which in time become recognisable.

Children's environmental and place values

Many young children are aware about waste and its disposal in bins, and some are beginning to understand about recycling. Even our youngest children appear also to be developing a sense of concern for our world, for example the need to protect natural features, such as trees and flowers. These beginnings provide the basis for viewpoints, values and attitudes. Wiegand (1992) reports that young children have positive and negative views about people and places that they have no information about, assimilated from home life, play with peers and the stories they hear. We must listen carefully to what young children say and be ready to challenge ideas they express which are partial, misconceived, inaccurate or negative to help them build a firm foundation for future place and environmental learning.

Imagining 'being in places and events'

Children's play is a vital element in their learning about the environment, whether this is through outdoor play (Tovey, 2007) or involves play with toys, through stories and imaginatively (Catling, 2006b). Consider the environmental and locational language in *We're going on a bear hunt* (Rosen and Oxenbury, 1989) and *The world came to my place today* (Readman and Roberts, 2002). Toy play and home corners provide opportunities for children to recreate experiences they may have had or witnessed. Guided and open play provide ways for children to imagine and act out people, place and 'environmental' events in large and small spaces using their imagination and props.

REFLECTIVE TASK

Reflect on why is it important that teachers are aware of and ensure they draw on, extend and challenge, as necessary, young children's developing place and environmental understanding?

Children's evolving direct experience of places

Children's opportunities in environments

Extensive research (e.g. Catling, 2003, 2005b, 2006b; Cele, 2006; Chawla, 1992; Christensen and O'Brien, 2003; Fog Olwig and Gulløv, 2003; Katz, 2004; Matthews, 1992; Pike, 2008; Spencer and Blades, 2006; Valentine, 2004) suggests that children's experience in the environment is essential to their appreciation of places and environments and of their spatial skills in using places. Through their experience in places children develop their sense of place.

Learning about places
Day (2007) argues that adults and children conceive the world differently. For children the world is new and their learning to come to terms with it involves making use of it in non-adult planned ways. Walls are for climbing; restrictions to be overcome; the street and open spaces for meeting and chatting; the mall for keeping warm and safe when there is nothing much else to do.

Opportunities to explore locally help younger children get to know an area, to make it familiar and to develop understandings of how they might be able to use it for their own interests in play and meeting friends. Place learning emerges from undertaking errands but is most strongly fostered through 'free exploration', outside adult control, enabling children to learn for themselves about places. Freedom of movement leads children to extend their 'home range', enables their wayfinding skills, and develops their competence in and styles of representation of the features, nature and spatial form of the familiar environment, as mental representations and in descriptions, models and maps.

Children's local knowledge
Place learning is about developing local knowledge. Children's locality knowledge depends in part on the constraints they place or have placed on their exploration (Bowles, 2004a; Cullingford, 1999, 2007; Fog Olwig and Gulløv, 2003; Matthews, 1992; Rissotto and Giuliani, 2006; Valentine, 2004). Their knowledge focuses on what is distinc-

tive for them. Play spaces are important, both formal playgrounds and games areas and patches of ground they designate as meeting places and 'games' places (Min and Lee, 2006; Pike, 2008). Their 'home range' in or beyond a neighbourhood – often more limited in cities – extends their environmental awareness, if only in passing. Between them children bring a variety of knowledge of the school's catchment area to share: personal geography becomes community geography. Such overlapping and cumulative children's everyday geographies provide information that includes:

- homes and gardens;
- shops, shopping streets, shopping centres;
- businesses;
- parks, play areas and other open spaces;
- places of worship, libraries, health centres, etc;
- roads, traffic and railways.

Children also bring their use, interests, feelings about and nuanced sense of place to school and class.

Sites of personal importance, place attachment and sense of place

Children's place learning provides opportunities to see the possibilities or limitations in using sites for their own interests, the site's functionality or 'affordance' (Kyttä, 2004, 2006; Min and Lee, 2006). The affordances that children most value relate to places to play, meet and spend time with friends (Cele, 2006; Henshall and Lacey, 2007; Pike, 2008; Else, 2009). Such valued places are complemented by places that are purely functional, such as particular shops in which to spend pocket money. Specific sites may be valued for their accessibility, because they are 'safer' from adult surveillance, they are interesting spaces or appropriate for particular activities. Other sites may be avoided because of traffic, older children or other potential interferences. Children personalise sites such as dens and 'desecration' is keenly felt when adults or rival children invade children's personal places. Their capacity to make use of places fosters their place attachment, the feeling of being comfortable – 'at home' – in a particular place, which has meaning, value and happiness for us (Catling, 2009a; Chawla, 1992; Tanner, 2009).

Neighbourhoods are ambiguous places, sites of pleasure as well as threat (Cullingford, 2007). Children's sense of place is based in the physical environment but constructed around the social environment and their feelings for places, evolving from their sense of the affordance of places, and is closely linked to their place attachment. It does not reflect attractiveness but focuses on interest to and for them. Senses of place may be positive, negative or ambivalent. Their home locale may be 'their place', but they may also be positive about a 'holiday' place, reflecting time there and escape from adult oversight.

RESEARCH SUMMARY RESEARCH SUMMARY **RESEARCH SUMMARY** RESEARCH SUMMARY

In her research into 8- and 11-year-olds' views of their local urban environments in Sweden and the UK, Cele (2006) used creative and interactive ways to involve the children. They annotated maps, walked a self-chosen route using them, and were interviewed about the area using photographs they took and drawings they made. The results provided a rich insight into how the children used their environment: what mattered to them; favourite places and places disliked or thought dangerous; how they enjoyed parks and green spaces as much as street spaces, and how their uses of them changed with the seasons; outdoor, unsupervised play was important to them and often related to what they found; they had fears and concerns about areas of their neighbourhood; they held views and expressed emotions about how places were treated by adults and adolescents; they noticed people and events; they might vary their choices of routes linked to friends or mood; and they were aware of environmental issues such as traffic. The children demonstrated evident knowledge of their environment, well developed spatial capabilities in the environment and the capacity to make use of the environment for their own interests, linked to play and socialising with friends.

REFLECTIVE TASK

What conclusions do you draw from the summary of research information above about middle and older primary children's views on their environments?

Environmental spatial understanding

Very young children readily learn their capacity for movement and begin to grasp the spatial layout of features in a room or floor layout important to them. Initial ideas about the spatial connections between places emerge through experience of journeys and travel in the local neighbourhood, with very early ideas about distance initiated through such experiences. Young children construct mentally the spatial layouts of familiar environments and build skills to begin to navigate places as they develop experience of them (Bell, 2006; Newcombe and Huttenlocher, 2000; Spencer et al., 1989; Uttal and Tan, 2000; Wiegand, 2006). This capacity to develop and use wayfinding skills and area layout is usually referred to as *mental mapping*. Key to the development of such mental maps is a child's independent mobility, being able to go out, to do errands or simply to explore places on their own or with friends.

Studies with children using vertical aerial photographs of familiar environments (Plester et al., 2006) show that children can use them in problem-solving activities in their familiar environments. This provides a basis for examining and deriving information from maps of other similar neighbourhood scale places. Map learning is a gradual process which involves appreciating the development of maps as spatial representations through their symbols alongside skills such as relating and aligning the map to the environment, understanding its scale, and appreciating the use of more abstract aspects such as direction and co-ordinates (Wiegand, 2006). Children draw map-like views of familiar areas from an early age, often pictorial in style and spatially informed. These improve in accuracy as children mature and draw on increased environmental experience (Mackett et al., 2007; Wiegand, 2006). Children will only develop cartographic formality through the use of published maps, which introduce conventions such as symbols and keys, grid references, compass points and scale. Using maps in the environment is vital.

Inhibiting children's exploration

Children's well-being is a charged notion, not solely about opportunities but also about care and safety across a range of domains, including environmental experience (Bradshaw and Mayhew, 2003; Guldberg, 2009; Layard and Dunn, 2009). Increasingly, limits are placed on children's free exploration of their locality. There are various reasons for this. What is evident is that children's experience of their localities is changing, some of this allied to increased access for more families to personal car transport, with children walking less (Hillman and Adams, 1992; Prezza, 2007), and in part to an adult-driven risk-averse approach to childhood outdoor experience (Gill, 2007; Guldberg, 2009; Layard and Dunn, 2009). Parents have become more concerned about children's road safety given ever-increasing traffic on roads, reflected in part through decreasing cycling (Cele, 2006), though road accidents involving children have declined (Cele, 2006; Cullingford, 2007; Else, 2009; Guldberg, 2009; Henshall and Lacey, 2007; Johansson, 2006; Katz, 2005; Mackett et al., 2007; Madge and Barker, 2007; Thomas and Thompson, 2004). Linked to this is concern that communities no longer look out for children, with parents feeling they need to keep their children under surveillance. Play spaces have become more confined and 'commodified' (Layard and Dunn, 2009; McKendrick et al., 2000). There are fewer 'wild areas' left for play, though these are valued by children as play spaces. Children do not decry what adventure playgrounds offer, but their security and structures inhibit the opportunities for children to create personalised and imagined places that untended areas provide. Forest schools are one of a number of formal approaches to try to counteract this situation (Knight, 2009).

Inclusion and exclusion

While children are beginning to feel more included and listened to (Madge, 2006), there remains a continuing sense of impotence in their communities (Moss and Petrie, 2002). Children are not always viewed favourably in the environment. They can find themselves viewed as 'out of place' if not accompanied by an adult (Valentine, 2004). They can be seen to be at odds with the norms of adult uses of places if they transgress by loitering too long or kicking a football about too noisily. Yet if older adults gather and chat in the mall or on the street corner this is appropriate. What concerns children is adults' unwillingness often to listen. The social distancing of adults from children in shared community places such as streets can create an atmosphere where children are unwittingly pressed to use liminal, or marginal, spaces (Nieuwenhuys, 2003). Children know when they are not wanted in places and not infrequently will seek out the places that adults pass by or miss to avoid their gaze and authority. This may explain why in some central urban public spaces children have absented themselves.

While these changes in children's place experience seem negative in Western societies, this is less so in other societies where children seem to retain greater freedoms and are more positively seen and valued when out and about (Chawla, 2002; Katz, 2004).

Teachers' knowledge of the school's locality

Many teachers do not live in the localities in which they teach, as a result knowing the area less well (Bowles, 2004b). Travelling in and out of a locality using specific routes limits what is noticed and appreciated about the school's neighbourhood. An inevitable result is that many teachers find themselves disadvantaged by not knowing the area in which the children live, not simply because they are uninformed of the features, layout and social life of the area but because they have no awareness or sense of place of their own to which to relate their children's perspectives on their area. Such a mismatch can inhibit confidence in developing effective geographical studies in a locality, in taking children into the streets for fieldwork, and in appreciating the experience that the children can and do bring into class. Where teachers explore their school's locality, they feel confident and can draw on children's knowledge, feelings and perspectives more fully, involving them in local enquiries more effectively.

PRACTICAL TASK PRACTICAL TASK **PRACTICAL TASK** PRACTICAL TASK **PRACTICAL TASK**

You may know the area around where you live well. Draw a sketch map. Mark on it the features you recall. Make notes on it about which features, services and sites you value, which you avoid, and indicate the areas you do not know. Now do the same exercise for the area around the last school that you spent some time at. What are the differences between your two sketch maps? Why is this? What action can you take?

Children's perspectives on school grounds

The common, shared place and environment in all children's and teachers' experience is the school itself. School is as much a place of children's geographical and environmental experience as is their local area. Research into children's experience of school as a place has proved informative (Catling, 2005c; Devine, 2003; Garrick, 2004; Holt, 2007; Titman, 1994).

Children are clear about the nature and quality of their school grounds. Where these are expanses of asphalt and grass with little variety, grounds are seen to be uninviting and 'boring'. Where there is variety in the features, with colour, with planted and wild areas, providing natural habitats as well as play spaces, they are regarded as 'cheerful' and interesting environments. Playgrounds offer opportunities for children to make use of them as they can. Titman (1994) identified playgrounds as vital places for children but that how they use and value them varies dependent on the child and their social context in the school.

RESEARCH SUMMARY RESEARCH SUMMARY **RESEARCH SUMMARY** RESEARCH SUMMARY

Holt's (2007) study of the socio-spatial reproduction of disability in primary school playgrounds highlights ways in which children's personal geographies are affected by others. When friendship groups play shared playground games, children not liked or with physical, learning or emotional disabilities may find themselves excluded from such uses of the playground space and even restricted to marginal areas in the playground. Teachers can affect these children's environmental experience by excluding them from parts of the playground or the playground itself because of problematic behaviour or for personal safety and health reasons. Children in such contexts find themselves on the margins of their school environment. It seems that this marginalisation in the environment is an unintended side-effect of decisions about who is viewed as able to behave sensibly in playgrounds and who is not. Children learn from such socio-spatial practices to include and exclude others in their wider society, assimilating perspectives, for instance, that 'other' or stigmatise those who are disabled in some way, which they then reproduce in their treatment of others during adolescence and adulthood. Where there are inclusive approaches, the reverse can be the case.

Children perceive that often adults do not value playgrounds or children's play in them, because of adult lack of interest, care and concern for quality grounds and play areas (Devine, 2003). There seems to be little recognition of the school's classrooms, building and grounds as environments in their own rights (Dudek, 2005) as well as being enticing and exciting places for learning. Research with children about their school play areas indicates that what they want bears little relation to what adults consider children want. Children have limited faith in adults' understanding of their own preferences, interests and needs. They want more varied playground settings, including 'naturalistic' spaces where they can play in stimulating ways, such as 'wild' spaces and materials they can use to build (Powell, 2007;

Tranter and Malone, 2004). Where organisations, such as Learning through Landscapes (see website), help improve school grounds, children enjoy more varied environments around the year through a variety of activities – quiet and personal, social, rowdy play, small group and large group games, etc. In some schools this has been the ethos, where a strong curriculum focus works alongside a playtime focus in using the school grounds (Jeffrey and Woods, 2003). Perhaps the real issue is involvement and trust, seemingly more evident in schemes involving children outside schools and in other parts of the world than in the UK (Adams and Ingham, 1998; Bellamy, 2003).

REFLECTIVE TASK

Consider your own playground experience, or if you have the opportunity spend time in a school playground and observe what occurs there. How would you describe your own and other children's personal geographies of the playground? Alternatively, what do you notice about children's use of the playground space, with whom they use it, what for, and what their demeanour is? Ask the children and reflect on how their explanation is like or differs from your own. What does this tell you about children's personal geographies?

Children's awareness of the wider world

Younger children's geographies include awareness and ideas about the wider world, of their homeland and of peoples and countries. Their awareness develops early, reflecting experience from various sources, including family, friends and peers, television programmes, and stories set in other places, such as *The day of Ahmed's secret* (Heide and Gilliland, 1997), *Kenju's forest* (Morimoto, 1992) or *Gregory Cool* (Binch, 1994). More recently new technologies are influencing children through their access to the internet and through texting, social sites and email. These sources inform children's ideas about and attitudes to people and places beyond their direct experience, positively and critically (Cullingford, 2000, 2007; Barrett, 2007). Children's knowledge and values develop more through chance than through directed attention, though this occurs linked to holidays, e-friends and homework.

Images of the world

Very young children develop a rudimentary awareness of the Earth as a globe but have little idea of countries and where they are. By 11 years old, many children have an idea of the shape and overall layout of the continents on the globe and can locate some countries within them (Wiegand, 2006). Seeing and using globes and world maps must be a factor here. Evidence suggests that travel helps develop children's ideas about distant places (Wiegand, 1992; Schmeinck, 2006), essentially holiday experience which provides only a particular type of experience of other parts of the world (Barrett, 2007). Images of places visited may well be partial and even misconceived. Contact with people in other places via email and the web may help to challenge misconceptions (Holloway and Valentine, 2003). By exchanging information about their lives, the places they live, what they do and like, among much else, older primary children can begin to recognise that children elsewhere are not unlike themselves. Utall and Tan (2000) noted that children's environmental experiences and understanding may become increasingly mediated through virtual experiences of other places – cyber-geographies – leading to shifts in children's global mental maps.

All too often children encounter only negative images of particular parts of the world, leaving negatively stereotypical views of areas such as southern Africa or Pakistan. Family connections with another country do not necessarily avoid this (Holden, 2004). If these misunderstandings are not challenged, children's ideas may remain heavily inaccurate. Some evidence suggests that children's positive images of places can become less strong with more information, while negative images may be made more positive because children become better informed (Barrett, 2007; Wiegand, 1992, 1993).

A sense of national identity

Studies of children's ideas about their own nation and identity and of people of other nations (Barrett, 2007; Barrett at al., 2006; Holden, 2004) suggest that children's knowledge of other parts of the world is variable, as is their knowledge of their own country (Catling, 2009b). Broadly children seem to identify with their home nation, giving it positive ratings and taking pride in it even where the level and nature of their knowledge about their country may be limited (Barrett, 2007; Barrett et al., 2006). Children in several nations develop a high sense of national identity very early in life while others come to this in adolescence. Children in many European countries think of themselves also as European, while British children are less inclined to think so. British children seem less well informed (Holden, 2004), to the extent of believing that areas of the UK are abroad and that some places abroad are in the UK. For many European children this dual sense of identity links to national political attitudes to 'being European' and an emphasis in their school education on Europe in geography, history and citizenship studies.

REFLECTIVE TASK

How did you develop your own sense of national identity? Did it emerge slowly or did you realise at a given point what it is? Is it important to you? Why is this? How does your sense of your nationality reflect a view of other nationalities? How do you think this might be the case for children in the UK?

Children in the wider world

We have concentrated on points that relate to children's personal geographies in local and distant places and environments. We now turn to geographies that impact on children (Catling, 2003). For children, place and environment are not simply about their personal geographies. They are also about the way the world affects them – geographies that impact on children.

Children live in particular places, and places differ

Whether rural or urban, suburban or inner city, island or wilderness locations, the places in which children live and the facilities, activities and access available to them impact on their opportunities and choices. For some life is very positive. For others poverty, lack of access to clean water and sanitation and being the victim of a natural disaster is the reality (Bellamy, 2004). More than half of the world's children are directly affected by such issues. Poverty has negative welfare effects, with children perhaps needing to work to support their families (Liebel, 2004; UNICEF, 2005; Weston, 2005), with impacts on health and welfare (Ansell, 2005; Brocklehurst, 2006), and through such life-shifting effects as migration (Waters, 2008) and press-ganging as child soldiers (Singer, 2006). Poverty, migration, welfare and well-being concerns are all aspects of many children's lives in the UK (Bradshaw and Mayhew,

2005; Vleminckx and Smeeding, 2003). They impact on children through their access to play, to resources and services, to healthy diets and family support. These national and international issues are not 'distant' from children but either realities for them or infiltrating their lives through local experience, the news media and aid appeals. We might feel that life in the Western world is relatively comfortable, but this not only hides issues of poverty and its impact in our midst; it can numb us to the lives of the majority of the world's children, only noticing them when their situation reaches extremes and hits our screen for a few minutes or for a few days. Children's personal geographies around the world are incredibly varied and not based on the assumptions that we make as part of our lives (Katz, 2004).

Children hear about various disaster-relief efforts, perhaps studying events such as the 2004 tsunami, and even collecting funds. They give generously (or encourage their parents to do so) to Children in Need or to Oxfam and many other effective charities to help people in the UK and around the world. Here the geographies of the Earth's natural forces and of survival and rebuilding, the geographies of water access and cleanliness, of poverty and wealth distribution, and the geographies of aid and generosity impact on children. Children learn that it is 'an imperfect world', an unequal world (Cullingford, 2007, p31; Layard and Dunn, 2009).

Children as a market

The focus of advertising at particular times of the day on television indicates the ways in which adults view and exploit children, as economic opportunities (Gunter and Furnham, 1998; Kenway and Bullen, 2001). The debate about the location of sweet counters in supermarkets (the geography of sales influence), the current concern about the healthiness and quality of diets and school meals, and the longer-standing concerns about the manufacture of a range of goods using cheap labour in economically developing parts of the world, where children can be a vital part of the labour force, are all elements of economic geographies that impact on primary age children. In this respect children have been commercialised as a key market by corporations, from clothes and toys to the food and entertainment industries (Mitchell and Reid-Walsh, 2002; Steinberg and Kincheloe, 2004). This influences what children purchase and the way they organise their spaces, such as their bedroom, to emphasise their interests. The television influences their perception of places through the programmes and films they watch. With age primary children become increasingly economically aware and autonomous (Webley, 2005) and have agency through their spending power. Their interests affect the ways in which shops select the goods they sell and the way they lay out the store. Children's economic strength has an impact on the geographies that affect them.

Increasingly, children 'travel' abroad

Alongside their real travel to other places, children see and encounter many places elsewhere in the world through television and, perhaps, the internet. Many of these are places in North America, western Europe and other scenic sites around the world, where they are settings for action dramas or documentaries. Places and environments are often the backdrop and may well be only subliminally 'noticed' rather than recognised as other realities to home. The geographies of adult vacations (it is not the children who decide on the holiday abroad) and the geographies propounded by edited visual media have an impact on children. This indicates that children's wider experience of the world is selected and selective, constrained and edited by adults. Place and environmental experience reaches children in these contexts unconsciously rather than intentionally. Today's globalised world makes some parts of the world seem just around the corner from our living rooms while other places remain determinedly far away or, quite possibly, hidden. Technologies are providing new opportunities about which we still know little of the impact on children's geographies (Catling, 2008; Glaser, 2007). Exploring conscious and unconscious personal geographies is important.

PRACTICAL TASK PRACTICAL TASK **PRACTICAL TASK** PRACTICAL TASK **PRACTICAL TASK**

Follow news reports for a week. Note when children are involved or affected by what happens in particular places. Consider news items where children go unmentioned but in which they are likely to be affected. Reflect on what these situations might say about these children's personal geographies and how being aware of them might affect our view of the wider world. What are the implications for teaching geography?

Children's imagined geographies

There is limited geographically and environmentally oriented research into children's imagined geographies, both as imagined and in virtual contexts. These are aspects of personal geographies in that they concern how we create the world, not only as perceptions of real places but also as imaginary places created for us or created by ourselves for personal interests.

Children's imagined places

Our imagined places are part of our 'private worlds'. Imagination is clearly stimulated in a variety of ways, not least through participation in and observation of real world experience but also through the stories children are told and read from an early age and through the opportunities to play and imagine and act through scenarios. The picture storybook, *Roxaboxen* (McLerran and Cooney, 1991) captures something of this. Illustrating the way in which a group of younger children acted out the life and activities in a stone model of their community, it connects both children's perceptions of life there and illustrates how children's personal geographies form the basis for imaginative activities. These occur daily in nursery indoor and outdoor areas, in the home corner and in the playground. For some children imaginary worlds go deeper. They create and develop their own small- or large-scale places, from neighbourhoods to islands, countries and continents (Cohen and MacKeith, 1991). Such personal imagined geographies often remain among the friends who invent and inhabit these worlds. While published authors indicate their inventiveness in creating places and lives within them, it seems that many more people create 'worlds of their own', particularly in their younger childhood. Children's geographies encompass not just the real world but imagined worlds.

Imaginary realism: places in films

Children's television and film viewing is often directed by their interest in drama and related programmes. An aspect of children's personal geographies that is under-researched is what they understand about the places they see – the settings of the stories – from the variety of ways in which they are depicted through soap operas, television drama and films. Animated films have long been favourites of younger children. They depict a variety of environments and habitats for people and wildlife. Whitley (2008) examined ways in which Disney films depict the 'idea of nature' and an ecological sense. Disney films portray a variety of environments from the tropics to the American wilderness, as well as European forests and the urban settlements of some fairy tales. What Whitley detects is their potential to raise questions about how we perceive and treat our natural environments, the role and issues around conservation and the meaning of nature. Watching such films may have an effect on how children perceive places and the environment, but this is an aspect of their personal geographies of which we know little.

Understanding places in virtual games

There is negligible research into younger children's ideas about virtual worlds. We are aware that children's use of virtual worlds impacts on them in some ways (Webber and Dixon, 2007). There are concerns about how adults might wish to control such experience (Aitken, 2001; Webber and Dixon, 2007) and the time that children might spend interacting in their virtual realities, but we lack studies about how playing in virtual worlds influences children's geographies.

A study of younger children's social engagement and interaction within the virtual game, *Adventure Rock* (CBBC, 2008; Gauntlett and Jackson, 2008) provides some insight. The virtual world is an island environment that allows players to play there supported by a friendly robot. Children select a variety of activities and use 'creative studios' to play games, use other children's inputs, create drawings and other features themselves, or tackle mysteries. It is *an online space where you can move around; you can have an impact on the world; and there are benefits from network effects* (Gauntlett and Jackson, 2008). Initial analysis of the ways children used *Adventure Rock* have identified eight types of player, three of whom seem to be engaged in different geographical dimensions (Catling, 2008). Others have overlapping geographical interests, including the following:

- *Explorer-investigators*: interested in 'being' outdoors, undertaking journeys and/or tackling quests and mysteries.
- *Life-system builders*: wanting to populate the area, add new elements to the environment and create new lands.
- *Power users*: focused on how the virtual world worked, spent time exploring and developed a considerable understanding of the environment's geography.
- *Self-stampers*: had an interest in making a home base and giving themselves an identity in the game.
- *Fighters*: took a destructive approach to the environment, focusing on power and its effect.
- *Collector-consumers*: interested in the economic system, wanting shops and consumerism, they accumulated value.

That children see the virtual world in relation to their different interests is not surprising. What is noticeable is the link beyond personal and social interests to environmental interests, where some want to know about this place not simply to use it but to enjoy the exploration of and journeys in it or to improve it as a place to be. This links with an informal geographical awareness, where some children create mental maps, and others have a sense of its future by taking responsibility for caring for the virtual world. Such virtual environments, while imagined, overlap with the various aspects of real worlds and may enable children to apply and explore their personal geographies through imagined places.

The area of virtual worlds is a contested one. It introduces the question of whether children might be able to make best use of a virtual world if they lack experience in the real world through outdoor exploration, making journeys, going shopping, using places and play.

REFLECTIVE TASK

We often ask children to write stories set in places, though we concentrate little on these, just as we rarely discuss the quasi-realistic and virtual worlds they see in drama and computer games. Why is this, and why might this be an area for research in children's geographies in future? Why might it be useful for geography teaching?

Children's environmental concerns and participation

A sense of environmental quality

Children are concerned about the quality of the environment and its future (Hicks, 2002). They are aware of the links between poverty and degraded environments and the issues of resource access for less fortunate members of societies (Cullingford, 2000; Layard and Dunn, 2009). They recognise the efforts people make to care for and improve the environment or the lack of such determination (Chawla, 2002; O'Brien, 2003). They are concerned about pollution and waste issues, derelict buildings and land, global climate change, and local concerns such as safety perceptions, rubbish, traffic problems and graffiti (Thomas and Thompson, 2004). They know about safe and unsafe places to play, and they value well-cared-for sites. They notice limited effective political action at local, national and international levels to address such human and environmental issues, though they want them tackled. While children wish to see a future world that reflects how they would like it to be, they are not unrealistic in considering what it might become and can be fearful of how it may turn out. Yet children are relatively optimistic about the future when they become involved in community improvement projects and school-based eco-initiatives linked to sustainability (Alexander and Hargreaves, 2007; Beunderman et al., 2007; Hicks, 2002; Steuer et al., 2006).

RESEARCH SUMMARY RESEARCH SUMMARY **RESEARCH SUMMARY** RESEARCH SUMMARY

In inner and outer areas of London and a comparison new town, older primary children were asked what they thought of their environment, about unsafe areas, and about its amenities (O'Brien, 2003). Homes were favoured places by inner-London children, but leisure and shopping centres were more favoured places by outer-London and the new-town children. For many across the three localities, places are drab and poorly looked after or too controlled. Of most concern to children were dingy and dark spaces in and around buildings. For outer-London and new-town children parks and woods could be unsafe places, while for inner-London children the street was seen to be as unsafe as walkways and stairwells. Children disliked graffiti and unkempt and poorly maintained streets. They saw maintenance as a key aspect of environmental improvement. Most important for them was that open spaces and play areas be considerably improved. While there was evidence that more inner-city children are staying indoors or near home, there was a strong desire by the children to be out-and-about more in places where they could play. They were concerned at the loss of unstructured and less regulated and supervised play spaces. What children seem to want is space in the public environment for their own use; not an easy request when parents want security for their children wherever they may be.

Children's active involvement

There seems to be more effort to listen to children, though not always effectively (West, 2007). Instances of children's active involvement in environmental improvement remain limited (Adams and Ingham, 1998; Hart, 1997; O'Brien, 2003; Spencer and Blades, 2006), some focused in school and others community based, usually around play spaces (Chawla and Malone, 2003). Too often involvement is tokenistic, but not always.

Several features characterise children's genuine involvement in school-based or local participatory activities (Hart, 1997; Olle, 2002; Titman, 1994). Children tackle improvement in a realistic way, state clearly what they want to have, and offer ideas for improvements that are straightforward. In the context of improving school grounds' quality they are not that interested in commercial equipment but want grounds that are varied, more natural in appearance and which offer challenges. They wish to see greater variety in resources for playtime activities, recognising the range of interests among their peers. In this and the wider context, children are happy to work with adults, recognising the skills, knowledge, etc., that adults bring. For children, participation is not about taking over the task but working with people. Not unusually, when they work on improvements they become involved in maintaining them.

This is a personal geography that is active and engaged. It is a committed geography. Alexander and Hargreaves (2007) found that where children are involved they feel they provide a positive input at a level at which they can act. The case is that children's involvement encourages a sense of ownership, for instance, of their play places (Mayall, 2008). It appears a small contribution to school and community improvement but it initiates active engagement in environmental improvement and sustainability.

Children's ideas about geography

It would seem that very many Year 6 children have an idea of what geography is about (Catling, 2001b). Very few muddle it with other subjects. This appears to reflect the timetabling of 'geography' topics, where geography is highlighted for children even in cross-curricular studies.

> Geography is to do with maps. Sometimes we draw maps and draw a key for them and we learn about different places. The type of book we use is an atlas.

> Geography is about countries and places in the world. We use maps to help us understand. Geography tells us all different things, like what soil is in that area we are studying, as well as how many people live there, and what is the most popular job. We do geography because it helps us to understand our world. If we did not have geography we would not know where we are.

The dominant association of primary school geography was with map work: map skills and using maps to find out about places and for following or creating routes. Children also identified geography as developing their awareness and understanding of the world and countries. This connected with references to knowing what places are like and what happens in them. These ideas indicate a traditional, indeed a public, sense of geography as being about the world and maps, which is not unlike that held by primary teacher trainees (Catling, 2004c).

A core aspect of primary geography is the study of localities, to which only a third of children referred, although locality studies are widely taught and include some of the best geography teaching (Ofsted, 1999, 2008a). Few children referred to fieldwork, which in other contexts children have noted they do too infrequently (Alexander and Hargreaves, 2007). Less than a tenth of children mentioned the study of environmental matters and issues, though this is a core theme that links with locality studies, or management and care for the environment and sustainability (DES, 1991; DfE, 1995; DfEE/QCA, 1999a). Ofsted (2008a, 2008b) have noted that sustainability is less well taught than it should be.

Research and evaluations appear to indicate that children's experience and sense of geography in school are disconnected with their personal, everyday geographies. It is as though primary geography in practice creates discontinuity between the geographies in and of children's own lives and of what and how they study geography in school (Catling, 2005c). This might account for the apparently 'boring' nature of primary geography for too many children (Catling et al., 2007; Robinson and Fielding, 2007), since it does not engage with: excite them, rarely engages their experience, perspectives and issues and is largely passively taught through over-reliance on structured geography units and worksheets (Ofsted, 2004, 2005a, 2008a). If primary geography has greater relevance and connection with children's lived experience, perhaps what children learn would come naturally rather than seem a burden for some.

PRACTICAL TASK PRACTICAL TASK **PRACTICAL TASK** PRACTICAL TASK **PRACTICAL TASK**

You have read and considered the ideas about geography in Chapter 2 and the perspectives on children's geographies in this chapter. Write a summary for yourself of what you understand geography to be and how this relates to your understanding of children's geographies.

A SUMMARY OF **KEY POINTS**

This chapter has:

> explained that children's geographies are significant to and for children;

> noted that their personal geographies are multifaceted and multilayered, encompassing environmental knowledge, sense of place and place attachment, and spatial awareness;

> considered that their personal geographies encompass their life in school but more so outside school;

> identified factors that are constraining and changing children's experience in the environment, linked to safety, travel and access;

> explored children's ideas about the world beyond their direct experience and their engagement with imaginative and virtual worlds, which may be changing their geographies;

> noted that locally and across the world geography affects children, whether directly through natural and human events or indirectly in relation to encountering such events through the media;

> noted that while children are concerned about environmental problems, they value and benefit from involvement in environmental activities;

> considered that children develop ideas about geography through their studies in school which may not make much connection with their personal geographies.

MOVING *ON* > > > > > > MOVING *ON* > > > > > > MOVING *ON*

Select from one or more of the aspects of children's geographies outlined in this chapter and follow up by reading one or more of the references to extend and deepen your understanding of that area.

FURTHER READING FURTHER READING **FURTHER READING** FURTHER READING

There are many books and articles about children's place and environmental experience and learning. Several publications have drawn together interesting research or provide overviews.

Ansell, N (2005) *Children, youth and development*. London: Routledge.

Christensen, P and O'Brien, M (eds) (2003) *Children in the city*. London: RoutledgeFalmer.

Day, C (2007) *Environment and children*. London: Elsevier/Architectural Press.

Matthews, H (1992) *Making sense of place*. Hemel Hempstead: Harvester/Wheatsheaf.

Spencer, C and Blades, M (eds) (2006) *Children and their environments*. Cambridge: Cambridge University Press.

Tovey, H (2007) *Playing outdoors: Spaces and places, risk and challenge*. Maidenhead: McGraw-Hill.

Wiegand, P (2006) *Learning and teaching with maps*. London: Routledge.

Key journals:
Children's Geographies
Environmental Education Research
International Research in Geographical and Environmental Education
Children, Youth and Environments, online at: www.colorado.edu/journals/cye

Occasionally research and review articles have appeared in:
Primary Geographer
Journal of Geography

Useful websites

Learning through Landscapes
    www.ltl.org.uk
National Children's Bureau
    www.ncb.org.uk
Play England
    www.playengland.org.uk
Sustainable Development Commission
    www.sd-commission.org.uk
The Good Childhood Enquiry
    www.goodchildhood.org.uk

4
Exploring places:
key ideas in understanding places

Chapter objectives

By the end of this chapter you should:

- **appreciate the idea of place as a core geographical concept;**
- **be aware that place is a vital component in your own experience;**
- **be able to explain why the study of places is a vital aspect in primary geography;**
- **be able to give examples of places to be included in children's geography curriculum.**

This chapter addresses the following Professional Standards for QTS:
Q10, Q14, Q15.

Introduction

In Chapter 2, one of the core concepts of geography, place, was introduced. We use the word 'place' variously in geography: objects being in their place; a city open space as a place to meet; your place of study or work; and 'no place like home'. These uses of place refer to position, site and to the nature of places. Children's experience of and in their own locality – their place – is a key element of their childhood; their knowledge of and ideas about places develop through their varied experiences. This indicates other notions of place in our list. Places hold meanings for us (Martin, 2006c). Their meanings encompass how and why we feel about and appreciate our familiar surroundings or the new places we visit; how and why we observe and understand places, both familiar and new; and how and why we use places as we do. These interacting notions of 'place' lie at the core of everyday geographies. Place is a complex, developed and potent idea geographically (Cresswell, 2004; de Blij, 2008; Roberts, 2003). Places can be personal and public, of varied size and scale, and real and imagined. This chapter examines these aspects of place.

Meeting places

A childhood place

Childhood places are important to us. We remember particular aspects of the places in which we lived in our younger and teenage years. From our earliest years places play a key part in our childhood everyday geographies. They help create our initial impressions of the outside world. They are where we played, the places we used; and how we felt about them remains with us. Such places may be small garden-size areas or cover a few streets, an area of countryside or a park. We recall people and features that were important to us. Family and friends are an important factor here, influencing us through taking us out, their experiences and their perceptions, and by giving permission to run errands and make journeys, allowing the possibility of exploring more widely. We construct our understanding of places and our images of place through our interactions with them, from our direct experiences. The places we know most about are those closest to us, emotionally and as physical sites. In her novel, *Blackberry wine*, Joanna Harris (2001) describes perceptively a child's sense of place, using her authorial license to explore in some depth the meaning of a place to the central character, Jay.

> Joe lived on Pog Hill Lane, one of a row of uneven terraces backing onto the railway half a mile from the station. Jay had already been there twice before, leaving his bike in a stand of bushes and climbing up the banking to reach the railway bridge. On the far side there were fields reaching down to the river, and beyond that lay the opencast mine, the sound of machinery a distant drone on the wind. For a couple of miles an old canal ran almost parallel to the railway, and there the stagnant air was green with flies and hot with the scent of ash and greenery. A bridle path ran between the canal and the railway, overhung with tree branches. Nether Edge to the townspeople, it was almost always deserted. That was why it first attracted him. He bought a packet of cigarettes and a copy of the Eagle from the station newspaper stand and cycled down towards the canal. Then, leaving his bike concealed in the undergrowth, he walked along the canal path, pushing his way through great drifts of ripe willowherb and sending clouds of white seeds into the air. When he reached the old lock, he sat down on the stones and smoked as he watched the railway, occasionally counting the coal trucks as they passed, or making faces at the passenger trains as they clattered to their distant, envied destinations. He threw stones into the clotted canal. A few times he walked all the way to the river and made dams with turf and the accumulated garbage it had brought with it: car tyres, branches, railway sleepers and once a whole mattress with the springs poking out of the ticking. That was really how it began; the place got a hold on him somehow. Perhaps it was because it was a secret place, an old, forbidden place. Jay began to explore; there were mysterious raised concrete-and-metal cylinders, which Joe later identified as capped pitheads and which gave out resonant breathing sounds if you went close. A flooded mineshaft, an abandoned coal truck, the remains of a barge. It was an ugly, perhaps dangerous place, but it was a place of great sadness, too, and it attracted him in a way that he could neither combat nor understand. His parents would have been horrified at his going there, and that, too, contributed to its appeal. So he explored; here an ash pit filled with ancient shards of crockery, there a spill of exotic, discarded treasures – bundles of comics and magazines, as yet unspoiled by rain; the hulk of a car, an old Ford Galaxie, a small elder tree growing out of its roof like a novelty aerial; a dead television. Living alongside the railway, Joe once told him, is like living on a beach; the tide brings new jetsam every day. At first he hated it. He couldn't imagine why he went there at all. He would set out with the intention of taking a quite different route and still find himself in Nether Edge, between the railway and the canal, the sound of distant machinery droning in his ears and the whitish summer sky pushing down on top of his head like a hot cap. A lonely, derelict place. But his, nonetheless. Throughout all that long, strange summer, his. Or so he assumed.
>
> (Harris, 2001, pp27–28)

A key feature of primary geography is helping children articulate and extend their awareness, knowledge, understanding and feelings about their own places through their study and exploration. It focuses on developing their appreciation of their own places, providing opportunities to express critical insights and positive perspectives, and to understand their place's present as well as to consider its future.

Exploring place

There are places that are part of our daily lives, and places we may visit. Being in and experiencing places provides the strongest sense of a place, but words and pictures can present an idea of how places may look, be and feel. Texts can describe and provide insight. Pictures provide information about and views of places that cannot be fully captured in words. Both provide, in their different ways, understanding and senses of meaning about places. The description below is of aspects of the old town, or medina, of Tunis in North Africa, taken from a tourist guidebook to the city. It provides information about and insights into the medina. A souk is a market, which may be in a building or a square or composed, as here, of narrow covered streets and alleyways. The photographs in Figures 4.1 and 4.2 illustrate features noted in the guide.

The Medina (Old Town)

*The **medina** of Tunis is probably the easiest to navigate in all of North Africa. At all the main gates you'll find a large map with all the streets clearly named, and there are small orange signposts pointing the way to the principal sights. The souks have their share of the usual hustlers, so be wary of anyone offering to show you a view, a museum or a special exhibition. These invariably lead to carpet shops.*

*The free-standing archway of the **Bab el Bahr** – also called the **Porte de France** (built 1848) on the Place de la Victoire – marks the entrance to the medina. It was once continuous with the thick medina walls, and stood on the shore of the lake of Tunis (the Arabic name translates as the 'Sea Gate') before the French built their own new town on reclaimed land. Walk through the Porte de France and then take the left hand of the two narrow alleys facing you.*

*This is the **rue Jemaa ez Zitouna**, the medina's main street, and it is lined with tiny craft shops and souvenir stalls. As you merge with the crowds that shuffle slowly uphill you will find yourself immersed in a world of heady sensations. Fragrant incense and exotic perfumes compete with the mouth-watering smell of roasting mutton and the aroma of freshly ground coffee. The tap-tap-tap of silversmiths' hammers and the scuff of sandalled feet on smooth paving stones almost drown out the muezzin's call to prayer from a minaret. The bright reds, blues and golds of flowing kaftans flash in the dappled interplay of sunshine and shade, and then the street disappears into a dark tunnel to emerge at the steps below the door to the Zitouna Mosque.*

(Wilson, 2009, pp30-31)

PRACTICAL TASK PRACTICAL TASK PRACTICAL TASK PRACTICAL TASK PRACTICAL TASK

Select a novel, children's book or a tourist guide which describes an urban or rural neighbourhood, or use photographs of somewhere you have been. What do you think the author or photographer (yourself?) is trying to convey about this place by writing about it and/or using pictures to show it? Now write about a place that you know well. How would you describe it to bring it alive?

Figure 4.1 The Porte de France in Tunis

Figure 4.2 Inside the souk

IN THE CLASSROOM

Their teacher introduced her Year 2 class to *Belonging* (Baker, 2004), a textless picture story. Previously, they had explored the neighbourhood around their urban school. Their teacher used *Belonging* to encourage them to think about changes that might have taken place locally. She asked the children to look carefully for changes they could see in the pictures, however detailed. The children quickly became adept at this. She took them through the story again, guiding them to think about how the place appeared across the pictures, over time, encouraging them to see the whole picture rather than its features. They discussed how it changed. They went through the story a third time – this time backwards – discussing why the changes happened and saying what they thought about them. She encouraged them to say how they felt about the place as it changed: What did they like or not like? What would they have changed and how? How would they feel if they were part of the family living there? She helped them understand what was happening to this area, as well as beginning to appreciate what it might be like to live there. She encouraged them to discuss what they knew about their own area from their personal experience and the fieldwork they had undertaken. Did they know about any changes? Some children brought in information from home about changes locally. She linked this with what they felt about living in the area, how they used it and what meaning it had for them. (Catling, 2009, pp194–5)

REFLECTIVE TASK

The examples above focus on localities, small-scale places: an extent of waste ground, the ancient city centre. What do they convey to you about the idea of place? Note the idea(s) of place that they stimulate for you.

What is place?

Geographers study place through people's use and impact and in people's minds (Matthews and Herbert, 2008; Cresswell, 2004). There are four important aspects to the idea of *place*.

- Where places are – the location of places;
- What places are like – the nature of places;
- What places mean to us – the meaning of places;
- How place relates to space in geography.

Locating places

Everywhere is somewhere. Location is centrally important in geography. It helps to know, understand and appreciate where places are, to find them, to refer to them, and – because this can be shared information – to anticipate that when we refer to particular places – countries, cities, mountains, resorts – others may know roughly where they are or be able to find out.

We collect and record locational information to help us, in street maps and national and global atlases. We use satellite-sourced websites such as Google Earth and Multimap to locate and view our place and others. Increasingly, car drivers, even walkers, use global positioning systems (GPS) to check where exactly they are and their own or alternative routes. We have used GPS in ships and aeroplanes for many years. While the earliest GPS were the dead-reckoning and local knowledge skills employed by sailors, the development of latitude and longitude to locate places uniquely on land and ocean (with the technology later to do so very accurately) enabled them to move precisely over the oceans and helped geographers and cartographers to state locations and make maps accurately. It is all about the core geographical question:

• Where is this place?

The sense of where is only the starting point for such studies. The location is important, but the place or feature itself is the reason for wanting to know.

The nature of places

Through the study of place, we try to describe what places are like and explain why physical and human features, such as lakes and towns, are where they are. Place studies focus on what the features are like, how they came to be as they are today, what continues to influence changes to them, and what impact such development might have on people and the built and natural environment in the future. Geographers ask about the character of places and their connections with and to other places.

• What is this place like?
• Why is this place here and like this?
• What use do people make of this place, and why?
• How is this place linked to and interdependent with other places?
• How is this place changing, and what causes this?
• What impact will changes have here and elsewhere, and why might this be?
• What is the future for this place, and why?

The focus of study here is on the human and physical, or natural, features and processes that create, characterise and change places. Places are dynamic, whether developments occur with some speed – a new housing estate or shopping mall – or over many millions of years – as the evolution of mountains or coastlines. Change may be dramatic, as with the floods in New Orleans in 2005 or the earthquakes in central China in 2008 and central Italy in 2009, and have major impact. Changes can be commonplace, such as new high-street shops or in-fill housing developments. Places are cultural creations, the result of human actions, like the 'idyllic' Cotswold village and landscape, or named through a sense of 'awe and wonder' at the natural environment, as is the aptly named Death Valley. A key aspect of places is what they might become, what possible and likely futures they have. Geographers examine the impact of changes in and on places, as well as on their future development, their preferred or probable futures.

Scale provides vital insights about places. Places encompass areas of differing sizes and complexity, from small localities to large regions covering a sizeable part of the globe, and, indeed, the Earth itself. We may focus on the minutiae of a shopping street or neighbourhood or study the relationships within a county or country, or even a large cross-national political region such as the European Union.

The meaning of places

We see places through two lenses: as real places and as imagined places. Our experience and knowledge of places is inevitably limited and partial, providing an image of these places. Our involvement in places creates a sense of that place which is personal. Yet much that we know of places through experience or via secondary sources is shared; we discuss traffic problems in the high street, and we know the shops we reference. Many places we are aware of we have encountered at second hand from a variety of sources: family, friends, TV news, holiday brochures, novels and films. We create our knowledge and understanding of the reality of places from the images of place that others provide. We may deal with multiple perspectives of the same place to create our own view. These 'place views' are partial and 'situated'. Place is not a simple objective notion but a matter of personal and collective meaning and interpretation.

Studying place concerns how localities have meaning for people. We all have sense(s) of place, the feelings about and appreciations of places with which we associate particularly: places we feel at home in, places we love returning to, places we feel are 'our' places, just as there are places we avoid. Geographers examine peoples' relationships with and to places.

- What is it like to live in this place?
- How involved do you feel in this place?
- What does this place mean to you?
- What is your reaction to change here?
- What do you want to see happen here?
- What do you want this place to be in the future?

Geography examines our knowledge and understanding of places and our emotional attachment to places. It explores how our identity interrelates with the places that have meaning for us. It examines why this is and what results from our views. Particular interest lies in the ways that the decisions we make might affect places, daily and long-term, their present and their future. In this context geography explores our values, interests and preferences.

Much of our understanding of places draws from our perceptions and images of places, our geographical imagination: how we organise our knowledge of places and imagine what they might be like from that understanding. We also imagine fictional places. Imaginary places are part of our experience, whether through television drama, novels, comics or poetry. We use our knowledge and perceptions of places to construct the appearance and sense of place we have before us. We may carry such creative images of places with us for many years from our favourite places and stories.

Place and space

Geographers study the spatial aspects of the Earth's surface, locally and globally, and try to understand and explain space. Places can be thought of as 'bounded space', a territory such as a neighbourhood or country (Matthews and Herbert, 2008) in space. Space encompasses the idea of location, where places are, and the relationships between locations, which links to such concepts as distance and scale. Geographers study spatial relationships between places, such as the locations and network of the leisure activities of children within a community or road, rail and air networks that connect places across continents. They are interested in explaining the spatial patterns they find in human activities and natural phenomena, such as the reasons why there is a relationship between pick-your-own farms, road access and urban areas. They look at the physical and human processes at work in the environment and develop notions such as location theory to explain why activities and developments, for instance schooling and shopping centres, appear where they do. This enables geographers to make predictions and proposals about natural and human activities. Geographers use a range of questions for doing this.

- Where do these features or events occur?
- Is there a relationship between these features or events?
- Can patterns be discerned, what are they, and how can they be explained?
- What processes are at work causing these relationships and patterns?
- What are the reasons for and the consequences of these patterns and processes, beneficial or otherwise?
- Can the patterns and processes be predicted and/or replicated or prevented?
- How can we adapt or use such processes for the benefit of people?

The interest in spatial relationships, patterns and processes lies in how we can foresee events. For example, the study of weather patterns and processes enables us to forecast the weather. Researching the best location for a new hypermarket or leisure centre might provide best access to the most people with least disturbance to the area in which it is to be sited. This is important because it concerns developing our awareness, knowledge and understanding of how the world works in order that as members of our communities and nations we might use these physical and social processes to improve the places we inhabit, use and enjoy.

REFLECTIVE TASK
BEELECLIΛE 1V2K

Read your notes about the concept of place. Consider how what you have written reflects the ideas about place expressed in this section. Add new points that have struck you about the idea of place. Identify why your ideas have developed.

Teaching about places

Why teach about places?

Studying places helps children understand and appreciate the location, nature and meaning of places and the importance of space. It gives them insight into how places work, what characteristics they have, what they mean to the children, and what it is or may be like for different people to live in and visit them. It draws on their personal experiences and understanding of places, at first hand or through indirect sources. Studying places expands their horizons from their places into the wider world. Their experience of picture stories, novels and drama helps develop their awareness and sense of place.

There are strong arguments for teaching about places implicit in the points made above and in Chapter 3. These draw on children's everyday geographies, their personal experiences in their environment and of the wider world through first- or second-hand encounters, perceptions and meaning. There are reasons that draw on the ways geographers explore, examine and understand places and people's activities in and meanings about them. Studying places provides opportunities for children to:

- use and develop their natural curiosity about places;
- examine and clarify their existing experience and awareness of places;
- develop their existing knowledge and understanding of their own and other places;
- develop their appreciation of their own and others' perceptions of their and other places, of why these places have meaning for and are important to those who live there;
- develop spatial awareness from the local towards a global scale;
- recognise their interdependence in their community, region and nation and with the rest of the world;
- build a global perspective from their local perspective, and use this to deepen their appreciation and understanding of the local;
- build positive attitudes towards other peoples, nearby and elsewhere, including those they will never encounter;
- value diversity in peoples, cultures and places;
- combat ignorance and bias, to challenge stereotyping and prejudice, and to raise their awareness of the partiality of and limits to our understanding of people and places, locally and far away;
- explore and develop ideas and skills and extend their place vocabulary and language.

Places to explore in primary geography

A variety of places can be studied during the Foundation Stage and Key Stages 1 and 2, including the school and its grounds, the local area, and other localities in the United Kingdom and other parts of the world. It is important to ensure that places are not studied in isolation but are linked into their regional and national context, that their global location is identified, and that connections to nearby countries and within their continent are noted, alongside a sense of their distance from and links to the United Kingdom.

School grounds
The school and its grounds are a shared aspect of children's lives. This small-scale place, whether of extensive or limited grounds, offers opportunities to examine its features and activities and the views and feelings of children and staff, among much else. Chapters 8 and 9 develop these and other approaches.

The school's local area and neighbourhood
The locality of the school usually is the area where most children live. It is the children's local area and is important in and to their lives. Whether an urban or rural environment, there is much to study locally. Approaches to studying the local area are considered in Chapter 10.

Places further afield in the United Kingdom
Studying other localities in the United Kingdom provides opportunities for children to explore another place similar in size to their own, where they can compare aspects with their place and community. Chapter 10 refers to the study of other localities in the UK, which should draw on much the same approaches as in the local area.

Places outside the United Kingdom
It is important that younger children develop some understanding of other places elsewhere in the world. Such studies best focus on similar-sized localities to enable valid comparisons. Recognising and appreciating the diversity across the world can be fostered through studying a locality in a less well-developed country economically, where similarities can be noted and contrasts considered. Such studies must be set in a global context. Some resources for and approaches to teaching are outlined in Chapter 11.

Where in the world

The public perception of geography concerns knowing where places are, though it is about much more than this. Knowledge of location is important: where features, places and environments are and where events happen in the world. Maps appear regularly in the media to locate places, to provide a sense of their relationship to our country. A basic idea of the whereabouts of the continents and oceans and of significant places and features in the world in our mental map helps us appreciate where events occur. We can, of course, look them up in an atlas each time we hear the news. This world knowledge is important, because what happens nearby or far away might affect each of us directly or indirectly.

In studying places children build up their mental map of their locality and other places they encounter through developing their locational knowledge (Catling, 2002). It is about locating where places are in the world as well as introducing children to globes and maps of the world, continents and countries. It supports their spatial awareness of the world. It is useful in primary geography to:

- enable children to identify and learn where significant places are;
- help children understand why having locational knowledge is useful;
- encourage them to find places on globes, atlases and maps, using appropriate skills, when they hear about them or are studying them, so that they construct their personal set of locational knowledge about the world.

IN THE CLASSROOM

In a Year 4 class there are always a globe and a world map accessible. Periodically the children are challenged to find and locate places to remind them where places they know are and to encourage them to locate 'new' places, taken from the news and children's interests. The children have become familiar with the continents and oceans and have drawn up their own set of significant places which are marked on a world wall map. They use circle time occasionally to discuss whether to add or remove places on their map. They also have a street map on the wall with their homes and other places they consider significant marked. Many have developed the habit of finding places in atlases and of bringing in obscure places for other children to locate. This reinforces and extends their evolving mental maps of their place and of the world.

REFLECTIVE TASK

What are your significant places? Make your own list. Which places in the world do you think are significant enough for children to be able to locate on a globe or world map. Why have you selected these places? Do they include natural features (e.g. mountains, rivers) as well as human features (e.g. cities)? Have you located events? Compare your list with the maps provided for the Key Stage 2 geography programme of study on the QCA website. Is your list similar or different? Why is this?

A SUMMARY OF **KEY POINTS**

This chapter has:

> examined places in terms of their location, their nature and their meanings and place as intertwined with space;

> noted that places are physical entities, perceived and imagined;

> considered the interrelationship of our experience of places and place as a central idea in geography;

> provided reasons for studying places and outlined a variety of places to include in children's primary geography;

> considered the value for children of developing locational knowledge.

MOVING *ON* > > > > > > **MOVING** *ON* > > > > > > **MOVING** *ON*

Choose a particular place you know. Google its name to find websites associated with it. What information and images are provided about this place? Which aspects of place are covered and which are not? Since it is a place you know, what can you add to the information, particularly about the meanings attached by you and others to this place? How would you help someone unfamiliar with this place see it as you do?

FURTHER READING FURTHER READING **FURTHER READING** FURTHER READING

The following are informative and accessible introductions to studies of place.

Cresswell, T (2004) *Place: A short introduction*. Oxford: Blackwell.

Matthews, J and Herbert, D (2008), *Geography: A very short introduction*. Oxford: Oxford University Press.

The following will help you develop your understanding and appreciation of place studies in primary geography and provide stimulating ideas for teaching younger children about place.

Catling, S (2002) *Placing places*. Sheffield: Geographical Association.

Halocha, J (2001) *Pocket guides to the primary curriculum: Geography*. Leamington Spa: Scholastic.

Martin, F (2006c) *Teaching geography in primary schools: Learning how to live in the world*. Cambridge: Chris Kington.

Palmer, J and Birch, J (2004) *Geography in the early years*. London: RoutledgeFalmer.

Scoffham, S (ed) (2004) *Primary geography handbook*. Sheffield: Geographical Association.

Read the magazine: *Primary Geographer*

Useful websites

Geographical Association: EY/Primary and ITT
www.geography.org.uk/
Geography Teaching Today
www.geographyteachingtoday.co.uk
Innovating with geography website
www.qca.org.uk/geography/innovating
NC curriculum PoS geography with maps for KS2
www.nc.uk.net
www.standards.dfes.gov.uk/geography

5
Exploring sustainability: environmental impact, sustainability and citizenship

Chapter objectives

By the end of this chapter you should:

- **understand what is meant by 'environment', 'environmental impact' and 'sustainability';**
- **know of the current government initiatives promoting sustainable schools;**
- **recognise the interrelationship in teaching sustainability, citizenship and controversial issues.**

This chapter addresses the following Professional Standards for QTS:

Q2, Q6, Q14, Q15.

Introduction

This chapter examines environmental impact and sustainability. This is a core geographical concept because the quality and nature of the Earth's and human's present and future depends on understanding the interactions in and between the human and physical environments. Geographers examine the uses and misuses of resources and technologies in our environments, people's access to resources and outcomes of unequal distribution, the cultural and social values held about the environment, the decision-making and decisions that affect the environment, and the extent to which the ways we live and use resources and the environment are sustainable. Geographers try to explain and evaluate what is being done and to offer advice about what needs to be and could be done. Geography is not a detached study; it is ethically informed, concerned and focused. Thus, connections with citizenship are noted, as are government initiatives for schools and education to help children take greater responsibility for their places, environment and future. This is an area of controversy, to be taught sensitively and inclusively, allowing children a sense of ownership and participation in their school and community and environment.

Environmental impact

Geography studies the physical or natural and human or social environment, investigating such aspects as natural features, processes and hazards and human settlements, population and transport. Central to these studies are the processes that cause and create changes in natural and social environments and the impacts that the outcomes have on environments, people and places. Children encounter the phrases 'environmental change' and 'environmental impact', usually in the context of destruction and degradation – the impact of flooding and high winds damaging homes and the local infrastructure, and families who find themselves living in run-down areas of boarded-up and vandalised housing and closed amenities. Yet, we must recognise and appreciate that environmental change and impact have a positive side, for example the redevelopment schemes in urban and dockland areas regenerating communities, tramway systems being built to reduce car usage and improve access to public transport, and the creation of natural habitats on wasteland encouraging the return of endangered species.

Studying changes that result from spatial and environmental processes leads to examination of their impact on the environment, people and places. The core focus is on the ways in which environmental impact is managed and enabled. Central to this aspect of geography is recognition that the environment is a resource to be used well, not mismanaged, inadvertently or intentionally. Environmental change and impact can lead to real improvements in or to the serious degradation of places and environments. For instance, the provision of paths and car parking areas in national parks helps the preservation of farmed and wild environments; the over-extraction of water leads to devastating impacts on water access and the livelihoods of farmers and communities. Geography studies, explains and may propose solutions to the management, use, replenishment and development of the environment. In particular, these studies concern the ways in which decisions are made about environmental use, who makes the decisions, why they are made and the impact they have in the short and long term.

A key topic in geography is the use of resources and how we live. There are finite resources, such as oil and other fossil fuels, which will run out. There are renewable resources, such as water and wind, though there is increasing debate about how we use, manage and sustain the Earth's renewable resources. There are regenerative resources, which include ocean fish stocks and the major areas of tropical forest, which if exploited rather than carefully managed and renewed through breeding and replenishment will be irreversibly damaged. Geography examines the activities and resulting outcomes and issues that affect people and the Earth, from the local to the global, including scarcity, misuse and exploitation, access, control and power, natural cycles and disasters, and environmental changes and impacts resulting from people's actions. For instance, geographers study climate change, its causes and effects, as they do the changes to city centres resulting from the building of out-of-town shopping malls, the impact of increased traffic in residential communities and the spread and effect of genetically modified crops. In doing so, geographers ask questions.

- How do people use and misuse the natural and social environment, why and with what impacts?
- Who makes the decisions that lead to effective use or misuse of the natural and social environment and their resources, why are they made and in whose interests?
- What can be done to create and ensure beneficial impacts from environmental changes and to reduce and minimise the negative effects of change?
- As citizens, what role can we play – and how – in making decisions that affect the environment, people and places?

Geographers' concern for environmental issues and their impact is important for children because they are the future. If children are to act responsibly in their stewardship of the world for coming generations, they need to develop their understanding of how to live in harmony with the Earth and how to come to decisions which are beneficial to and balanced for people, locally and globally. Geography plays a vital role in developing children's environmental awareness, knowledge, understanding and values, so that they may act as responsible local and global citizens.

> **IN THE CLASSROOM**
> Year 5 children were introduced to Brian Patten's (1990, pp110–11) poem 'The River's Story'. This challenging poem, rich with images and unusual vocabulary, depicts the life of a river and introduces issues about people's impact on it through industrialisation, buildings, agriculture and pollution. Through the poem the river's course is brought to life. After reading, discussing and understanding the poem, the children worked in groups, using the text and artwork, to produce their own river 'viewpoint'. This provided excellent consolidation of their work on rivers. A display was created to show the children's views, and they debated their different interpretations of people's impact on the river and its effect on people's lives.

PRACTICAL TASK PRACTICAL TASK **PRACTICAL TASK** PRACTICAL TASK **PRACTICAL TASK**

Find a poem or story about ways in which people affect a place or the environment (see Appendix 1). Use the headings, 'features and processes' and 'impact and response', to note the natural and human features and processes involved and to identify how the people and environment were affected and what happened in response.

Sustainability

Sustainability is complex and contentious and has various meanings. Its everyday meaning describes the capacity to maintain ways of life and usage of particular resources at current levels. The widely accepted definition provided by the Bruntland Commission (United Nations, 1987), which examined the use of the Earth's resources, states that a 'sustainable' way of life is one that:

> ... meets the needs of the present without compromising the ability of future generations to meet their own needs.

Ofsted (2008b, p6), in its review of sustainable development in schools, reiterated but slightly modified this view.

> The goal of sustainable development is to enable all people throughout the world to satisfy their basic needs and enjoy a better quality of life, without compromising the quality of life of future generations.

Sustainability emphasises using resources such that they are self-renewing or carefully replenished, and with working finite resources so as to manage a smooth transition from declining resources to new – hopefully renewable and regenerative – resources. How we use resources and live is a matter of future sustainability. This concerns the distribution of resources between and their use by people, with the goal of enabling all to live comfortably rather than a few to live well while the majority live in poverty. Geography reflects on the practical and ethical uses and misuses of the environment and of people and their places and communities. Examining environmental impact and sustainability involves concern with social and environmental justice.

It seems contradictory to talk about sustainability as maintaining the *status quo* while implying suggestions of expansion and advancement. Commonly, we perceive development to mean economic and lifestyle progress. This has been manifest in developing technology to improve material possessions and using increasing amounts of energy to do so. Environmental sustainability implies the need to steward renewable and regenerative resources such that while we use them they remain available in future. It implies that we develop alternative sources to replace finite resources. However, both contexts are now viewed as highly problematic and not necessarily possible. We need to think about environmental sustainability and sustainable development in terms of improvement not materially but for our environment, societies and communities, as *environmentally friendly growth* (Huckle and Martin, 2001). Only then can we have real sustainability globally and understand that *we are here for good and not just the weekend* (Patten, 2000). Martin and Owens state that sustainability is less a product than:

> *...a process: thinking about ourselves, thinking about others and using our knowledge to make responsible decisions and actions.*
>
> (Martin and Owens, 2008, p6)

Sustainability challenges the way we live. Its focus is on developing solutions that can improve the environment in which we all live and, thus, people's and communities' lives. It encourages us to think about how we can improve public services and facilities and how we can reduce, reuse and recycle to preserve the precious resources we have and utilise them in more effective and economical ways. Geographers are concerned to ask the following questions.

- What do sustainable lifestyles and environments look like?
- What creates, aids, damages or prevents the potential for sustainability?
- What options are there to enable a balanced, equitable and just use of the environment and its resources for a sustainable future, and how might the best options be identified and implemented?
- How can decision-makers be encouraged to adopt environmentally, people friendly and just strategies and actions to improve the lives of people across the world?

With an increasing focus on climate change and general environmental degradation, we are seeing a shift in attitudes towards tackling issues around sustainability. We must address this with children for they will carry forward the new initiatives to tackle environmental and social problems. Consequently, government and non-governmental organisations have attempted to inject concepts of sustainability into the curriculum and the ethos of schools. The emphasis is to develop children's understanding of their carbon and ecological footprints, for our actions affect the climate mechanisms of the globe and the Earth's whole environment, its ecosystems, the built environment and the global community.

REFLECTIVE TASK

Sustainable and ethical living is fraught with dilemmas. Consider where you stand on this dilemma. What would be your responses to children who asked you about it?

We are constantly being made aware of the detrimental effects of food being transported across the world, for us to eat whatever we like at any time of the year, irrespective of seasonality. Changing this is seen as positive and environmentally conscious. How do we square such change with the farmers in other parts of the world, perhaps in a fair trade business, who, to meet our insatiable demand, have developed their agriculture such that their survival depends on the production and sale of their cash crops to our market all year round? Which option do we choose: the reduction of food miles to support the planet, or supporting communities in other parts of the world reliant on us for their income? What other factors do we consider? Do we see this as good economics and supportive or as injurious and socially unjust?

Sustainable schools

The government has been increasingly concerned about the sustainability of schools and mindful of the impact of the school community on the environment. Because of this the government has committed to sustainability, requiring all schools to be 'sustainable schools' by 2020. It has promoted its Sustainable Schools programme (DfES, 2006a, 2006b). Ofsted (2008b) has noted that much work remains to be done. Few schools have developed co-ordinated and coherent approaches, integrating sustainability throughout the school and curriculum. Work to promote sustainability in schools is supported through the Sustainable Schools website.

The Sustainable Development Education Panel (Holland, 1998) argued that sustainability education develops the understanding, values and skills to enable us to take up the challenge provided by the Bruntland definition of sustainability. It outlined seven key concepts for Education for Sustainable Development [ESD] (see Table 5.1). These reflect the ideas implicit and explicit in the geographical concept of environmental impact and sustainability. Their role is to be interpreted and used more widely, but it is evident that they are both geographically informed and inform geography teaching.

Table 5.1 The key concepts of education for sustainable development

ESD concept	Developing the knowledge, understanding, values and skills to:
Inter-dependence	understand the connections and interrelationships between people, places and environments at local and global levels, and that decisions taken in one place have an impact elsewhere
Citizenship and stewardship	realise our rights and responsibilities to participate in making decisions that affect people, places and environments, and that everyone is entitled to a say in what happens in the future
Diversity	understand and value the importance of diversity in our lives, culturally, socially, economically and biologically, and that we are impoverished without it
Quality of life, equity and justice	recognise that for any development to be sustainable it must provide equitable benefit to people, improving their lives and welfare
Sustainable change	appreciate there are limits to the ways in which the world can develop, and understand that the consequences of unsustainable growth are increased poverty, hardship and environmental degradation, disadvantaging everyone
Uncertainty and precaution in action	realise, through our continuous learning about the Earth, to be cautious in our approach because our actions may have unforeseen consequences for people, places and environments
Needs and rights of future generations	learn to lead our lives considering the needs and rights of others, and recognise that what we do now has direct implications for what life is like in the future

Source: Adapted from www.nc.uk.net/esd/index.html; Holland, 1998; Martin, 2006; Martin and Owens, 2008

The Sustainable Schools agenda provides guidance and a range of resources for a national framework to promote sustainability. This framework is based around the 'eight doorways' which schools are encouraged to use to develop their approach and children's understanding and appreciation of and commitment to sustainability (see Table 5.2).

Table 5.2 The 'eight doorways' of the Sustainable Schools Strategy

The doorways	Focus of interest
1. Food and drink	access to and supply of food and drink; sustainability of supply from local producers; environmental impact of drink and food production and consumption.
2. Energy and water	issues of increasing water and energy demand; approaches to sustainable conservation and reduced use.
3. Travel and traffic	examining journey and travel decisions and practices and traffic concerns; creating sustainable travel and transport to school, and reducing congestion and accidents.
4. Purchases and waste	evaluating the 'throw-away' culture, actions and impacts; exploring sustainable resource purchase use and practices; examining recycling, reuse, repair and reduction.
5. Buildings and grounds	appreciating how physical environments affect well-being; reviewing the nature and use of built and natural spaces in school and locally to improve environmental quality and sustainability.
6. Inclusion and participation	evaluating the inclusive nature of the school community; creating places and actions that respect human rights, cultures, freedoms and creative expression; enabling children to participate in place and environment decision-making and development.
7. Local well-being	schools as centres for change and enhancement of the local community and environment; understanding local issues and needs, with active engagement in school and locally.
8. Global dimension	recognising and valuing local–global interconnections; taking an international outlook and understanding the impact of personal and community values, choices and behaviours, as global citizens.

Source: DfES, 2006a, 2006b

The framework of the 'eight doorways' is linked to the context of the '*4Cs*'. Here the *Child* is at the core of the interlinked spheres of the school *Campus*, the *Curriculum* and the local *Community*, the three key elements involved in providing and enabling the study of sustainability (see Figure 5.1). While this programme involves embedding it into the ethos of the school to create a holistic learning experience, geography has a central role to play (Catling, 2007).

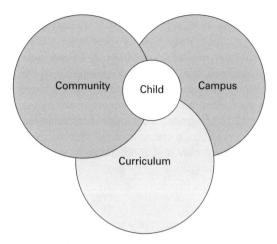

Figure 5.1 The '4Cs'

Source: DfES, 2006b, p11

Recognition of the constraints placed on children's freedom of movement and play has led to the realisation that we need to encourage and facilitate children's increased interaction with and contribution to their environment and community. This reflects the increasing reliance on schools to provide a focus for children's interaction with the local community. Essentially, this can only happen through the curriculum and with guidance. The sustainability framework provides a structure to facilitate this. Through geographical studies of the local area, involvement in environmental schemes in school – recycling, school garden initiatives and such like – children can be encouraged to connect again with and contribute to their community. Similarly, through the extended schools initiative, communities are being developed and children given greater opportunities with people and spaces within them. One key initiative here is the Eco-Schools Scheme (see website), which recognises the developments within a school towards sustainability. Schools can apply to receive an award at three progressive levels: bronze, silver and the most coveted 'green flag'. This scheme has proved popular, with schools across the country taking up the structure using guidelines and targets to embed sustainability throughout their school community.

Environmental well-being

Environmental well-being (Catling, 2007; Collins and Foley, 2008; DfES, 2006a) concerns our state of happiness and contentment within our environment, natural and built, and is underpinned by the concept of care (Noddings, 2005). Two criteria used to measure well-being are satisfaction with life and personal development (NEF, 2005). Many of the issues concerning environmental well-being lie in sustainability. For many people the natural environment is a key factor in their contentment with life (Countryside Commission, 1997) and that engagement in it encourages better social ties and sense of community, improved physical and mental health, strengthened economic prospects, reduced crime rates, and enhanced children's play and learning.

This can, however, create the tension that the more we strive to search for and reconnect with nature, the greater our negative impact on the environment as we drive and fly to access it, holidaying often in modern facilities (NEF, 2005). We seem reluctant to reduce our choices and constrain our economic growth, though these do not seem to equate with well-being (Shah and Marks, 2004). Brown and Kasser (2005) noted that, when given the opportunity, children are keen to take greater responsibility ecologically and consciously and show a more stable and contented state of mind when thinking that they are able to help and be effective, reflecting similar findings from the *Community Soundings* report for the Primary Review. *Where schools had started engaging children with global and local realities as aspects of their education they were noticeably more upbeat*, and that *the sense that 'we can do something about it' seemed to make all the difference* (Alexander and Hargreaves, 2007, p12). It is, undoubtedly, our responsibility in this unsettled world to give children the opportunity to take ownership of their future and allow them to be active, effective citizens, with a role to play and a difference to make, not least to foster their sense of environmental well-being.

IN THE CLASSROOM

A Year 2 class examined in their geography topic what happened to waste at home and in school. They identified the variety of types of waste produced at home and school and surveyed classrooms and other parts of the school to see how much waste was produced over a week and what became of it. They considered what they found through the *4Rs*: *reduce*, *recycle*, *reuse*, *repair*, and added a fifth: *replace*, looking for more sustainable resources to use. They offered some ideas about changes that could be made in their own and other classes. They produced posters to encourage their ideas about the *5Rs* which they placed around the school and used drama in an assembly to demonstrate changes in behaviour to support a sustainable environment.

REFLECTIVE TASK
REFLECTIVE TASK

There are many sustainability concerns and issues that we encounter on a daily basis, including refuse and waste disposal; access to clean water and to nutritious and sustaining food; providing shelter and hygiene; poverty and inequality; climate change; environmental degradation; and rising demand for energy. Can you add to this list? Choose one issue and use the web to find out more about it. Try the Oxfam, ActionAid, Save the Children, Christian Aid or other websites. What might be effective approaches to developing children's understanding?

Sustainability and the futures dimension

Children want to be involved in doing something to help improve life and the environment. Such an approach reflects a sense of the future and being a positive part of it. Huckle (1990, p159) argues that:

> If we are not to overwhelm pupils with the world's problems, we should teach in a spirit of optimism. We should build environmental success stories into our curriculum and develop awareness of sources of hope in the world where new and appropriate technologies now offer liberation for all.

Education incorporating the futures dimension is beneficial. In an education where the majority of time and consideration is spent looking at and analysing the past and the present, it is increasingly pertinent to enable children to consider the future and begin to understand how they might plan for and shape it. Hicks (2002) argues that the future is the *missing dimension in the curriculum*, and that if we are to live sustainably we must give children the opportunity to consider their future. Geography is ideally placed to provide this, using its enquiry-based learning and real-world problem-solving approaches.

Hicks (2002, pxiii) identifies three different kind of futures.

- The *possible future*: what could happen, considering all eventualities.
- The *probable future*: what is most likely to happen.
- The *preferred future*: the one that we would most like to happen, but that will take a conscious effort, through planning and vision.

Children should be encouraged to explore different environmental futures and be able to discuss them openly and safely. They often feel unsure about their future. With a regular diet of despondency via the media, this is not surprising. Children think a great deal about the future but are rarely given the chance to discuss or explore it and, even less often, the empowerment to feel that they might be able to do something to influence it. There are many ways to encourage children to consider the future and at different scales. They can be encouraged to think about how things are changing locally, nationally and globally, for other people and themselves, and project their ideas into the future. Issues of environmental change and impact and of sustainability provide obvious focuses for this approach, about what could happen, might occur and they would prefer to happen.

It is important to emphasise that change is not just about what happens to us but is also about how we contribute to change – how we can effect change and what its impact might be. This can feed effectively into geography topics, for example, considering both the immediate impact of a new shopping development and the long term implications locally, of continuing development at such scales and about how we can make our voice heard.

Geography, citizenship and controversial issues

Geography and citizenship

Geography's key concept of environmental impact and sustainability links directly with active citizenship. This serves to strengthen and enhance both curriculum areas. Local and global citizenship are about finding ways to become increasingly aware and responsible in relation to people's lives, communities and the environment (Young with Cummins, 2002). Geography and citizenship education help develop younger children's knowledge and understanding, values and attitudes and skills. There are various opportunities to develop children's awareness as citizens in their local and national communities (Osler and Starkey, 2005). The range of mutual interests between geography and citizenship provides opportunities to consider the responsibilities which everyone, including children, has in every community. The guidance for citizenship education in primary schools (DfEE/QCA, 1999c) notes several aspects to develop (see Figure 5.2), linked to the following broader contexts:

- identifying likes and dislikes, fairness or unfairness, right and wrong;
- considering social, environmental and moral dilemmas;
- researching, discussing and debating issues, problems and events;
- sharing opinions and explaining views on issues and making choices and decisions;
- resolving differences by looking for alternatives.

- Involvement in communities.
- Awareness of the range of jobs carried out by people in places.
- What improves and harms the local natural and built environment.
- That resources can be allocated in different ways and these choices affect individuals, the community and the sustainability of the environment.
- Knowledge of different people's needs and responsibilities and that these can sometimes conflict with each other.
- Respect for differences and similarities between people, and realising they arise from factors including cultural, ethnic, racial and religious diversity, gender and disability.
- How the media present information selectively and create images about people, places and environments.
- The role of voluntary, community and pressure groups.
- The decision-making process affecting local decisions.
- Topical environmental and place issues as they affect people.
- Different people's responses to environmental and place changes and issues and their impact on them.
- Interdependence, the world as a global community, and challenges affecting the world.

Figure 5.2 Mutual aspects of geography and citizenship

There are clear links that can be made between sustainability and the global dimension, connected through global citizenship. These are explored in Chapter 11.

Controversial issues

Many geography and citizenship topics examine matters of controversy. There can be reluctance or concern to tackle controversial issues. It takes confidence in the children and yourself, but younger children are interested in issues and controversy (Claire and Holden, 2007). However they rarely involve straightforward solutions. It is frequently difficult, if not impossible, to conclude whether something is 'right' or 'wrong' – the issues are complex and there are differing, valid viewpoints (Oxfam, 2006b). The importance lies in enabling different views to be heard and respected. This involves developing the following skills, abilities and attitudes in children:

- listening to others;
- distinguishing between fact and opinion;
- recognising and accepting other points of view;
- arguing a case;
- dealing with conflict;
- understanding and accepting there may be alternative solutions.

Controversial issues have a number of elements, concerning personal, social, environmental and/or political impacts, that can arouse strong feelings, relate to genuine concerns, and deal with questions of values and belief. We all – children and ourselves – encounter controversial issues in our everyday lives and, consequently, in the everyday geographies we pursue in teaching geography. Figure 5.3 lists several of these. Such issues possess the potential to generate differing and contradictory opinions, some valid and others less so but in need of consideration and being weighed on merit. This should be facilitated when teaching about controversial issues by adopting specific approaches.

- Children are involved in establishing ground rules for and behaviours in discussion and debate.
- There is balance in the variety of perspectives considered, with children engaging with more than one set of issues.
- A balanced range of evidence and viewpoints is provided to children, using, where possible, information and claims from the different sides and interest groups involved.
- Views and arguments should not be ignored or discounted because they are challenging or minority perspectives.
- Children should offer other interpretations to those provided, including contradictory perspectives.
- Children should consider carefully what the evidence informs them about, and be encouraged to distinguish fact from opinion, values and belief.
- Children are allowed to decide the extent to which they express their own opinions but be explicit when doing so.
- Children are aware that they are not the sole authority or arbiter on matters of opinion or information.
- Conclusions should take account of minority perspectives.
- Children are challenged when they present assertions as fact or without care or viewpoints too speedily arrived at.

- Changes to traffic management, e.g. road humps, narrowing roads.
- The impact of traffic, e.g. traffic congestion, parking charges, safety.
- Building on farmland, e.g. for housing, industry or commerce.
- The loss of essential local services, e.g. shop and service closure, reduction of buses.
- Littering, e.g. in local streets, dumping in the countryside.
- Failure to improve residential and industrial areas, e.g. derelict housing; factories.
- Pollution of water, e.g. effluent discharged into rivers.
- Atmospheric pollution, e.g. fossil fuel burning, ozone damage.
- Poverty and the unequal distribution of resources, e.g. clean water, food access.
- Destruction of the rainforests, e.g. forest clearance in Amazonia and Canada.

Figure 5.3 Examples of controversial geographical topics

Various strategies can be employed to teach controversial issues, providing safe contexts through which to tackle the potential for bias and subjectivity.

- *Role play*: taking on the roles of different participants in the issue and arguing the case from the perspective of your 'character'.
- *Hot seating*: questioning individuals about the views of their 'character'.
- *Preparing a balance sheet*: listing and balancing against each viewpoint the evidence, perspectives and conclusions.
- *Debate*: groups putting forward the cases for different sides in an issue.
- *Drama*: writing a play script and acting out with the variety of viewpoints examined through different 'characters'.
- *Enquiry*: identifying the questions, deciding on the approach to investigation, evaluating the initial findings, continuing the investigation, drawing conclusions.
- *Conducting a 'public enquiry'*: inviting the different sides arguing about an issue to present their arguments.
- *Conducting interviews*: arranging to interview a variety of people who have different perspectives on a particular issue.
- *Proposing a change*: putting forward proposals for change to an area, looking at the possibilities and alternatives, seeking advice and different viewpoints, balancing ideas and arguments, and making proposals based on evidence and argument.

These approaches can be stimulated in various ways. Figure 5.4 highlights several topics in which two or more perspectives need to be considered and about which judgments need to be made. The approach is based on raising awareness of a problem or issue, considering ways in which it might be resolved and becoming involved in making it happen, itself a controversial approach, yet one in relation to environmental impact and sustainability that the primary geography curriculum includes by encouraging children to consider what action they would take (DfEE/QCA, 1999a). Geography's ethical dimension is reinforced.

Heightening awareness
- Use **poetry** about an environmental matter to stimulate debate about care for the environment.
- **Photograph** 'attractive' sites and sites of 'concern' in the local area, create a display and encourage children to write captions for the photographs to express their views, and say why.
- Examine an environmental issue in the media, and create a **radio or TV programme** to describe and explain the causes and consequences of the issue.

Proposing ways forward
- Identify a local issue and **plan** a way to improve it.
- Use **role play** to identify possible solutions to an environmental issue.
- Develop an **exhibition** of drawings, text, maps, models, digital photographs, charts and labels to describe and explain how an area might look in the future.

Taking action
- Design and create a distinctive area in the school grounds, such as a wild area, a garden (even simply with growbags) or a quiet area.
- Put into **practice** improved ways to reduce waste and increase recycling.
- Meet a local environmental action group and **join in** with their activities to improve the environment.

Figure 5.4 Nine examples of approaches to environmental impact and sustainability

There are rarely clear-cut 'answers' to controversial issues. The teacher's role is to enable learning rather than transmit knowledge and information. Many issues contain various dilemmas and possible outcomes. It is essential that we understand this complexity to overcome a tendency to oversimplify and look at issues in dualistic and clear-cut terms, stating for example that 'fair trade is good' or that 'driving is bad'. We must encourage children to question and consider, and to reflect critically and with balance, if not impartially. Organisations and initiatives such as Oxfam, Philosophy for Children and Open Spaces for Dialogue and Enquiry provide help to do this (see websites).

REFLECTIVE TASK

Read Oxfam's (2006b) advice on teaching about controversial issues (see the Oxfam website). What are the most important points made about the role of the teacher?

A SUMMARY OF **KEY POINTS**

This chapter has:

> considered the key concept of environmental impact and sustainability;

> noted how sustainability is being incorporated into the fabric of our schools;

> identified several examples for consideration in the classroom;

> noted the connections between environmental well-being and sustainability;

> introduced the role of a 'futures dimension';

> noted the links between geography and citizenship;

> outlined strategies for teaching controversial issues.

MOVING *ON* > > > **>** **>** **>** MOVING *ON* > > > **>** **>** **>** MOVING *ON*

Develop your reading about environmental change and impact and sustainability, why this aspect of geography is often controversial, and why it is an important aspect of geography and citizenship.

FURTHER READING FURTHER READING **FURTHER READING** FURTHER READING

The following books provide useful follow-up reading about the topics considered in this chapter.

Claire, H and Holden, C (eds) (2007) *The challenge of teaching controversial issues*. Stoke on Trent: Trentham Books.

Martin, F (2006c) *Teaching geography in primary schools: Learning how to live in the world*. Cambridge: Chris Kington.

Martin, F and Owens, P (2008), *Caring for our world: A practical guide to ESD for ages 4–8*. Sheffield: Geographical Association.

Young, M with Cummins, E (2002), *Global citizenship: The handbook for primary teaching*. Cambridge: Chris Kington.

Useful websites

Citizenship education
   www.citized.info/
Eco-Schools
   www.eco-schools.org.uk/about
Geographical Association
   www.geography.org.uk/
Oxfam Education
   www.oxfam.org.uk/education/
TeacherNet: Sustainable Schools
   www.teachernet.gov.uk/sustainableschools/index.cfm

6
Understanding geographical enquiry

Chapter objectives

By the end of this chapter you should:

- understand the importance of using enquiry as an effective model for learning in geography;
- understand there are various approaches to developing children's enquiry-based skills and how to structure effective enquiries;
- recognise how enquiry can feed into the studies of places and environmental impact and sustainability;
- be able to make connections between geographical and philosophical enquiry.

This chapter addresses the following Professional Standards for QTS:

Q2, Q6, Q14, Q15, Q25, Q30.

Introduction

The enquiry approach is specifically referred to in National Curriculum geography (DfEE/QCA, 1999a). It states that children must be taught to ask and answer geographical questions, investigate their questions and draw conclusions and viewpoints in a reasoned and measured way. The focus is on real-life issues that have relevance and meaning to them. Enquiry is a very effective way of investigating the world by tapping into children's unbounded curiosity, inquisitiveness and excitement about all that is around them. It is an active ingredient in children's learning and understanding of the world. It is closely aligned to scientific investigations and historical enquiries. It is about children being engaged actively in their own learning, and, in so doing, develop as self-motivated, independent learners.

What is enquiry?

A straightforward view of geographical enquiry states that:

> Enquiry is the process of finding out answers to questions. At its simplest, it involves encouraging children to ask questions and search for answers, based on what they might already know from data sources. As their skills develop, children can move to a more rigorous form of enquiry involving the development of testing of hypotheses.

(NCC, 1993, p27)

Enquiry enables children to find out about the world through:

- observation and research;
- critical evaluation;
- putting forward solutions;
- considering values and attitudes.

By its nature enquiry involves the enquirer. It is an active, not passive, approach to learning. As Martin states, enquiry necessitates that:

> *Children are actively engaged in the creation of personal and shared meanings about the world, rather than being passive recipients of knowledge that has been created or selected by the teacher.*
>
> (Martin, 2006c, p9)

Martin argues that children must be both physically and mentally active when engaged in enquiry. It is essential that they are not just doing the activities but are intellectually and emotionally stimulated by and engaged in them (Martin, 2006c). To achieve this, children need to be able to generate effective and stimulating questions, which will encourage them to explore the complexities of the world about them, start to make links between geographical concepts and begin to recognise the patterns and processes that exist.

Enquiry is embedded in robust pedagogical theory. Roberts (2003) states that, in the context of social constructivism, children learn most effectively not directly from teacher to pupil but by making sense of the world for themselves. This focuses on the difference between what they are able to do themselves and what they can do when supported by others. Through supported enquiry, children learn within but are enabled to move beyond their zone of proximal development (ZPD) – the point of distinction between what they are able to do for themselves and what they can do when supported by others – fostering achievement and progression. Vygotsky (1962) advocated the teacher's crucial role in supporting children's learning (Roberts, 2003), arguing that whenever children worked within their ZPD they would need a teacher, facilitator or mentor to help them to achieve higher levels of thinking. The word 'scaffolding' has come to represent what he meant by *light assistance* and building up children's knowledge and understanding. It is the interactions in which children and adults engage so that children's thinking is guided, promoted and enhanced (Webster et al., 1996; Wood et al., 1976). Scaffolding is about rather more than teachers' assistance; it involves teachers in playing a collaborative role with children and is the *crucial link between the teacher and child* (Webster et al., 1996, p96). The teacher has a vital role to play in developing effective enquiry learning, to support and guide the children's own learning from the initiation of their questions to researching and analysing their findings and coming up with reasoned and meaningful conclusions.

Geographical enquiry in schools

Ofsted recognises the vital role that geographical enquiry has to play and reinforces the view that enquiry is a process of active learning (Roberts, 2003), arguing that activities such as fieldwork are vital components in a meaningful geographical enquiry process. Ofsted states that:

> *Geographical enquiry encourages questioning, investigation and critical thinking about issues affecting the world and people's lives, now and in the future.*
>
> (Ofsted, 2008a, p31)

Geographical enquiry enjoys variable success in primary schools (Ofsted, 2008a). However, there is good evidence that in a number of situations enquiry can be particularly advantageous, such as:

- in developing observation and investigative skills when working out of the classroom, particularly for very young children;
- when employing increasingly complex questions to develop children's geographical understanding;
- where the children are involved in generating an enquiry through their own questions because it is relevant and meaningful to them and their lives;
- when children are involved in real-world enquiries, linked to their own environment, involving engaging fieldwork, analysing and using the results, e.g. to run a 'public enquiry' where they work collaboratively, and express their own feelings, attitudes and views;
- being provided with opportunities to articulate their preferred future for a development and to have their say in determining what places should look like;
- using enquiry skills to investigate what is not always immediately obvious and so look for the interconnections between seemingly disparate issues and link them together to gain a more holistic and coherent understanding – this has the bonus of stimulating their curiosity and encouraging them to find out more.

Ofsted (2008a) identifies constraints in developing children's experience and skills in using geographical enquiries, where they are limited in the scope of their enquiry and set prede-termined questions and too prescriptive boundaries, often to make it logistically more straightforward for the teacher or linked to the school's over-structured geography units of work. A further criticism is that many teachers lack awareness of the range of skills to use in enquiry learning and are reluctant to merge them rather than employ them in isolation, perhaps because they lack confidence in their own and the children's capabilities.

Developing geographical enquiry

Traditional approaches

Traditional place and environmental enquiry has often focused on five key questions, used by teachers to provide structure, sequence and stimulus for children's studies (Storm, 1989, 4).

- What is the place like?
- Why is this place as it is?
- How is this place connected to other places?
- How is this place changing?
- How would it feel like to live in this place?

These questions have served their purpose well, though concerns have been raised about their use to guide pre-constructed geographical enquiries, such as through the QCA geography scheme of work units (DfEE/QCA, 1998/2000), where children's questions are minimised when used 'off-the-shelf'. Other concerns include the limited ways in which geographical questions have been used by less confident teachers, for instance when asking why a place is like it is and focusing on the natural and built environment while excluding exploration of people's lives and the social, cultural, political and economic aspects of communities. Rowley (2006) noted similar limitations when considering 'what it may feel like to live in' a particular place, a focus which requires considerable information for it to be answered in an insightful and empathetic way. Rigidly used, such questions have tended to create a 'strait-jacketed' approach with less confident teachers not encouraging children to propose and pursue their own questions.

Developing geographical enquiries

If we want to initiate innovative, problem solving enquiries, we need to broaden the base and move beyond these *deductive* styles of questions and enquiries, which promote description and limited analysis, to more evaluative and empathic enquiries as found in *inductive* enquiry approaches. The tendency has been to be overly descriptive with younger children and more analytic with older children, but this needs to be superceded by a balanced approach adopted for all ages. Children are never too young to start thinking about *why* things happen nor to offer their ideas about what might or should happen in future.

Rowley (2006) argues that enquiry provides opportunities to develop more considered and creative investigations into our environment and that we need to use them to develop a greater sense of awe and wonder in children's learning as well as to provide our learners with ways of looking, thinking and problem-solving with greater ethical awareness. He acknowledges that although enquiry is one of the most advantageous and effective forms of learning, it is also one of the most complex and demanding, since it asks much of the teachers using it, particularly when such enquiries are initiated by children's curiosity and planning the work cannot be prepared for and undertaken in a formulaic way – that is, it can not be controlled, though it can be managed. Such 'unknown territory' can be uncomfortable, with the possibility of the unexpected emerging. This can cause anxiety when curriculum planning, a situation some teachers find challenging to engage in with their children, or, when they do take it up, are far more controlling and didactic using carefully prepared questions and known and safe answers. Such a teacher-dominated approach constrains children's ownership of their learning, and it does not develop the crucial skills of problem-solving. It inhibits children's creative and principled investigations and solutions to some of the complex and intricate problems facing us, effective though children can be seen to be in carrying out small-scale, local enquiries and in beginning to see how solutions can be applied to the bigger picture (Ofsted, 2008a).

Structured geographical enquiries have most consistently been used to find out about places and environmental concerns – what Rowley (2006) describes as what we learn – and has been an effective approach – how we do it – supporting information-oriented learning. Such an approach has inhibited children's engagement both with what matters to them and with real-world problems and issues, where they might have opportunities to make proposals or even take action, in other words, be involved in creating realistic 'outcomes', enabling them to gain a sense of greater responsibility, becoming more active participants in their own futures. This connects directly with children's everyday geographies in their places and the wider world and with providing opportunities to examine environmental impact and ways to live more sustainably and equitably within their environment. This requires developments in the approach to geographical enquiry, which are illustrated in Figure 6.1 below. An example of this enquiry approach in practice is shown in Figure 6.2 below.

By its nature, this type of enquiry is open-ended and fairly unbounded. It is essential that the geography is rigorously retained and the overall enquiry maintains a clear purpose as to why it is being carried out, its focus and what the desired objectives are to be. This issue-based enquiry requires real and meaningful input from the children. It involves them thinking about and discussing the issue and devising their own questions. It requires them to structure their enquiry and encourages them to think in creative and empathetic ways, so developing their values and attitudes alongside their knowledge of the issue. They may then begin to see how

---

Raising awareness

Children consider an issue that is relevant and pertinent to them and which has meaning for them. They ask questions to find out more about it and develop a structure and plan for their enquiry.

↓

Investigating

Children research their questions using primary and secondary sources to find infor-mation and answers to their self-generated questions. They draw up and communicate their findings.

↓

Raising concern/taking action

Children articulate feelings, attitudes and values about what they have found out and begin to want to take responsibility and, possibly, action in order to change or improve something they have identified.

Source: Adapted from Morris (u.d.)

Figure 6.1 An enquiry sequence about a place or geographical issue

---

Raising awareness

Local headlines announce bids for the development of the only remaining wharf area remaining on the Grand Union Canal in Berkhamsted, Hertfordshire.
Children generate questions, plan their enquiry and begin to investigate the story.

↓

Investigating

Children research their questions through primary and secondary sources, finding information and responses to their questions. They interview town planners, local residents and concerned business parties, and survey the area and local environment. They analyse and draw conclusions about what they have found out and heard.

↓

Raising concern/taking action

Children weigh up the different viewpoints and realise that they are able to have a say about the proposal and in the outcome. They write letters to concerned parties, produce a display at school and in the local town hall to raise awareness, express and demon-strate their feelings and opinions, and feel a part of the eventual planning decisions made.
(As a result of similar local action and community protests, the residential development company was not awarded planning permission. The site is to be taken over and developed by a community-run organisation, promoting education and enterprise on this previously derelict area of the canal.)

Figure 6.2 An example of the enquiry sequence in practice

they can take some responsibility in what is happening and propose possible solutions. This allows them to think about and possibly affect what their 'preferred' rather than just the 'probable' future in that place might be (Hicks, 2007). Figure 6.3 presents the structured enquiry framework which encourages children to develop and agree their question, to investigate it collaboratively, draw conclusions and come to their own justified views.

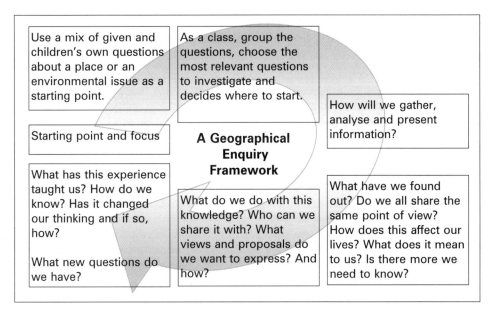

Use a mix of given and children's own questions about a place or an environmental issue as a starting point.	As a class, group the questions, choose the most relevant questions to investigate and decides where to start.	
Starting point and focus	**A Geographical Enquiry Framework**	How will we gather, analyse and present information?
What has this experience taught us? How do we know? Has it changed our thinking and if so, how? What new questions do we have?	What do we do with this knowledge? Who can we share it with? What views and proposals do we want to express? And how?	What have we found out? Do we all share the same point of view? How does this affect our lives? What does it mean to us? Is there more we need to know?

Source: Modified from a curriculum-making tool developed by Paula Owens and Wendy North for the Action Plan for Geography, Geographical Association, 2006

Figure 6.3 An enquiry framework

Geographical enquiry can be used in a variety of different ways and with a range of different concerns.

- Geographical topics, to explore topics focused on water and rivers, the local weather, how we feel about the place where we live, and identifying changes that are taking place in different places which we compare.
- Environmental impact and sustainability problems, such as how to relieve parking congestion, ways to improve a particular area, access to places for everyone.
- Controversial issues, such as the impact of pollution, decision-making about a change in land use, conflicting views about climate change.

Children's geographies and the enquiry process

The example in Figure 6.2 above draws on children's geographies, more specifically the geographies that affect children: change and impact in their local area. Geographical enquiries should draw on children's geographies in the early stages, possibly throughout and towards the end of their investigations. Developing children's skills in undertaking geographical enquiries requires children to be inducted through their primary school years into enquiry approaches. The approach outlined in Figure 6.4 offers a structured development for this: the 'three Es' approach (Catling, 2003). This structure initiates the process of geographical investigation in which questions are raised and selected by the children, and their teacher takes the role of the facilitator for the ensuing discussion – an approach consistent with that advocated in Philosophy for Children – and, with the children, for co-planning, organising and the carrying out of their enquiry. The classroom example below illustrates how one class undertook such an enquiry. Using enquiry in geography should encourage children to look at places and environmental interests and concerns from more than one angle and share and reflect on these, as this class did.

Enabling enquiry: Children are inducted into an enquiry approach, drawing on their sense of exploration and inquisitiveness. While structured by the teacher to enable young children to develop a sense of focus and for ordering their enquiries, it should enable children to put forward their own questions, which they begin to investigate systematically to identify their own responses.

Enhancing enquiry: The role of the teacher is to encourage children to take an increasing level of responsibility for identifying the questions to investigate, within a disciplined framework. The teacher challenges the children's questions and approaches, to focus them consistently on matters of geographical relevance, in relation to places, the environment and environmental spatial understanding.

Empowering enquiry: Children are encouraged to take direct responsibility for identifying, refining, using and evaluating their enquiry questions and process. This is not only about children structuring the way they work to an increasing extent, but also about them selecting their approaches and methods and identifying with their teacher their needs, to be able to achieve the challenge they set themselves. Their teacher continues to act as a critical mentor.

Source: Catling, 2003

Figure 6.4 The 'three Es' enquiry structure

IN THE CLASSROOM

A Year 4 class began a study of their local area with group and then class discussions about what they knew about it, what they thought about it and how they felt about it. It became clear that they had a wide range of knowledge of the area between them, that they related differently to it and that they had differing views about the state of the area. Drawing out their ideas and questions the teacher encouraged the children to work in four teams, each one focusing on a different perception of the locality, and each of which producing its own report. The four mini-topics were:

What is good about our place?
A clean neighbourhood?
What can you do here?
What do we like here?

A variety of investigations developed. Opportunities for fieldwork were organised and many of the children were able to draw on their local knowledge and to follow up lines of enquiry outside school. Fieldwork and other investigations involved interviews with family, friends and other local people; taking and analysing photographs of places liked and thought 'scruffy'; mapping local shops and other useful services; and sketching particular features and views. The children were encouraged to be creative in preparing their reports. The teams drew on items such as leaflets and posters that they had come across for inspiration. One team produced a brochure to attract people to the area and emphasised what a good place it is to live in. Another provided a 'clean up our neighbourhood' poster with photographs of unkempt sites and advice on what to do. The third team made a presentation of their own and other children's favourite places using maps and photographs to show the sites. The fourth team produced a map leaflet to show what services were available and where they were. The outcome of the enquiries was insightful, in that it provided four differing but overlapping perspectives on the children's geographies of the area. The children's favourite sites did not mesh with the views of a range of adults and younger people on what was good about the locality, though there was some overlap with other people's ideas of what was scruffy about the area, such as the waste ground, and about how the area was valued.

Catling, 2009c, p193

REFLECTIVE TASK

Think of an enquiry that you could do or have done with children and consider how it might enable, enhance and empower children's enquiry skills and ultimately their geographical understanding. Relate this to the approaches illustrated in Figures 6.1, 6.2 and 6.3.

Philosophy for children

Enquiry is about asking and examining questions and, importantly, getting children to ask and investigate their own questions. This motivates them to seek the answers – rarely do we ask a question that we are not interested in finding the answer to. Often, though, we are asked questions that we are not terribly interested in investigating. Child-generated questions are, therefore, the most effective and inspiring and are being given increasing attention and consideration.

One approach encouraging children to ask questions and discuss what they raise is the Philosophy for Children (P4C) movement. It encourages children to reason and to be reasoned with, asking and discussing questions about very real issues in a safe, critically enquiring environment (see the SAPERE website). P4C was developed to encourage children to become more 'reasonable' and thoughtful through asking 'Socratic' questions on the path to the ultimate educational goal of practical wisdom and good judgment (Lipman, 2003). Using approaches adapted from social constructivism, P4C emphasises that we learn to think just as we learn to speak. Its approach is based on the notion of 'communities of enquiry' in which teachers and children work together to cultivate understanding not only about the material world but also about their personal and ethical world. It is an enquiry-based approach. This development and refining of enquiry skills enables, enhances and empowers children's enquiries (Haynes, 2002) and can be a stimulating and effective starting point for geographical enquiries (Rowley and Lewis, 2003). P4C aims to develop and improve children's thinking skills, encouraging them to engage in the thinking process and to go beyond simple information retrieval to gaining insight and understanding through analysis and reflection. This can lead to positive action being suggested and taken in the light of understanding, reinforcing children's capacity to take greater responsibility and participate in creating their preferred futures.

IN THE CLASSROOM

P4C can be used to stimulate debate about real-world geographical issues, such as climate change. P4C sessions are initiated by a stimulus to generate children's questions. This approach is used from the Foundation Stage through Key Stage 2. A photograph of two polar bears atop a melting iceberg was placed in front of Year 5 children sitting in a circle. They were asked to come up with questions about the picture that could be discussed. Open-ended questions, such as *Why can't they be on a bigger piece of ice?*, rather than closed questions, such as *Where are the polar bears?*, are encouraged to involve the children in thinking around the wider issues and understanding the 'big' questions. The children put their questions on the floor and voted on the one that interested them most. They spent 30 minutes discussing and answering the question. Not only did this encourage them to generate meaningful questions but it also initiated real consideration of the myriad issues around concepts such as climate change and the geographical reasons and implications of it.

PRACTICAL TASK PRACTICAL TASK PRACTICAL TASK PRACTICAL TASK PRACTICAL TASK

Visit the Philosophy with Children (PWC) forum on their website and, if appropriate, contribute some thoughts and ideas that have been raised from reading about philosophy, enquiry and thinking skills in the context of geographical enquiry. You might follow this up by visiting the Open Spaces for Dialogue and Enquiry website (www.osdemethodology.org.uk) to explore further concepts around enquiry and questioning.

Broadening children's enquiry horizons

Expanding children's geographical enquiry horizons depends on encouraging them to ask their own questions, as much as expanding the questions that we ask them. To prompt children and to develop their questioning, we, as teachers, have a responsibility to challenge their questioning to higher levels. In this set of questions the italicised questions are those that encourage and allow children to move on in their understanding and to developing greater insight and deeper understanding and examine their feelings, attitudes and views.

- *What is it?*
- *Where is it?*
- *What is it like?*
- *How did it come to be like this, and why?*
- *How is it changing, and why?*
- *How and why might it change and what are the alternative possibilities?*
- *What different viewpoints and opinions are there, and why?*
- *What impact is change having, and why?*
- *What should happen next, and why?*
- *What do I think/feel/do about this, and why?*
- *How is it like/different from other examples, and why?*

These questions help us to think about what useful – or effective – geographical questions are. The following criteria can help us focus on encouraging children to articulate good questions, whatever their age. Some examples are provided in Figure 6.5.

- It stimulates and motivates – you want to investigate and answer it.
- It is challenging – not straightforward to answer.
- It will be about a concern or an issue, not just provide information.
- It is about why, not just what.
- It involves analytic and creative thinking skills alongside values.
- It produces informative and interesting (and perhaps, realistic) responses – not always solutions.
- It encourages proposals for action, and possibly their follow up.

- Why can't we play on the grass all year round?
- How can we waste less in our classroom?
- Where is the best place in school?
- Can we organise the dining hall in a more attractive way?
- Where would we locate a pond in the school grounds?
- How can we make the school more accessible for a wheelchair user?

Figure 6.5 Effective geographical questions based in a school environment

At its core, geographical enquiry is about facilitating children to be:

- *connected* – children's geographical enquiries have relevance for and are of interest to them;
- *involved* – children are actively engaged in their geographical learning, and feel valued as participants in the process of their learning;
- *aware* – children are able to internalise meaning from their geographical enquiries, connecting with their senses, feelings and thoughts;
- *motivated* – the geographical topics and the styles of teaching are stimulating and engaging, involving a variety of teaching and learning strategies and activities;
- *challenged* – children are challenged to think and, so, to apply, adapt and develop their geographical understanding, knowledge, values and skills in continuing and new enquiries;
- *geographers* – while using a variety of methods and tasks, the approaches to teaching and learning about places and environments are through geographical skills, knowledge and understanding;
- *citizens* – children are enabled to develop and express their views and ideas through the enquiries they undertake, including being able to promote and even act on their considered judgments and proposals.

PRACTICAL TASK PRACTICAL TASK **PRACTICAL TASK** PRACTICAL TASK **PRACTICAL TASK**

Drawing on the examples in Figure 6.5, try to write four or five useful geographical questions of your own. Base them in the local area where you live. Select one and write a plan to outline how you would set out to investigate your question.

A SUMMARY OF **KEY POINTS**

This chapter has:

> **considered what is meant by the term 'enquiry' and outlined its role and potential in teaching geography in the primary curriculum;**

> **explored the rationale for the practice of enquiry, demonstrating why it is such an effective way of developing children's geographical understanding;**

> considered traditional enquiry questions and processes and introduced more contemporary foci for developing and delivering enquiry, encouraging children's greater participation and involvement, taking into account their own geographies;
> considered the role and potential of pursuing enquiry in greater depth and with broader outcomes through asking more open questions involving initiatives such as Philosophy for Children.

MOVING *ON* > > > > > > MOVING *ON* > > > > > > MOVING *ON*

You might follow up the last practical task by carrying out your enquiry to build up a picture and an understanding of your immediate locality, and to consider how enquiry helps us to understand our environment, develop a sense of place and recognise local issues.

FURTHER READING FURTHER READING **FURTHER READING** FURTHER READING

The following books all contain useful sections on and examples of geographical enquiries.

Martin, F (2006c) *Teaching geography in primary schools*. Cambridge: Chris Kington.

Rowley, C (2006) Are there different types of geographical enquiry?, in Cooper, H, Rowley, C and Asquith, S (eds) *Geography 3–11: A guide for teachers*. London: David Fulton.

Rowley, C and Lewis, L (2003) *Thinking on the edge*. Morecambe: Living Earth.

Scoffham, S (ed) (2004) *Primary geography handbook*. Sheffield: Geographical Association

While Roberts's book is written for Key Stage 3, it is the clearest examination of geographical enquiry and presents strong arguments for and approaches to enquiry.

Roberts, M (2003) *Learning through enquiry*. Sheffield: Geographical Association.

Examples of geographical enquiries are published regularly in *Primary Geographer*.

Useful websites

Geographical Association
    www.geography.org.uk
Geography Teaching Today
    www.geographyteachingtoday.org.uk
Open Spaces for Dialogue and Enquiry
    www.osdemethodology.org.uk
Philosophy with Children (PWC)
    www.childrenthinking.co.uk/forum.htm
QCA Innovating with Geography
    www.qca.org.uk/geography/innovating
SAPERE
    www.sapere.org.uk/

7

Experiencing and visualising geography: fieldwork, photographs and maps

Chapter objectives

By the end of this chapter you should:

- **appreciate the importance of outdoor learning and undertaking fieldwork with children of all ages;**
- **understand the value and role of photographs and maps in geographical learning, and know some ways to develop children's understanding;**
- **appreciate that children learn through 'virtual' environments.**

This chapter addresses the following Professional Standards for QTS:

Q2, Q6, Q14, Q15.

Introduction

Geography is founded on investigation of the real world. It is, therefore, vital that children engage in learning outside the classroom and undertake fieldwork as a key element in their studies. We cannot always take children out, but it is possible to bring the outside world into the classroom, through the use of photographs, film, artefacts and maps. These are key resources in geographical learning as are new technologies. They provide the potential for children to engage in active learning, through their enquiries and linked to field studies. This chapter introduces these aspects of primary geography.

Engaging in fieldwork

In one of the Primary Review's studies, children contrasted their classroom-based experience of learning revolving around paper, books, the computer and virtual environments with their limited experience of going outside to learn. They considered the latter of real value *because you're seeing things, feeling things,* real *things* (Alexander and Hargreaves, 2007, p13).

The importance of fieldwork

Ofsted's report on *Learning outside the classroom* strongly endorses experience for younger children in the outdoors, stating that it:

> ... *can help to make subjects more vivid and interesting for pupils and enhance their understanding. It can also contribute significantly to pupils' personal, social and emotional development...*

> (Ofsted, 2008c, p7)

One of the enduring memories many people claim to have of their geography at school is of fieldtrips they undertook. Fieldwork brings subjects alive, involves younger children in investigating and exploring real places and environments, and develops their interpersonal skills. This approach to 'out of classroom learning' engages pupils' interest and provides a relevant, real-life stimulus for geographical questions, setting up a sequence of focus, investigating, collecting, recording, presenting, analysing and evaluating evidence as part of geographical enquiry (Richardson, 2004a). In doing so, it provides opportunities to promote higher-order thinking skills and is a useful vehicle for developing and applying decision-making skills based on real places and issues, while appreciating other people's values and attitudes. It contributes to children's social learning, to changes in their behaviour 'for the positive', and to *their resilience to be able to respond to changing conditions in their environment* (Malone, 2009, p6).

Fieldwork is a required component of the statutory primary geography curriculum from the Foundation Stage through Key Stages 1 and 2 (DCSF, 2008c; DfEE/QCA, 1999a). While it is not always easy to organise fieldwork, particularly beyond the school's grounds, there is clear endorsement to provide a variety of outdoor learning and fieldwork experiences and activities for children in the government's *Learning outside the classroom manifesto*, which states that:

> We believe that every young person should experience the world beyond the classroom as an essential part of learning and personal development, whatever their age, ability or circumstances.

(DfES, 2006c, p2)

IN THE CLASSROOM

Ofsted (2008a) has described various examples of good practice in fieldwork studies. Two examples are summarised here.

Undertaking fieldwork children completed an audit of the school and grounds to ascertain their sustainability, embedding the work in the eco-school ethos. This work prepared the children for a visit to a landfill site where they considered both the potential hazards at the site and ways to reduce the carbon emissions and improve general recycling facilities in the area. Back in class, the children then used software to manipulate and analyse photographs that they had taken on the fieldtrip and presented their findings to the rest of the school to improve safety on future visits. They produced a safety pamphlet which they presented to the landfill operators and which was subsequently used for other primary schools visiting the site. This gave real meaning and relevance to the trip which was stimulating, inspiring and productive. (pp35–36)

At the start of a topic investigating the pedestrianisation of the local high street children thought primarily of their own interests and attitudes to the idea. It was not until they engaged in meaningful, qualitative fieldwork, conducting surveys and interviews, that they recognised and understood that other people had vested interests in the proposals and began to value these viewpoints. Sketching and photographing the proposed site allowed the children to draw up detailed and annotated maps of the area which they used to argue their case, in different interest groups for and against the proposal. They devised their own risk assessment for their fieldwork by identifying and minimising potential hazards. This gave them a heightened sense of awareness and responsibility for their own well-being and safety. Further work involved them writing up the arguments for and against and submitting them for publication in a local newspaper, so developing their communication and persuasive writing skills. (pp36–37)

REFLECTIVE TASK

Reread the two classroom examples above. Focus on the role of fieldwork in the topics described. What are the elements of good practice in planning for and making use of fieldwork that are described? What was the role of the teacher in the planning? What was the role of the children?

Where to carry out fieldwork

Fieldwork can be undertaken in a wide variety of locations and sites. Figure 7.1 indicates the range of 'nested' distances from school where fieldwork can be located.

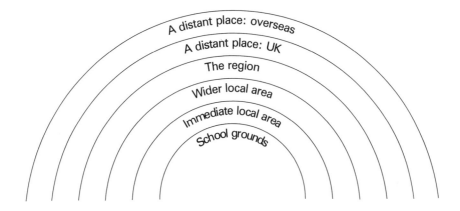

A distant place: overseas
A distant place: UK
The region
Wider local area
Immediate local area
School grounds

Source: Richardson (2004a, p137)

Figure 7.1 Locations for fieldwork activities

Many different sites can be used for fieldwork. Figure 7.2 provides examples of the variety of features and places that might be visited. They vary in type, size and scale. It would be usual to include several different types of features, within one site, in one fieldwork visit. Sites might be chosen to stimulate an enquiry, with the fieldtrip taking place early in the topic. It may occur later, planned by the children, coming at an appropriate point to gather the data desired. It is possible that more than one visit takes place during a geographical enquiry, so that findings from a first visit can be followed up and developed on a later fieldtrip. This is most likely when using the school grounds and the local area of the school.

The school building and grounds
Park, playground, green spaces
Buildings, housing areas and estates
New developments
Local improvement schemes
Shopping parades, streets and malls
Shops, supermarkets, markets
Business park, small businesses
Leisure centre, library, sports facilities
Local services, fire station, police station, doctors' surgery
Roads and pavements, railway station, bus depot, airport
Wasteland
Hills, valleys
Water features, stream/river, pond/lake, reservoir, canal
Sewage works
Refuse depot, rubbish tip, recycling plant
Coast, sea
Woodland, open spaces, country footpaths
City centres, suburbs, villages
Bridges
Rural and city farms, livestock market

Figure 7.2 Some possible sites and features for fieldwork

Usually fieldwork is pre-planned and well organised, for good reasons, but sometimes stimulating out-of-classroom learning occurs spontaneously. It can be as down-to-earth as taking children into the playground and asking them questions such as:

- What can you see?
- What can you hear?
- What does it feel like to be here?
- What do you think happened here yesterday and what might happen tomorrow?
- What changes would you like to see made here?

Fieldwork should be well focused and planned and, if going further afield, children need organised investigations, either teacher-led or from child-generated questions and enquiries. Links can be made to other curriculum areas so that the children have a holistic experience of the area and recognise and appreciate the interrelationships in the environment around them. Connections between geography and history are obvious ones to make (Catling, 2006c; Martin, 2004;).

Fieldwork should develop thinking and feeling and discussion of attitudes and values. It should encourage children to take a fresh and creative look at their environment and enable them to consider explanations for and resolutions to problems. This requires thorough and meaningful preparation, inclusive, innovative and participatory activities and considered, significant follow-up work. It is most effective as part of an enquiry approach where the children have initiated and developed the questions and investigations. Ofsted (2008c) reinforces the importance of preparatory work for successful fieldwork, commending a well-focused lesson in which children analysed photographs and maps of the area that they were to visit, allowing them to draw on their previous geographical knowledge. This enabled them to decide how they would collect and analyse the information on the fieldtrip and to evaluate and draw conclusions from it on their return.

For the youngest children fieldwork will use the nursery and school grounds and into parts of the immediate area. During Key Stages 1 and 2 the area will be widened and older children may travel further distances. This may include for one or more year groups a school journey based in another locality for several days. It is important to give all children a variety of scales to study, for instance taking Foundation Stage children out to a local farm. Similarly, Year 5 or 6 children can study their own locality intensively.

Organising successful fieldwork

Organising fieldwork successfully means that you must take several things into account. Invaluable advice and guidance are provided in various places (e.g. Catling, 2010; Scoffham, 2004). A key website is Learning Outside the Classroom (see end of chapter). The following points are a guide to key considerations and decisions that you need to appreciate and make.

- Check the school's requirements for the adult/pupil ratio for taking children out of your classroom into the grounds and off the school site. This is a health and safety matter which must be adhered to (DfEE, 1998). Adult helpers can be school support staff, parent helpers, governors and anyone else with an up-to-date Criminal Records Bureau (CRB) check.
- Be clear about your objectives for the visit and your expected outcomes. Ensure the work you prepare with and for the children can meet these. Fieldwork must be a meaningful and productive learning experience for the children.
- Organise the class into groups and allocate them particular tasks. This is essential with younger children who need a higher ratio of adults, but its key purpose is to enable children to work together and focus on the tasks they undertake.
- You must undertake a thorough recce and check of the area that you visit, even if it is local. You should carry out a risk assessment (see Table 7.1) to ensure you have considered all eventualities and taken appropriate precautions to minimise risks. Complete your school's risk-assessment proforma. There may already be one for your site but you must check it. If you go to a managed site or field centre, they have partially completed risk-assessment forms you can complete. Doing this, you must consider inclusion, particularly any children who might have difficulties accessing the areas that you visit. You must state how you will provide for them. Involving children in making risk assessments, using photographs and maps alongside their knowledge and common sense, is beneficial.

Table 7.1: Example of risk assessment
Risk assessment
Area to be visited:

Location	Hazard/Event	Risk	Action to be taken to reduce risk	Action to be taken in event of occurrence

Risk coding: L – Low – unlikely to occur; M – Medium – could occur; H – High – could well occur if inadequate caution taken

- The school's Educational Visits Co-ordinator (EVC) should advise and support you and help you complete the necessary paperwork. You may need to complete a school checklist, such as that in Table 7.2, when you go off site.
- Ensure you have the *resources* you need to make the learning experience as effective as possible. As well as the educational resources, such as clipboards, pencils, paper, digital cameras, maps and photographs, you need to have contact numbers for the school, relevant medical information about your children, a list of your helpers, first aid kit and items such as bin liners, collecting boxes, tissues and spare waterproofs.
- After your visit complete an *evaluation* to inform your teaching and planning and to reflect on any lessons learnt and adaptions for future trips. Debriefing and thanking your accompanying adults is also essential.

Table 7.2 School trip details

Off-site school visit details

Date of visit:	Time of departure:	Return time:
Venue:	Telephone no.:	Mobile phone no. of group leader:
Year group:	No. of pupils:	Adult/Pupil ratio:
Group leader:	Accompanying adults:	First Aiders: First Aid Kit:
Transport booked:	Name of coach co.: Name of coach driver:	Risk assessment: Date completed: (Copy attached)
Packed lunch: Lunchtime supervisor notified:	Consent letter sent out: (Copy attached)	Consent forms: Medical information:
Cost per head: Money collected/given to office: Initial payments made:	Resources to take:	Plastic bags, tissues, etc.:
Additional information:		

Bringing the outside in

We cannot go out all the time, but 'learning outside' opportunities can be provided in the classroom. We can introduce children to places and environments that they might not have the opportunity to experience through fieldwork. A story of a cancelled leisure visit to the seaside because it rained, *The inside outing* (Laird, 1994), illustrates imaginatively a way to have an 'outing' and an 'outdoor' adventure 'inside' with young children by being creative with some accessible resources. The children imaginatively create various environments they would have liked to have visited, drawing on their everyday geographies of elsewhere, 'creating' the beach, tropical islands, various sea creatures and adventurous travel using everyday home resources. Such explorations can be recreated in the classroom using ordinary objects, allowing children to experience and articulate through play activities places, activities and feelings that they would not otherwise encounter.

Travel to a new place or environment can be simulated and recreated with, for example, the children buying tickets, showing their passports and boarding an 'aeroplane' – pairs of chairs lining either side of an aisle – to 'fly' to a new destination. This might present an opportunity to discuss the impact of flight, of carbon emissions and alternative forms of transport – perhaps an imitation train carriage or coach could be arranged for an imagined journey. Once the children have reached their 'destination', there are many ways to bring it alive. Resources to use include photographs, photo packs, artefacts, maps, brochures, leaflets, simulated activities on the computer, internet-found information sources, films, audio recordings, food and cooking, music and invited visitors familiar to the area.

REFLECTIVE TASK

Think of somewhere you would like children to visit and experience. How might you create that environment in your classroom? What resources would you need? How would you arrange and organise them? What would children do to help create it? Older children might plan and manage this 'place play' creation for themselves or younger children, identifying the resources they need, where they can obtain them, how they will arrange them, and what they plan to do on arrival in the 'new environment'.

Virtual fieldwork

An alternative approach, when not able to experience somewhere directly, is to use virtual fieldwork. Preparing a series of digital photographs of an area, including specific features you would like the children to focus on, can bring a distant place to life. You can enhance this by encouraging children to superimpose themselves onto the photographs, so that they begin to imagine what it might be like to be there, and what they would see, feel, hear and do in that particular place. They can examine details in the photographs, imagining what is happening, whether it is the powerful erosive force of river water flowing against the outside of the river bend or the ways in which people might be buying and selling items in a market.

Undertaking a fieldtrip and sequencing events can be experienced through the use of hyperlinks on a PowerPoint presentation. Presenting sequential photographs of an environment and having 'stopping-off' places to ask and answer questions can recreate the sense of discovery and exploration on a journey and be highly motivating and engaging. Google Earth and Google's Street View, among many other sources, provide opportunities to access photographs to use to create such 'tours' and investigations (see Appendix 2).

Using photographs

The importance of photographs

Visualisation is a key skill for children to develop their understanding of places, environment, events and lifestyles which they have not seen with their own eyes. It allows them to use their imagination in order to build up their own picture of something or somewhere that they are not able to experience. Some children, for example, may never have been to the coast, so when we talk about cliffs they may not have any visual image of them. We need to help children 'see' phenomena through photographs, diagrams, film, and so on to provide them with opportunities to observe, interpret and make meaning out of images, developing their understanding of the world around them. Mackintosh (2004) notes that just as we interpret meaning from written words (literacy), spoken words (oracy) and numbers (numeracy), we interpret meaning through pictorial forms of spatial information (graphicacy). Graphicacy often receives less recognition and attention, yet it is a very potent, indeed essential and effective, skill to develop, particularly to enhance use and critical awareness of our increasingly visual forms of communication.

Research indicates that rather than seeing pictures holistically, younger children perceive the different parts as apparently disconnected details and need to learn how to see both the parts and the whole picture, as well as to 'read' and appreciate scale and dimension. There is progression in the interpretation of images from very young children who identify mainly the 'big' details to more sophisticated, merged and holistic understanding of the whole picture by Year 6 (Mackintosh, 2004).

Using photographs

When children look at photographs they ask questions to understand more about what they see, what is going on, and why it looks the way it does. Photographs are a snapshot and need to be 'read' carefully to consider what might have happened before or comes after. Consequently, children ask questions to fill in the gaps. It may be that no specific answer can be given. It is the discussion and the asking of effective questions that allows the development of observational and interpretational skills (Bowles, n.d.).

Many activities can be used with children to enable them to 'see' and interrogate photographs. An effective initial stimulus is to give them a photograph and encourage them to ask questions about it, as Figure 7.3 below illustrates, writing the questions in speech bubbles around it.

Figure 7.3 Asking questions of a photograph

The following four approaches to using photographs indicate further possibilities. Photographs for these activities can be ones you have taken in the school grounds, the local environment or somewhere else that you have been. They can be selected from a pack of photographs produced for the study of a UK or non-UK locality.

- Ranking photographs. Use straightforward criteria such as like/dislike, or more sophisticated criteria such as damaged/improved environments. Ask the children to explain their decisions.
- Captioning photographs. Children either match captions provided to photographs or create captions for photographs which capture their essence and context and demonstrate their understanding of what is shown.
- Stimulate a story. Give the children a scene and ask them to write about what happened before and what might happen next, weaving geographical vocabulary and understanding into their story and keeping their tale as realistic as possible.
- Where is it? Show photographs of views and scenes in one particular urban or rural environment in the UK or elsewhere. Ask children to say where they think they show and to justify their choice. At the end explain that the photographs show the same place, though there seem to be various different features, views and activities which the children associated with different places.

Short, focused excerpts from films and videos can be effective ways to enhance children's virtual experience and allow them to visualise places and scenes that would otherwise remain inaccessible. Television programmes about journeys around or to distinctive areas of the world, about natural processes and spectacular events or about particular places and environmental issues are excellent sources of high quality visual geography. You might use programmes made to support children's geographical learning. An effective approach is to watch short, selected parts of a film or video and then discuss and interpret what has been viewed. Film introduces dimensions and senses that photographs do not, such as the sounds and dynamism of a place or the processes occurring during a river flood, the building of a shop or road, or the impact of an event or development on a place. Animations can be informative about processes such as river erosion and deposition and of the sequence of events in an earthquake or volcanic eruption.

Photographs and films have their limitations, because they are chosen, edited media. We need to be wary that children do not assume or take away images that the whole of the continent of Africa, for instance, is as depicted in the few photographs of a village or city that they have seen. Visual images can be powerful creators of negative stereotypes if all children see, via the television 'special' or Oxfam/ActionAid/Save the Children 'appeal', is a view of poverty, shanty settlements, arid lands or war-torn places. It is vital that children see a representative and versatile range of different photographs and types of footage, showing the considerable range and variety of life.

In the Classroom

A group of Year 1 children discussed with their teaching assistant the different features, animals and activities shown in three photographs of a farmer feeding his cattle. Children used their awareness of 'farms' and what farmers do, from stories that had been read and seen, to describe what the farmer was doing in the photographs and to sequence the photographs in the correct order.

Using artefacts

Using artefacts helps to bring places and people's lives alive. Geographical artefacts are the items that we can collect from places we visit daily or on holiday which are in daily use, such as postcards, local newspapers and street maps, but they include a variety of other items (see Figure 7.4). Artefacts allow children to touch, feel and even smell things and so get a sense of what they are like *in situ*, introducing a wider range of senses. Using and interpreting artefacts is a popular and effective teaching strategy in historical enquiry (Hoodless, 2008). Similar approaches can be used in geography. Asking questions of the artefact, discussing what its use is or might be, what it tells us about the activities in a place, who does or might use it, how it got there, and so on, are all important questions in the search to find out more about the place it came from. Artefacts are an invaluable component of the study of local and distant places, allowing children to engage with places, affording them a fuller, overall picture of what life is or might be like to live there. (Catling, 2009c, p194)

Photographs taken in the area
Postcards
Tourist brochures and guides
Local newspapers
Local street, tourist and other maps
Ordnance Survey maps
Bus, coach and rail timetables
Tea towels and other mementoes showing the area
Restaurant and take-away shop menus
Items made locally
Paper and plastic bags provided by local shops
Shop till receipts of purchases
Food ingredients and samples
'Home' items, e.g. cooking utensils
Clothes
Local directories
Advertising leaflets and posters
Local parish or council magazines
Rock samples
Local publications, factual, stories and poetry
Other collectable items, such as sheep's wool

Figure 7.4 Examples of 'geographical' artefacts

REFLECTIVE TASK

Drawing on the points made about the value and role of photographs, make a list of reasons why 'geographical' artefacts are important resources for studying places and environments and what children might learn about a place by using them.

Using maps

The value of maps

Making and using maps and plans are fundamental components of good geography teaching and learning. The interpretation of maps is one of the essential skills that children should develop. Wiegand (n.d.) states: *whether conventional or digital they [maps and atlases] capture the essence of geography more than any other resource*. Maps allow children to record and pass on information about places that they know and to 'read' an environment which they cannot visit. Maps are selective but still provide very considerable amounts of useful information remarkably concisely.

Essentially maps show what is where. They provide information about the features or places they show, or the themes they portray, such as damage to environments. They show the spatial layout, distribution and pattern of these features. From maps we are used to, such as local and national street maps, we can see where places are and the road networks connecting them. We can find our way around, something which increasingly Sat Nav devices also help us do. We can develop, from a large-scale Ordnance Survey map, an idea of what may be in a place – a pub or a post office – whether it is small or large and, perhaps, what type of place it might be, a coastal resort, an industrial area, etc. As we learn to 'read' and interpret the map we may also be able to develop a sense of what a place may be like and plan what we might do there, for instance, on holiday. We can use maps to indicate how we might like somewhere to look in the future. They can help us make predictions of the impact of particular activities on places and the people who live there, such as the building of a new road or housing estate.

Map use and making enables children to learn how to describe where they are and to record information in an accessible way. Children can use maps to plan and record routes around the classroom, the school, or to and from school and elsewhere. As they develop these skills, children encounter maps from the globe and atlas maps to maps of their country and local area. Effective use of maps, whether creating or interpreting them, allows children to understand better the world around them and develop their sense of place and relative location within it.

IN THE CLASSROOM

A Year 3 class used a large uncluttered picture map of a rural area to develop their awareness of maps and what they communicate. The children worked in groups of three, using a large sheet of sugar paper and a set of felt pens. They numbered themselves 1, 2 and 3. First, the #1 from each group came out to look at the picture map, observing it carefully for a minute. They returned to their groups and described what they had seen, with #2 drawing what #1 described for two minutes. Next #2 came out and repeated the observation for one minute looking at what was on the map that had not been included. #2 returned to the group and gave #3 further information to draw for two minutes. Finally, #3 to went out, repeating the process, with #1 drawing for one minute. The completed maps were displayed. The children discussed what they had done and how their map looked, what they found easy and difficult, and so forth. They discussed the features of the area, its spatial layout and what sort of place it was.

Different types of maps

There are myriad types of maps. These are just a sample of the range. What they have in common is that they show what is where.

- Picture maps.
- Street maps and road atlases.
- Ordnance Survey maps.
- Architect's plans.
- Sketch maps.
- Shopping centre plans.
- Atlas maps.
- National and continental wall maps.
- Thematic maps.
- Globes.
- Old, 'historical' maps.
- Postcard maps.
- Tourist fold-out and brochure maps.
- Bus and railway maps.
- Shipping charts.
- Maps in newspapers and on websites.
- Maps in board and virtual games.

To these you can add:

- Satellite images.
- Aerial photographs, vertical and oblique.

PRACTICAL TASK PRACTICAL TASK **PRACTICAL TASK** PRACTICAL TASK **PRACTICAL TASK**

Build up a collection of as many different types of maps as possible. Use the list above as a guide, but extend it. Create a display of them in class to discuss what maps are like, what they show, how they show places, information and feelings. This might be a settling-down or circle-time activity, not necessarily part of a geography topic.

Map skills

There are a number of characteristics of maps which children need to be introduced to so that they can learn to use them effectively (Wiegand, 2006). By doing so they develop various map skills, such as using a map key to interpret the symbols or using a grid reference to find a location. These skills need to be developed through active experience using maps both outside and in the classroom in place and environment based tasks.

Symbols: including shapes, lines and colours to show the variety of features and networks on maps. Symbols can help to avoid clutter on maps. They can be informed by words and numbers, e.g. street names and contour heights. Initially symbols may be pictorial, only later with plan shapes and more abstract symbols being used, as children come across these on commercial maps. Children enjoy devising and using their own symbols. Do remind them to make their symbols 'accessible' for others to understand so that it is clear what is shown on the map. Children must be encouraged to provide 'keys' for their maps.

Location: stating where features are on maps and finding your way around the map. Initially using phrases such as 'next to' or 'beside' provide relative locational information. Later children learn to use alphanumeric grids, development of which can be linked with mathematics, moving to increasing complexity with four and six-figure grid references used on Ordnance Survey maps.

Direction: encompassing relative direction such as behind, in front, left, etc., and cardinal directions, such as north, southeast and so on. Children can be unsure of directions. It is a useful ice-breaker and reinforcement to have children go to different parts of the room or playground (north, south, east and west) according to their name or some other criterion. It helps to build awareness and knowledge. Continue to familiarise the children with the points of the compass using a compass and compass rose (increasing complexity with age to include the 4, 8 and even 16 points of the compass) to which they can refer, allowing them to construct an habitual sense of direction. Always encourage the use of correct and accurate directional vocabulary to describe and locate directions and places.

Scale: a vital understanding allowing places to 'fit' onto the map as well as to give an accurate idea of the size of features and places and their distance in relation to each other. Children should be encouraged to think about relative scale and relative size and distance to begin with, then move on to measurements and absolute scales. This is a difficult concept for young children and needs to be built up gradually, with clear and obvious scales initially, becoming increasingly fine as children's skills develop. Useful links are effectively made with mathematics.

A variety of maps can be used with all children at all ages. Foundation Stage and Year 1 children can be introduced to the globe and an outline world map where the focus is on the major shapes and areas, such as the continents and oceans, the names of which can be introduced. They can also use a simple plan of their room spaces and walk around noting what is in the room, relating it to what is shown on the plan. With children in Year 3, plans, street maps, atlases and globes may all feature, as they will with Year 6 children in their studies. What develops over the period of their learning is a move from using relative directions to compass directions, from relative sizes and distances to measures and scales. It is the increasing complexity and demand that is made, alongside the use of greater awareness and knowledge of places and environments to be able to interpret more from maps and to make their own maps more appropriately relevant to their topics. Young children will identify and talk about features, while older primary children should be noticing patterns on maps, such as the distribution of fields around a village or the network of streets in a suburb. Wiegand (2006) provides a detailed account of the development of younger children's map understanding and of approaches to teaching.

The same approach is appropriate with children being introduced to and using aerial photographs. Both oblique aerial photographs – showing the view from above but looking down at an angle – and vertical aerial photographs – where the area is shown looking down directly from overhead, as in a map – can be introduced in the Foundation Stage, where children can identify features they see and recognise, particularly if the aerial photograph shows their school and the area round about at a large scale. Large-scale aerial photographs should be used throughout the primary school, with demands increasing on children to find features on both oblique and vertical photographs and to relate the two to each other and to simple and, later, Ordnance Survey maps. Children can use aerial photographs alongside local and other maps to look at patterns, to identify information the map does not show, such as vehicles on the road and car park use. They can consider the time of year and look for changes shown by comparing the two sources.

The use of maps and aerial photographs should always be linked with other aspects of study, such as an enquiry in the local area into a particular topic or concern or into another locality (which might be found on Google Earth), or related to a particular environmental theme or issue. Children should use them alongside ground level photographs and the other information that is available, so that by connecting photographs and information with what is shown on maps, they gain deeper insight into how a place is today, how it may have developed in the past and what it might become like in the future.

Using maps with children

Introduce young children to 'plan view' by looking down on familiar objects in their class-room and playground, photographing and drawing these, full size and in reduced size. Such photographs or plans of features in class and around school can be given to children to find. Children might be asked to imagine what a feature they cannot look down on looks like from above, such as their playground or a school building and to draw a plan of it. This might be compared with an aerial photograph or a map. These activities can be part of a topic on 'exploring how our school looks', as one of the 'angles' at which to look at the school. While using teacher-prepared and commercially available maps with children, it is equally impor-tant for them to create their own plans and maps whenever possible. This develops their mapping skills, helping them to recognise how maps work and how important they are in communicating information that we want to get across. Starting with simple plans of the classroom and using them to navigate their way around helps to develop several mapwork skills. Working in small groups, they can make their own plan and get each other to follow it,

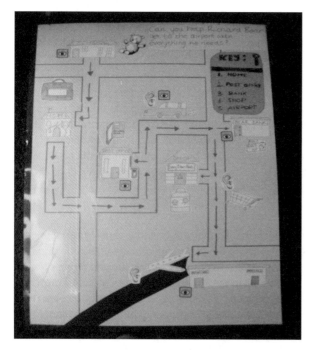

developing accuracy and clarity. Similarly, children can make their own maps from information about their local area or another place they study. Roberts (2003) argues that children should also be encouraged to use 'affective mapping', recording their feel-ings about particular places and environments.

Trails are an excellent way of engaging children and devel-oping their orientation and mapwork skills (Figure 7.5). These can be designed for any level and can include clues to be found in order to complete the trail. Trail maps can be informative and also explore emotional responses.

Figure 7.5 A handmade trail for children to follow looking for clues in the local area

Using a more '3-D' approach, map-lines and journey sticks can be used. Map-lines originate from the Native American Indian tradition of collecting memorable natural objects such as leaves from a specific tree, stones from a river bed and grasses from a meadow and tying them onto a piece of string so that the journey can be remembered and retraced on the way back. Children can go on a similar journey in the school grounds, their local area or further afield, collecting objects on the way to remind them of where they have been. It might be that these objects are less natural and include crisp packets, old rail tickets and so on. For younger children, it is easier and more rewarding to use a piece of card with some sticky tape, onto which they can stick their memorable objects. As well as string, sticks can be used, with children encouraged to choose a stick that they like from a wooded area and stick their objects onto those, hence a 'journey stick' (Whittle, 2006).

As children's map skills develop, they can begin to use increasingly complex maps with more detail and can also begin to use more sophisticated vocabulary, referring to the points of the compass, grid references and scale (Bridge, 2004; Catling, n.d.). This will give them increasing access to a wider range of different maps which they can use in conjunction with local area studies, understanding the locational context of places, patterns and processes in the environment and of distant place and global themes.

IN THE CLASSROOM

A Year 4 class used maps to become more aware of their school grounds. Working in small groups they were given three or four different photographs. In their classroom they discussed where they thought each photograph was taken. They were given a map and sent out to find the different locations/features shown on the photographs in the grounds, which used and developed their observational skills. On the map they marked where the photograph was taken from, the direction of view, and anything that had changed since it was taken. They used a digital camera to take a similar photograph. Returning to class, they located their retaken photographs on a prepared map of the school grounds on the computer, noting its orientation and listing changes. Displaying the whole map on the interactive whiteboard, they discussed the changes they found as a class and identified similarities and patterns in their findings.

In cross-curricular contexts, maps can be an excellent enhancement to stories (Bridge, n.d.). Drawing maps and plans, children can create an imagined world for their stories. Many storybooks have a map or a plan of their imagined world and these can be read and shown to stimulate children's imagination. Classic examples include Katie Morag's adventures, *Treasure Island*, and *Winnie the Pooh*. Children might draw maps for those stories which do not include a map, interpreting and describing the environment. In history enquiries into how the local area has changed over time requires the use of old maps. The use of local large-scale maps and of the relevant Cassini maps can be particularly effective here. Atlas maps will be used in studies of other times and places.

PRACTICAL TASK PRACTICAL TASK PRACTICAL TASK PRACTICAL TASK PRACTICAL TASK

Create your own affective map of your local area using the information at the following website and consider how to adapt this for different ages of children.

www.geography.org.uk/projects/valuingplaces/cpdunits/thinkmaps/#924

New technologies for geography

There have been and will continue to be considerable advances in the provision and range of new technologies supporting geographical learning. Two areas that have benefited particularly from the plethora of software and hardware are mapwork and fieldwork. The use of digital cameras, videos and other mobile technology, such as hand-held digital recorders and mobile phones, have created great advances not only in the efficacy of the work but also in the children's engagement and interaction with their own learning. This has allowed them to connect with what they are doing and become excited about doing it. A variety of sources for maps and ground and aerial photographs are now available. Some are referred to in Appendix 2. Others are included in the list of websites in Appendix 3. Software, such as *Local Studies*, which can be used to create maps, is also available. You can keep up to date with developments through the websites for the Geographical Association, Geography Teaching Today, and the Staffordshire Learning Net, as well as through *Primary Geographer*. There is a variety of good advice provided by Rodgers and Streluk (2002), Pickford (2006) and Williams and Easingwood (2007). Sources for applied contexts include Sharp et al. (2007) and Barber et al. (2007).

A new area to explore involves the use of new technologies at personal and societal levels to record information and to enable communication, such as mobile phone photography. This raises questions about not just using new technologies in geographical learning but of investigating their impact as geographical topics. One example would be the nature of communications locally and globally through email and related systems, text messaging and the use of Facebook and MySpace-type websites. Another is the nature, purpose and ubiquity of surveillance in society, provided through the use of overt and hidden cameras in shops, high streets and along roads across the nation, as well as the capacity to locate individuals through the use of the mobile phone signal network. Technologies are not only tools to use; they are used to respond to and shape our interests and lives as consumers – a point not lost on the national supermarkets with their interconnected computer systems linking stores, warehouses and production companies, to ensure the goods people 'want' are in the stores when they 'need' them. As a growing element in our everyday geographies we must investigate their impact in primary geography as well as use them.

REFLECTIVE TASK

Consider how advancing technology is enhancing children's geographical thinking. The link below could help to get you started.

/www.geography.org.uk/projects/gtip/orientationpieces/usingict1/#top

A SUMMARY OF **KEY POINTS**

This chapter has:

> **advocated the importance of outdoor learning and fieldwork in geography and outlined approaches to organising fieldwork;**

> **provided ideas for carrying out fieldwork and developing relevant skills both outside and inside school through virtual means;**

> considered the importance of photographs, film, artefacts and maps in geographical learning, and outlined some approaches;

> noted opportunities for using new technologies.

MOVING *ON* > > > > > > MOVING *ON* > > > > > > MOVING *ON*

When you are next in school find out how often children work outside the classroom and undertake fieldwork. Which geographical studies do they undertake fieldwork in? To what extent do they use maps and photographs outside the classroom as well as in class in geographical and other studies? When and how are artefacts used in geography teaching? What role do new technologies and ICT play?

FURTHER READING FURTHER READING **FURTHER READING** FURTHER READING

The following books provide further insight and ideas about fieldwork, mapwork, and the use of photographs and ICT.

Council for Learning Outside the Classroom (2008) *Out and about guidance*. www.lotc.org.uk/out-and-about-guidance

Hoodless, P, Bermingham, S, McCreery, E, and Bowen, P (2009) *Teaching Humanities in Primary Schools*. Exeter: Learning Matters.

Pickford, T (2006) *Learning ICT in the humanities*. London: David Fulton.

Scoffham, S (ed) (2004) *Primary geography handbook*. Sheffield: Geographical Association.

Wiegand, P (2006) *Learning and teaching with maps*. London: Routledge.

Look for further teaching approaches in issues of *Primary Geographer*.

Useful websites

Council for Learning Outside the Classroom
    www.lotc.org.uk
Geographical Association
    www.geography.org.uk/
Geography Teaching Today
    www.geographyteachingtoday.org.uk/
Google Earth
    http://earth.google.com/
Ordnance Survey maps
    www.ordnancesurvey.co.uk/oswebsite/getamap/
Real World Learning
    www.field-studies-council.org/campaigns/rwl/index.aspx
Staffordshire Learning Net
    www.sln.org.uk/geography/

8
In the beginning: geographical learning in the Early Years Foundation Stage

Chapter objectives

By the end of this chapter you should:

- be aware of the 'geographical' aspects of the Early Learning Goals in 'Knowledge and understanding of the world';
- have explored a variety of play approaches and activities which support young children's geographical learning;
- know of activities to use to develop young children's understanding of place and sustainability.

This chapter addresses the following Professional Standards for QTS:

Q1, Q10, Q14, Q15.

Introduction

This chapter explores opportunities available in the Early Years Foundation Stage, in nursery environments and classes, to enhance young children's geographical experiences and understanding. A key element of provision and practice in the Foundation Stage is play, which lies at the heart of the learning environment inside and outside (Bilton, 2005; Bruce, 2001, 2005; DCSF, 2008c; White, 2008). The play environment, its space and resources, its accessibility and its planned use are central to developing early geographical learning. This is enabled and supported through the Early Learning Goals, particularly 'Knowledge and understanding of the world', which includes a geographical dimension, though some aspects are covered in other goals.

The 'future' starts here!

Geography is not directly mentioned in the Early Learning Goals but the premise of various elements in 'Knowledge and understanding of the world' is that the *child is a young geographer* (Owen and Ryan, 2001). A variety of evidence was outlined in Chapter 2 showing that very young children develop their geographical and environmental awareness from their very earliest years, through their everyday geographies. They bring this developing and evolving background into the Early Years setting at 2, 3 and 4 years old. Their early lives have been lived in places, and place lies very much *at the heart of children's geographical understanding* (Milner, 1996, p7). This provides a strong rationale for developing their geographical experience during the Foundation Stage (Conway et al., 2008; Cooper, 2004a; Heal and Cook, 1998; Martin, 1995; Martin and Owens, 2004; Milner, 1996, 1997; Palmer and Birch, 2004; Spink et al., 2008). Several good reasons underpin this.

- *Children's play experience*: Children's experiences of and in places, and of their features, is enhanced through providing a variety of play and other learning opportunities in the nursery indoor and outdoor areas. The nursery environment becomes a part of their everyday and personal geographies.

- *Children's direct experience*: Taking young children into the local area to walk interesting routes and visit particular places to discover more about them and make use of them develops their experience of real places, enhancing their personal geography.
- *Children's imaginations*: Reading a variety of story and other books to and with children, which introduce them to a wider range of places and environmental matters, develops their awareness of their own places and brings new places to them, particularly where stories focus on events and people's lives and activities.
- *Children's mental maps*: Children's play and exploration in the nursery, as well as through guided walks locally, supports the development of their awareness of places as the foundation of their 'mental maps'. This is vital for understanding how our world works, for way finding and for understanding pictures, maps and artefacts.
- *Children's awareness of the 'wider world'*: Young children's knowledge of the world about them and further afield, of people's lives in places and of environments will be partial, inaccurate, even stereotypical and biased. This is expected, since their experience is very limited and evolving. Misunderstandings and prejudices can become embedded at an early age. Through play, activities and talk, children may exhibit their understandings and feelings, which can be responded to and tackled.
- *Children's curiosity and sense of wonder*: Young children are naturally curious about the world around them. We can encourage their asking of questions and provide opportunities and resources to respond to them. We should foster their fascination with the world, their sense of awe at the new places they encounter, at the variety and incredible nature of the natural world, as well at people, their lives and activities, landscapes, features and urban environments.
- *Children's active participation*: Their experience of and engagement with the world at hand should be active, through helping to look after and put away the resources used daily. It can occur through discussion and choices about which place and environmental activities to undertake. It can involve suggesting ways to enhance activities in the nursery outdoor area. Children learn through active participation in contributing to decisions that affect their environment.

IN THE CLASSROOM

A group of 3- and 4-year-old children were read and shown the story, *Rosie's walk* (Hutchins, 1992) by their nursery assistant (QCA, 2005). They talked about the characters and the farmyard shown in the pictures. Several of the children had seen farmyards in other stories and on television. They were encouraged to recognise the locational language in the story. They went outside to enact the story. The assistant retold *Rosie's walk*, encouraging the children to act out the different roles as they went around the outside area, pretending that various features were different parts of the farmyard scene. This resulted in much merriment as the children tried to imitate Rosie's 'journey' and her encounters. When the re-enactment was completed, the assistant used a variety of relative positional and distance language to involve the children in looking around the outdoor area, so that they began to use terms such as 'beside', 'behind' and 'close to'.

PRACTICAL TASK PRACTICAL TASK PRACTICAL TASK PRACTICAL TASK PRACTICAL TASK

Find a suitable storybook to read to 3–4 or 4–5 year old children based in a place or an environment. Try *We're going on a bear hunt* (Rosen and Oxenbury, 1993), *Not so fast Songololo* (Daly, 1987), *Babylon* (Patton Walsh, 1992) or *The lighthouse keeper's lunch* (Armitage and Armitage, 1994) (see Appendix 1).

Consider how you would use it to develop one or more activities for young children to do. Which 'geographical' and 'environmental' language would you encourage the children to practise and understand through a play activity?

Knowledge and understanding of the world

The Foundation Stage recognises that young children learn about the world around them through exploration, from their family and friends, through the media and the places they visit through what they see, hear, smell and touch. The Early Learning Goal 'Knowledge and understanding of the world' (DCSF, 2008b) encompasses some of the basic aspects of scientific, technological, historical, geographical and social awareness and understanding, as well as the skills, values and attitudes associated with these areas. It encompasses ideas to do with places, the environment and communities and helps develop the foundations of young children's geographical learning. There are three geographical dimensions in 'Knowledge and understanding of the world' for young children:

1. encountering accurate information about the world, including about how people live, various ways of life, its processes and the local neighbourhood;
2. learning to value and respect people, to develop caring and positive attitudes, and to avoid developing negative views and ideas of others and the environment;
3. making investigations and explorations to find out about their world, and to begin to learn to apply the knowledge, understanding and skills they gain.

The various aspects of geographical learning are set out in the *Practice guidance for the Early Years Foundation Stage* (DCSF, 2008c, pp77–89). They are supported by elements in each of the other Early Learning Goals. Drawing on reviews of children's developing geographical and environmental awareness during their early years (see Chapter 3 above; Catling, 2006b, p72), it can be argued that two further 'early learning goals' should be included, because they are invariably aspects of children's experience. These 'goals' draw on children's 'world awareness' at an early age (see Cooper, 2004a; Glauert et al., 2003; Palmer and Birch, 2004) and support those goals that explore cultural awareness and environmental feelings. Young children should:

4. find out about the world they inhabit, its varied environments and the lives and activities of peoples in places similar to and different from their own;
5. find out and talk about environmental concerns and ways to care for the environment.

REFLECTIVE TASK

Refer to the section on 'The youngest children coming into school' in Chapter 3. Consider how the Early Learning Goals for 'Knowledge and understanding of the world' reflect and build on young children's geographical understanding. Is it justifiable to add two further goals?

Young children, geography and play

Learning through play is vital to children's effective early learning (e.g. Bruce, 2001; 2005; DCSF, 2008c; Filer, 2008; Wood and Attfield, 2005). Play offers children opportunities to develop their sense of their world but it requires contexts within which children can *explore, develop and represent their learning experiences* (DCSF, 2008c, p7). Both physical and virtual places, such as those in Table 8.1, can be such play contexts for young children, providing opportunities to play out aspects of their place and environmental experience.

Table 8.1 Environmental contexts for geographical play

Play environments	Context of geographical play	Examples of environments
Real environments	Places which are part of the 'normal' or adult environment, used by people of many ages and not necessarily intended for children's play or other use. They are sites which children may subvert or manipulate for play activities.	Rooms, gardens, playgrounds, parks, the beach, waste/derelict land, overgrown areas, woodlands, fields, paths/alleys, streets, shopping malls, garage plots, car parks, 'out-of-the-way' spaces in playgrounds and around buildings.
Miniature environments	Places designed for younger children to play in, adapted to younger children's sizes. Places created for play and games rather than for physical exercise.	Playgrounds, adventure play areas. Child-sized buildings, 'forts', walk-ways, playground street markings, with cars, pushchairs. Small-scale furniture: tables, chairs, cookers, cupboards, beds, and 'home' equipment such as cutlery, crockery, cooking utensils, model foods.
Toy environments	'Small-world' play equipment. These can be realistic and replicate the world children see or can be fanciful. Their role is to enable children to create their own 'real' and imagined places.	Model buildings, furniture, equipment, people, animals. Place/environment playmates, road layouts, buildings, street furniture, vehicles, people, trees, fences, domestic and farm animals, railway tracks and rolling stock.
Virtual environments	'Places' created using computer software for children. These might be based on TV or film animations or created to be explored, 'inhabited' or played within by children, and to which they might be able to add features from sets of icons.	Simulated 'real' places, fantasy 'worlds'. Pictograms to move and position in extant 'worlds' or to create new places and scenes.

Source: Adapted from Catling, 2006b, pp69–70

Children make sense of their place and environmental experiences through a variety of means. The areas of learning and development in the Early Learning Goals illustrate that children learn through sensory experience as much as through the journeys they make with their families, through their imitations of adult activities they observe as much as through their physical exploration of places they are allowed some freedom of movement within, and through their own imaginative play with models as much as through sources such as television and stories. Table 8.2 outlines five aspects of play that support geographical learning (Catling, 2006b).

Table 8.2 Five aspects of place play that support young children's geographical learning

Aspects of play	Opportunities to support children's geographical learning	Geographical illustrations
Sensory play	• Encounters and examinations of the environment through the senses: sight, touch, sound, smell, (taste), mobility.	• feeling the texture of natural and built features; • identifying different types of smell in the locality, and their source; • discriminating different sounds locally and their sources; • cooking/eating different foods from various parts of the world; • talking about favourite and disliked places locally, elsewhere and from stories and television programmes.
Exploratory play	• Movement about the environment to develop spatial awareness. • Investigating places to find out what is there, in familiar and new places.	• in the outdoor area, journeys around road layouts and obstacle courses; • journeys to the local playground or park, to shops and other sites; • talking about play areas, seeing what shops sell and asking why and to whom, buying resources for cooking; • using a simple map to locate places in relation to each other in school and beyond.
Imitative play	• Role play used to begin to grasp ways that adults act in and use places and what is in them.	• use of free imaginative play in the 'home bay' set up as a type of place, e.g. a shop, hut, etc; • role-playing staff and customers in a layout for a bus, aeroplane, etc.; • being people debating what to do with waste items, the use of an empty shop, about cutting down trees, etc.; • pretend play as children/adults in their own and other communities locally and across the world; • setting up a play building or tent for free-play activities.
Representational play	• Model making, drawing and writing involved in activities in places, to recreate them and to extend the play.	• using play mats to make journeys and identify routes and activities; • using pictures, maps and aerial photographs to find objects/features in and outside; • making drawings of objects and features in and out of school; • using toys to make models of places, locally and imaginatively and to people them with activities.
Fantasy play	• Creation of imagined places and environments, realistic or fantastical, which might be acted out, drawn or written about.	• using play materials and toys to make buildings, sites, etc., for free play; • using natural and artificial materials in the outdoor area to create features and places for imaginative play.

Source: Catling, 2006b, p68

PRACTICAL TASK PRACTICAL TASK PRACTICAL TASK PRACTICAL TASK PRACTICAL TASK

Use Tables 8.1 and 8.2 to plan a play-based activity for a group of 4- or 5-year-old children. How will you organise the activity? Which aspects of geographical learning are you introducing to children? What resources will you need?

The 'outside classroom'

The outdoor area is a vital learning environment for young children. The essence of a good outdoor area is the variety of environments for the children to use (Bilton, 2005), including:

- a creative area, for painting, rubbings, music making, craft activities and other such activities;
- a quiet area with seats and shelters, books and pictures;
- an environmental play area where there are a wide variety of resources including a sandpit and water tray; model vehicles and buildings, toy animals and people; path or road markings, mobile child-size buildings or building fronts painted on walls, wheeled vehicles, and similar play resources; ground to dig, and a garden area to grow plants in; a wild area and natural objects to make things with;
- an open space area with equipment to make off-the-ground climbing, balancing, swinging, sliding, etc. activities, with small apparatus.

Outdoor areas such as these reflect the Reggio Emilia approach to young children's experience and learning in pre-school environments (Cadwell, 1997; Thornton and Brunton, 2007). The message is that, as high quality environments and places in themselves, much can and should be made of and developed in the outdoors within this secure and safe setting. These areas have much potential for geographical learning, through investigations, exploring, making and building, enacting and role play, small-toy play, the use of language, imagination and much more. These activities are not exclusive to particular outdoor 'spaces'. Creativity can occur in any one of them through imaginative role play or the use of laid-out apparatus, which might as readily be the source for explorations and investigations as might the wild area, a street scene or a set of photographs.

The use of play implies that children have both the right and opportunities to make choices about their activities outdoors (and inside). These choices are constructed by the resources available to children, what is provided on the day and how it is set up. Permanent features such as climbing frames and small-scale huts can be used regularly for environmentally oriented play. When provided with a variety of 'environmental' toys children have the chance to direct their own learning in relation to the event, place and environmental experiences they have had or imagine.

OUTSIDE THE CLASSROOM

In the nursery sandpit two 4-year-olds used a variety of toy vehicles and buildings. They moulded the sand to create smoothed out 'roads'. One child used a bus to make journeys, stopping at points along the 'road' to pick up passengers. After a while both children began to put buildings alongside their 'roads'. The other child parked two cars and a van by the 'homes' he had placed. They both played close by each other and became so engrossed that they ran their vehicles along each other's 'roads', moving around each other to play in the larger area. This overlapping activity became a co-operative activity when they added new roads and buildings to join up and extend their 'town'. At different times they concentrated on each other's homes and cars for people to make journeys to go to the shops and the garage.

REFLECTIVE TASK

REFLECTIVE TASK

Consider the activity in which the two 4-year-olds were involved. It was not a structured activity but was initiated by them. How did their play in the sandpit support their geographical learning? What was the role of the resources in this play? If the nursery staff had intervened, how might they have enhanced or inhibited the learning?

Activities for early geographical learning

Providing opportunities for geographical learning means setting up areas with particular resources, inside or outside, organising particular activities in specific bays, choosing the focus of the story to be read, and observing and spending time with particular children to encourage their learning in a specific direction. There is much advice on the range of geographical activities that can be provided in the nursery environment (Ashbridge, 2006; Conway et al., 2008; Cooper, 2004a; Glauert et al., 2003; Heal and Cook, 1998; Martin and Owens, 2008; Milner, 1996, 1997; Owens, 2004a, 2004b; Salaman and Tutchell, 2005; Simco, 2003; Thwaites, 2008). These examples illustrate indoor and outside activities and a journey into the locality. Figure 8.1 below outlines other activities to use or adapt.

The view from the window

Inspired by Jeannie Bakers' (1992, 2004) books *Window* and *Belonging*, create a large window frame on a wall. Use cut-out drawings to create a scene viewed through the window. Every day or two introduce a change to the scene, e.g. a building added or something removed. Children might make the new features. Continue until the view has changed very much. At different points in the 'development', discuss with the children what is happening. Take photographs of the changing window view. Use these to talk about the changes that have taken place, showing children the changing views over time. This approach helps young children to see what is changing in a place and how those changes have an impact. They can talk about why the changes are happening and what they feel about them. As the area develops, different children might become 'residents' in the new development, giving them a stake in their views on environmental change. Later, arrange a proposal to make another change which they must discuss and agree before it can be made. What will their views be? Will they all agree? Why will they hold the views they do?

'In the den'

Children love dens and places they can make into their own 'bases' in bushes or woods, in alcoves or under stairwells in or outside buildings (Tovey, 2007; White, 2008). While the nursery area may not provide such opportunities, there may be a 'play hut', small-scale 'buildings' or tents that children can use as play spaces for imaginative games, or crates, boxes, frames and drapes which with adults they can use to create dens (Cooper, 2004b). These should be allowed to be the children's own 'secret places' (Dixon and Day, 2004). A variety of 'home' resources, such as furniture, crockery and cutlery and toys, can be provided for the children to use in their play hut or den, but they must decide what to use. Children can be encouraged to talk about what they play, perhaps even to take digital photographs of their special place and activities, though they may be reluctant to let adults into their world. The adults responsible for supervision can provide prompts and ideas to extend the children's own 'den' play, to encourage photographing it across the year, talk about how to care for it, and discuss ways the children might improve it. It can be a source for role play, for storytelling and modelling, to *show me what it is like because I cannot go in there*, or a context for talking about how it 'feels like home' and 'what I like about it', exploring ideas about a sense of place at a young child's scale.

Going to the park

Taking children out of the nursery and school area is always stimulating. Various possibilities can be pursued in the local urban or rural environment (Conway et al., 2008; Milner, 1996; Salaman and Tatchell, 2005; Simco, 2003; Thwaites, 2008). Walking to the local park or play area offers several possibilities for young children to observe and use appropriate vocabulary to name features and discuss what they see along the street and in the park or play area.

- Focus on the children's view of the 'world', at their eye-level. Features can be noticed, including street names; service covers in the pavement; entrances to drives and gardens; fences and walls; seats; different surfaces; worn areas; pavement and road markings about parking and where to cross the street safely.
- Looking up reveals street signs giving directions and warnings; street furniture, such as lampposts and bus stops; home and shop fronts and entrances; and further up, the heights of buildings, roofs and chimneys.
- They pass people making journeys, shoppers, and others working in the street.
- In the park the children observe various features, including signs and seats, but also find pathways and natural elements, the grass, trees, plants and shrubs, and birds, animals and mini-beasts. A park keeper might answer children's questions about the park, how it is looked after and who uses it.
- Young children associate parks with play activities. They should play in the open spaces or fenced-off areas available. Encourage them to talk about what they like to play and when they might come.

Children can take digital photographs to record selected features and views that they see or record their comments and thoughts for use back in the nursery. During their walk they might talk about what they like or dislike, about favourite places or that people drop litter; use directional language when they turn corners or to indicate where features are in the park; and indicate features they would like to see added to or removed from the street, the park and play area.

Taking young children out of the nursery and school grounds requires good organisation and careful management, as outlined in Chapter 7. A visit should be introduced to them before going so they know the purpose of their outing (Salaman and Tatchell, 2005).

Caring for our place

Developing children's caring for the environment requires active engagement (Martin and 38; Owens, 2008). There are many opportunities to involve the children in maintaining and improving the quality of their indoor and outdoor nursery environments. Children can:

- take resources out and put them away carefully, discussing why this helps, what they learn about care and what others should do;
- be responsible with adults for looking after particular areas in the nursery to see that everything is in order and is being cared for;
- walk around the nursery outdoor area periodically to see what is there and to talk about how plants grow, the needs of mini-beasts, birds and other creatures, to check the fencing, to see that paths are looked after, to check for litter or fallen leaves;

- observe whether something seems 'shabby' and in need of repair or painting – they can discuss who would do this, and how to improve the look and use of the resources and area.

Through such foci and activities, young children learn about environmental care and concern, using observation and discussion, appreciating who helps to keep places clean and tidy, and about using safe practices when doing so. They can record what they see and hear, and discuss what care for the environment is and why people think it is important. They can consider when it is important to tidy up and when and why some things may be left untidy, such as a wild area in the grounds or if we leave off part way through an activity to come back to it later.

Journeys

Hide and seek: Use outdoors or inside to play hide and seek. Talk about good and bad places to hide and why they are.

Along the street: Use child-size vehicles in the playground for play journeys along marked-up 'roads' in the playground (use playground chalk or have them permanently marked). Plan and make journeys to stops along the routes. Use large boxes or make large cut-outs of features, like shops, to stand along the route, for children to visit. Make road signs to be followed: one-way, stop, no entry, etc. Involve pedestrians and drivers. Link this to road safety. Children use the road to act out and talk about what happens there. Role-play shopkeepers and residents.

Places

Model playhouse: Provide a model house (with a removable roof and floors) with model furniture and people. Encourage children to sort furniture into rooms and to create layouts. Look down on the floor and room layout. Talk about what is where, why furniture has been put in specific rooms, the spatial arrangement, and the view from above. Take photographs from above of the layouts.

Changing places: Use a play mat showing a town or country area. Talk about what is shown on the 'map' and what the area is like. Propose that an area of the town, village or farm is to be changed and developed. Ask the children what they would like to put there and why. Using appropriately sized pieces of paper, involve the children in drawing or making models of the features they would build. Fix these to the 'play map'. Discuss the effect of the changes.

Shops and food

Shopping: Chose an item to buy that the children like, such as baked beans. Talk about where to buy it, types of food shops and supermarkets. Discuss where nearby shops are and how to get there. Encourage children to mention shops they are taken to. Visit a local shop to buy something. Observe and talk about other items sold there.

On the farm: Use farm toys (buildings, fences, animals, vehicles) or make farm features. Use a farm play mat or design and make the layout of the farm. Sort the animals and locate them on the farm. Talk about where different animals live and vehicles are kept. Discuss what farms are for. Compare different areas around the farm and their uses: how the land is used and what happens at different times of year.

Environments

Creating new environments to explore: Make a variety of different environments in one or more nursery bays. Create a jungle with materials and imagine walking through it; think about how you would get there and what you would see, hear and smell. Use chairs

---

to create a plane, bus or train. Decide where to go on your journeys, locally and around the world, and 'visit' them.

Dressing up: Use clothes to talk about and enact what to wear for different activities: play, dirty work, clean work, etc. What are we going to do: where are we going, for how long? Discuss what to wear to go out in dry or wet weather, when it is hot, cool or cold, to play in the mud or in a wild area, to wear on short or long journeys, or if you are expected to 'look smart'.

Mapping

A treasure hunt: Hide familiar toys outdoors or inside for children to find. Say 'hot', 'warm' and 'cold' as clues, or give instructions or other clues, such as pictures or pictorial symbols, for the children to follow. Alternatively, mark the locations on a large aerial photograph of the outdoor area which children use to find them (Plester et al., 2006).

Earth from space: Use postcards or posters of views of the Earth from space (of the continents and oceans) and a globe. Create a spaceship for children to imagine they are astronauts orbiting the Earth. From time to time they must spot and identify the postcard views of the Earth by looking for them on the globe, which is placed outside the 'space-ship' window and rotated during the play to help simulate the spacecraft orbiting the Earth.

Figure 8.1 Examples of activities to develop geographical awareness in the Early Years

PRACTICAL TASK PRACTICAL TASK **PRACTICAL TASK** PRACTICAL TASK **PRACTICAL TASK**

Select three of the activities outlined in Figure 8.1. Using Tables 8.1 and 8.2 identify the aspects of play and the contexts for play that are involved.

A SUMMARY OF **KEY POINTS**

This chapter has:

> **provided a rationale for developing young children's geographical and environmental experience through play and emphasised its importance;**

> **described a variety of contexts for and aspects of place-based play to develop geographical learning and understanding;**

> **noted the role and value of the 'outdoor classroom' in the nursery environment;**

> **provided various examples of activities to use with young children to foster experience of geographical ideas, skills, values and attitudes.**

MOVING *ON* > > > **>** **>** **>** MOVING *ON* > > > **>** **>** **>** MOVING *ON*

You may have visited or have the opportunity to visit a Foundation Stage setting in a nursery or primary school. Consider the approaches and opportunities the nursery teacher uses to develop young children's geographical and environmental experience and learning. What does the outdoor area offer for children's play? Note the variety of equipment that is available to encourage place and environmental play and that children might use and adapt to create environments of their own.

FURTHER READING FURTHER READING **FURTHER READING** FURTHER READING

There are many publications on Foundation Stage school environments but only a few that discuss providing geographical and environmental experiences through play and other approaches for learning.

Bilton, H (2005) *Learning outdoors: Improving the quality of children's play outdoors*. London: David Fulton.

Catling, S (2006b) What do five-year-olds know of the world? Geographical understanding and play in young children's early learning. *Geography*, 91 (1), 55–74.

Conway, D, Pointon, P and Greenwood, J (2008), 'If the world is round, how come the piece I'm standing on is flat?' Early Years geography, in Whitebread, D and Coltman, P *Teaching and learning in the Early Years*. London: Routledge.

Cooper, H (ed) (2004) *Exploring time and place through play*. London: David Fulton.

Palmer, J and Birch, J (2004) *Geography in the Early Years*. London: Routledge.

White, J (2008) *Playing and learning outdoors*. London: Routledge.

See relevant issues of *Primary Geographer* and *Nursery World*.

Useful websites

Early Years geography
www.geography.org.uk/eyprimary
Early Years Teaching Ideas
www.teachingideas.co.uk/earlyyears/contents.htm
Forest Schools
www.forestschools.com/earlyyears.php
Learning through Landscapes
www.ltl.org.uk
Playing with sand, water, etc.
www.communityplaythings.com/c/resources

9
Investigating the school and its grounds

Chapter objectives

By the end of this chapter you should:

- **be able to explain the value in using the school grounds for learning and teaching geography;**
- **recognise the opportunities the school site provides;**
- **be aware of geographical topics and activities you can undertake in the school grounds.**

This chapter addresses the following Professional Standards for QTS:

Q7, Q8, Q14, Q15, Q22, Q25.

Introduction

The school is a key site in children's everyday geographies. It is the place which they share as members of its community, users of its buildings and grounds, participants in its activities, routines and rules. They can describe and discuss what life there is like, how, where and why things happen, what they think and feel about this, and how they might like it to be in the future. The school provides a geographical site to explore, and the children who investigate it are active participants in the social and physical environment they study. They can both observe from the outside and provide insight from the inside (see Chapter 3). Exploring the school's geography creates opportunities to develop children's enquiry and research skills (Kellett, 2005).

Why study the school building and grounds?

Studying the school's geography enables children to explore how it works as a place, and to enquire into key aspects of its environment. Studies in the school and its grounds link geography with science, history and art (Hare et al., 1996). A few schools use their school environment as the focus of their curriculum; it is their 'place of learning' and their 'learning environment' (Jeffrey and Woods, 2003). That it is a living place in which children are its *raison d'être* and prime participants is the core reason for using the school as a geographical focus for study. It provides a key context for active learning. Fieldwork is essential to exploring its current and future geographies – from mapping what is where to identifying ways in which the school grounds could be landscaped to provide more varied environments for playtimes and for learning and teaching. These lead to the obvious reason – it's there!

It is accessible

The school building and grounds are readily accessible, the place to take children for out of classroom learning. There are few constraints on access around the school – areas 'out-of-bounds' or best not used if the weather is poor. Children might investigate which areas of the school are accessible or not, when and why, whether accessibility changes during the day or the year, and who decides whose access.

It has 'immediacy'

Aside from particular school requirements, it is relatively straightforward to arrange fieldwork, given the usual need to plan appropriately and to bear in mind that other classes may be working outside too. You can respond to spontaneity, to take opportunities to use the grounds, and to develop learning that was not planned for.

It stimulates and generates motivation

There is ample evidence from geography inspection reports (Catling et al., 2007; DES, 1989; Ofsted, 1999, 2008a) that investigations in the building(s) and grounds stimulate children's interest and engagement, particularly when examining what their school is like, what happens in it, its features and layout, what people do, the uses made of it at different times and in different parts, and by examining energy use or dealing with waste and how to reduce these.

It is a site to study and use key geographical ideas, concepts and content

The school is an excellent environment for developing children's geographical understanding. It provides a space, a place, and an environment for study, considering the sort of place it is, how space is designated and used, what changes occur and with what effect, and of sustainability of practices around the school. Its external connections provide insight into where the school obtains its resources and pupils and about its local impact. Physical and human processes, such as local weather patterns and how people respond to these, can be studied. Through its school community cultural awareness and diversity can be examined.

It provides the context to use and develop geographical skills

Children can use enquiry and fieldwork skills, planning an investigation, for example, of the use of water in the school or the location for a new feature. They will use skills such as mapping, gathering, analysing and presenting data, taking photographs and making sketches.

It is invaluable for introducing and following up geographical topics

The school building and grounds provide opportunities to initiate new ideas. The different uses of a large space might be explored first by identifying and mapping land use around the school site. An environmental issue might be illustrated by looking at waste and its disposal in the school.

It is possible to have an impact on the school site

Geography as an ethical subject leads to active involvement in finding ways to care for places and environments and to make improvements. One way to achieve this is by identifying ways in which the school can be more sustainable, for instance, through energy reduction or by collecting rain water to use in the school's garden area.

REFLECTIVE TASK

The reasons given above referred to the school building and grounds. You can, as easily, undertake geographical studies in the classroom. List reasons for using the classroom for geographical study. Consider some of the points above to guide you.

What are the school and its grounds?

Schools contain three key physical and social spaces. These are:

- the classroom;
- the school building(s);
- the school grounds.

The classroom

This includes not just the physical features of the room, fixed and movable, but also the people who work in the room. The classroom's geography includes the variety of features, its layout, why it is laid out as it is, its 'routeways', access to it, how people use it, how it might change in layout or use regularly or from time to time, and who creates or makes the decisions about the 'sense of place' that a classroom has. Other rooms around the school can be considered similarly.

The school buildings

There may be more than one building on the school site, other teaching blocks and outbuildings. Its geography includes the layout of the building(s), the floors and rooms and their uses, the range of activities that happen inside, how what occurs is affected by its layout, shape and community, the corridors and routes around the building(s) including stairs up and down, which rooms are accessible to whom, the times of day when rooms are used, by whom and what for, the 'atmosphere' of the school provided through the teaching and other activities, the decor and displays, its rules and regulations, explicit and implicit, and how it feels as a place. It includes the exercise of control and order over spaces in the building, what is in or out of bounds, and who decides, for what purpose and with what effect.

The school grounds

The school grounds include all the features that are within the territorial boundary of the site. Its geography covers its physical and natural features: the shape of the site, the lie of the land which may be flat or on a slope, its landscaping such as terracing, the nature and sites of its plant and animal/insect ecology, its weather, its buildings, access roads, car park, paths and routeways, its boundary wall or fence, edges and borders (which in a few schools even includes a stream) and its entrances. Its social and cultural geography include the designation of the spaces in the school, the roles and activities of the people there, the nature of its community, its regular and occasional visitors, whether parents, grounds maintenance staff or drama groups. Its geography includes the quality of the site, the 'feel' of the place at playtimes and during lesson times as well as in the evenings and during school holidays, the ways in which it is cared for and maintained, how people treat the site and its features from its users to the local authority or independent owner, and the sense of place that its users develop.

The 'everyday' environment and experience of the school is more than its physical environment. It is the community and social and cultural life in the school. Its geography concerns the social ethics of space and place, who can go where and do what in which parts of the school, why this is so, what differences there are between what children and adults can do where, how they subvert these positively and negatively, inside and outside the rules, who is consulted over the uses of spaces and the activities in them, and who decides on the regulations that organise space, set expectations of behaviour and allow activities. In many ways a school is a microcosm of the neighbourhood and the community, with its variety of features and people, of relationships and activities, of possibilities and constraints. It is this physical and human world, this place and environment that are the everyday geography of the school and its grounds.

PRACTICAL TASK PRACTICAL TASK **PRACTICAL TASK** PRACTICAL TASK **PRACTICAL TASK**

Recall a school site you know, from a school experience or from your own schooling. List features of that site that you recall. Draw a sketch map of the school grounds and of a floor of the school building. Annotate your maps about the physical and social geography of the school. Consider how easy or challenging this has been, and why. Identify how you will become well acquainted with your next school's geography, its buildings, grounds and social and cultural life.

Core resources

Investigating school geography requires resources. While children will develop their own resources during investigations – sketch maps of their classroom or the school grounds, digital photographs, questionnaires and checklists – there are resources to acquire.

- School site plans and maps.
- An OS map (c.1:1250 scale) of the school site.
- Access to Google Earth, Multimap or similar vertical aerial photographs of the site.
- Prepared plans of the school building floors and classrooms.
- Photographs of various features around the school.
- Old photographs and maps of the site.
- School rules and codes.
- Documents from the head teacher, the governors and others, such as past plans for changes, records of meetings, reports, log books, etc.
- Children's information books about schools and people who work there.
- Directional compasses, tape measures, trundle wheels, a clinometer, and weather-recording instruments.

IN THE CLASSROOM

A Year 4 class became concerned about the overuse of the school car park area. Often visitors parked, blocking staff cars which might be needed in an emergency. They studied this problem by considering if the space could be reorganised so more cars could park. When this proved impractical they looked for car parking spaces in the streets outside and nearby. They identified and drew up plans for parking spaces for visitors to be marked on the road outside school and noted alternative nearby parking areas. They outlined their plans to the school's governors, including the local councillor.

Investigating geography in school

Investigating the school and its site should use an enquiry approach. A problem-oriented enquiry is a useful focus for investigating matters on the school site. It goes beyond simply identifying information and presenting it; it focuses on a concern to understand better and even resolve. Such an issue might be the study outlined above or the best location of litter bins in the playground areas. A problem-oriented approach is not a problem-solving approach. Too often children can be given the impression that by undertaking a study and making recommendations, the problem they have studied will be resolved. Some problems can be tackled and changes made; others cannot be, perhaps for resource reasons, or because there are competing interests, or regulations override the children's proposals, or because the scale of the change is too demanding in the current school context. This is how the everyday world works. By engaging in problem-oriented enquiries children meet everyday problems and outcomes (or the lack of them) and learn to deal with such situations that they might encounter out of school as citizens in the local, national and global communities. In selecting with children geographical problems to investigate, ensure from the start that they realise that their geographical learning comes through the investigation and by making proposals.

Almost all school building and grounds investigations will involve fieldwork. This should be effectively planned and draw on the advice in Chapter 7. It can be included within a classroom-based lesson. Good quality learning is more likely to occur during well-organised fieldwork. Even in school you should always undertake an informal risk assessment of the area(s) you intend to use. An example of a lesson plan is included in Chapter 12 in Figure 12.3. It outlines a fieldwork session in the school building and grounds undertaken during a lesson which also includes class-based work.

PRACTICAL TASK PRACTICAL TASK **PRACTICAL TASK** PRACTICAL TASK **PRACTICAL TASK**

Identify a particular aspect of your campus and a concern or problem associated with it. Use the advice on organising an enquiry in Chapter 6 to plan, undertake and report on your geographical issue. Include how you could adapt it to use in school.

Topics to investigate

There are many possible geographical topics to investigate in school. The following are used quite often, investigated in their own right, or in an early lesson in a topic that focuses on the local area or more widely, to familiarise children with the topic and ideas being studied and enquiry approaches and methods to be used.

- Wayfinding and routes.
- Location of features and activities.
- Room, building and land uses.
- Access, movement.
- Attitudes to the community, building and grounds.
- People's jobs and activities.
- How people use and affect the site.
- The 'natural' environment.
- Its layout, spatial patterns.
- Microclimate, weather and its impact.
- Water and weathering.
- Impact of litter and waste disposal.
- Damage on and to parts of the site.
- Energy and water use and conservation.
- Changes to the environment.
- Caring for and improving the site.

The geographical topics, questions and activities outlined below cover five themes: the school as a place, its physical environment, patterns around the school, sustainability and the school's wider world connections. The common feature is that they link into the every-day life of the school and the everyday geographies of the children and staff. They involve a problem or concern to investigate, are initiated by geographical questions, and require active fieldwork to be developed effectively. Two examples are given for each theme. Each can be adapted to year groups in both key stages.

School as a place

There are many ways to study schools as places, from their features to the types of community they are. Two topics illustrate this: how the school site is used, which explores aspects of its community role; and what those in the school think and feel about it as a place, focusing on affective responses to places.

Topic: How our school is used
Suggested enquiry questions: Who uses our school, what for, when and why? What types of jobs and activities are done? Can changes and improvements be made?

Possible activities:

- Monitor who uses the school buildings and grounds during the school day from observation and experience, and what they do.
- Ask the children and staff about the activities and jobs they do, where and when.
- Investigate who uses the building and grounds for what, outside school hours.
- Map the school areas used, for what activities, by whom and when.
- Create a timetable to show the use of the school across the day and week, in terms and holidays.
- Identify the benefits of the different uses and users, and any limitations.
- Consider improvements and/or additions to the use of the school site.
- Report to the head teacher on the use of the school.

Topic: How we think and feel about our school
Suggested enquiry questions: What do we think of and feel about our school and its grounds?

Possible activities:

- Develop criteria for evaluating the quality of the school buildings and grounds.
- Survey sites around the school using the criteria.
- Involve children and staff to find out what they think of the school site and how they feel about the school as their place.
- Report your findings with proposals about what could be done to develop positive views and attitudes further or to address negative feelings and views.

IN THE CLASSROOM
A Year 1 class discussed what they liked about their school. Top of their list were the people they worked with, adults and children. Second were the resources they could play with at playtimes. Third was the landscaped area where they could go to sit, talk or play quiet games with their friends. They liked to be able to run about from time to time but they were concerned about the older children not always noticing and

bumping into them. This raised a question about whether everyone in the school liked the same things. A sample investigation took place with small groups of children, working with their TA, asking five children in each other class what they liked or did not like about their school. They found a mixture of responses with playtimes being popular with some but not with others, most children liking the variety of places to play around school, and a general view that their school was a nice place to come to.

The school environment

There are many aspects to the school's physical environment, including its built features and its ecology. There are factors that impact on a school, though, that are not of its own making. The topics below illustrate these. One concerns the weather and its effect on people and life in school; the other considers the problem of damage through human activities and natural forces to the school's fabric. These topics link geography and science, through undertaking scientific investigations (Sharp et al., 2007) for weather recording or to observe and record erosion in the school grounds (Bowles, 2004c).

Topic: **How the weather affects us**
Suggested enquiry questions: What is the weather like on our school site? How does it affect us? How do we respond?

Possible activities:

- Observe different aspects of the weather.
- Discuss how the weather feels: cold, hot, warm, cool, etc.
- Observe and discuss how people respond to different types of weather: what they do, what they wear, etc.
- Estimate and measure aspects of the weather, e.g. rain, wind direction and speed, amount of cloud cover.
- Make weather records.
- Find out about what processes cause different weather elements and effects, e.g. rain, wind, cloud.
- Give a daily weather report and forecast.
- Report patterns in weather and people's responses over time, e.g. a week, a month, a term.

Topic: **Damage around the school**
Suggested enquiry questions: Is there any damage to features around the school? What types of erosion occur to school buildings and in the grounds? What can be done to stop or limit such damage?

Possible activities:

- Discuss the idea of damage to the environment, e.g. through graffiti, broken windows, broken plants/trees.
- Find out and discuss what erosion means and includes.
- Observe, describe and map areas where there is damage or erosion around the school, e.g. worn areas on grass, damage to plants at the edge of the playground, graffiti, and to buildings such as worn stairs or wall bricks or paintwork through human or rain or wind action. Take photographs.
- Examine how this has happened. Consider how serious it is.
- Identify ways to reduce and/or prevent damage to the buildings and grounds.
- Report on your findings and proposals.

REFLECTIVE TASK
REFLECTIVE TASK

Consider how the topics outlined above support the development of children's geographical understanding of key concepts. For instance, 'Damage around the school' illustrates environmental impact and sustainability and physical and human processes. Which key geographical concepts can be developed through the other three topics?

Patterns around the school

Understanding how space is used within the school site means studying the distributions of features and activities and their resulting spatial patterns. The first topic examines the distribution of litter bins around the school site, focused on their location in appropriate places and whether their distribution is the result of considered thought, guesswork or whim. The second considers the ways rooms are designated and used, the distribution of these uses and the impact of this pattern.

Topic: **Litter bins around the school**
Suggested enquiry questions: Where are the litter bins? Why are they there? Can they be better located?

Possible activities:

- Discuss the use of litter bins and the reasons why they might be located in particular sites.
- Map their location.
- Observe and record littering and throwing away and the effective use of litter bins.
- Interview children and staff about attitudes to dealing with litter, the use of bins and about their location.
- Make proposals, with plans, for locating litter bins effectively, and if changes are needed.
- Report on what has been found out and request your proposals are implemented.
- Trial and evaluate relocating bins and amend as necessary.

Topic: **Room use in the school building(s)**
Suggested enquiry questions: How is the use of rooms in the school best arranged?

Possible activities:

- Map the use of rooms in the school building and identify the patterns of use.
- Identify the relevant accessibility of different rooms, e.g. the library, from classrooms, and find out times of use and flows of movement.
- Note which rooms/services can be changed and which cannot, e.g. toilets or a music room.
- Consider whether there are more practical locations for particular services, related to use, need, room size, etc.
- Report on whether the best use is made of the rooms in the school and on your proposals for change.

A sustainable school

The Sustainable Schools agenda uses the 'eight doorways' approach (see Chapter 5). This has created an impetus for schools to develop their sustainability (DfES, 2006a, 2006b), even aiming for eco-school status and the 'green flag' ranking (see the eco-school website). This offers a rich opportunity to develop the quality of the school's approach to sustainability and to its social and physical environment. The topics below provide ways to connect sustainable schools' activities with geographical studies, focused on environmental impact and sustainability. The litter bin study can be complemented by studying recycling in school. The use of and understanding access to water in school is another 'doorway' topic.

Topic: **Recycling in school**
Suggested enquiry questions: Do you recycle? What and how? Why? Enough?

Possible activities:

- Discuss and find out about the various types of waste produced in school.
- Undertake interviews to find out about waste produced in areas such as the kitchen.
- Invite the school caretaker into class to talk about waste disposal.
- Within health and safety limits, observe, examine, categorise and weigh types of waste products found in school.
- Find out about recycling practices used in school.
- Propose ways to extend, improve or initiate recycling waste to the head teacher.

Topic: **Our water use in school**
Suggested enquiry questions: Where does our water come from? Who uses it? How can we be more careful in its use?

Possible activities:

- Consider why water is so important, how we use it and how much we use.
- Map the location of water access around the school.
- With the help of the caretaker investigate where water comes into the school and how it is distributed around the school.
- Survey who uses water, what for, when and why during the school day.
- Investigate how much water is used through sample surveys.
- Ask a representative from the local water board into class to talk about water provision and use. Prepare questions beforehand.
- Consider the necessity of the amount of water use and ways to reduce consumption.
- Make proposals for measuring and reducing water usage.

IN THE CLASSROOM

A Year 5 class proposed various geography topics to investigate. The class voted to explore energy issues. This topic developed from comments by children that lights were often left on in classrooms when no one was there. This initiated a survey and linked with science to develop further their understanding about electricity, light and energy use. It led to proposals for classes to monitor their use of lights and to turn them off when possible. It examined the heating of the school, the class inviting local electricity and gas officials to talk to them about ways to make savings. With the caretaker's help they learned about the electrical and heating systems of the school. The outcome was a poster campaign encouraging energy saving. Complementing their school site studies the children examined their use of energy at home and noticed how energy was used in their local area. They became much more conscious of the role energy plays in our everyday lives, how much we use and depend on it, and why efforts are made to encourage people to save energy.

Connections beyond school

Schools recognise their interconnections with their local community, not least through their pupils, and with the wider regional, national and global world. Geography provides an effective focus to explore such links. An obvious connection is children's travel to school, focused on the local links. Schools are connected with the wider world through such diverse forms as the internet, the origins and delivery of resources, and the variety of places children visit with their families and on school fieldwork and other activities.

Topic: **Travel to school**

Suggested enquiry questions: How do we travel to school? Are there travel to school improvements that can be made?

Possible activities:

- Survey the ways in which children and adults travel to school, and why.
- Map the catchment area of the school to see where people travel from and the routes they use. Link this to their modes of travel.
- Monitor and map the ways children arrive at the school 'gates'. Include the collection (e.g. walking, bus) and drop-off points, use of particular entrances to the grounds and buildings and times. Consider local travel risks, including road crossing.
- Create a display showing the variety of ways travelled to school, collection and drop-off points, and where and when people enter the school.
- Consider and propose ways to improve travel safety, reduce car journeys and ensure safe access into school.

Topic: **Connected to the wider world**

Suggested enquiry questions: With where are we connected? How? Why there and with what impact?

Possible activities:

- Investigate the links people in school have and that the school has with other parts of the local region, country and wider world.
- Select a variety of sources to survey, e.g. children's personal links, links through the internet, where some of the resources in school come or are delivered from, places visited on fieldwork and school journeys, holiday destinations. Map them.
- Explain why these links exist, their value and benefit.
- Consider which links are most useful, whether others might be developed and which could be ended.
- Create a display to show the school's connections to the wider world.

REFLECTIVE TASK

Select one of the geography topics outlined above and consider how you might introduce it to a class. What would be the main geographical concepts and skills you would want to develop? How would you start your topic? What would you do next? What would be the focus for fieldwork in the school? Plan it as an enquiry.

MOVING *ON* > > > > > > MOVING *ON* > > > > > > MOVING *ON*

In your next school look around to familiarise yourself with its geography. Walk the school's grounds and observe it from the different angles. Use your phone camera to photograph building and grounds features, large and small. Walk around the school building(s) to see how inside spaces are used. Make a sketch map of the grounds and building(s). Annotate the map with what you see happening in the school. Take account of activities at different times of day. Reflect on and note the aspects of geography you have encountered as you made your observations and maps. Think how you could use them to help children learn geography.

FURTHER READING FURTHER READING **FURTHER READING** FURTHER READING

Views and ideas about using the school grounds appear in several publications.

Foley, M and Janikoun, J (1996) *The really useful guide to primary geography*. Cheltenham: Stanley Thornes.

Hare, R, Attenborough, C and Day, T (1996), *Geography in the school grounds*. Southgate.

QCA/DfEE (2002) *A scheme of work for Key Stages 1 and 2: Citizenship*. London: QCA/DfEE.

Scoffham, S (ed) (2004) *Primary geography handbook*. Sheffield: Geographical Association.

Titman, W. (1994) *Special people, special places*. Winchester: Learning through Landscapes.

See also *Primary Geographer*, 59 (2006), Focus on outdoor learning.

Useful websites

Eco-schools
   www.eco-schools.org.uk
Growing Schools
   www.teachernet.gov.uk/growingschools
Learning outside the Classroom
   www.lotc.org.uk
Learning through Landscapes
   ltl.co.uk
Let's walk to school
   www.walktoschool.org.uk
Safe Kids Walking
   www.safekidswalking.org.uk
Sustainable Learning
   www.sustainablelearning.info/

10
Exploring locally and further afield

Chapter objectives

By the end of this chapter you should:

- **understand the meaning and importance of locality studies and the links to children's geographies;**
- **know and appreciate key aspects of the geography of a locality;**
- **recognise opportunities for children to investigate localities;**
- **be aware of connections between local studies, sustainability, citizenship and local environmental participation;**
- **be able to identify opportunities for local enquiries and fieldwork;**
- **know of the range of resources to use in locality studies.**

This chapter addresses the following Professional Standards for QTS:

Q14, Q15, Q25, Q30.

Introduction

The study of a locality provides opportunities for children to develop some understanding of a smaller-scale place. The local area of the school is an excellent place to investigate, not least because it is most children's home area. The local area offers various possibilities, such as studies of physical and human processes in the environment and of environmental impact and sustainability. Studying localities has long been recognised as essential in primary geography teaching. It is a key element in the primary geography curriculum for this reason. This chapter examines some aspects of local area studies, looking particularly at the immediate locality of the school, but noting that similar studies can be made of other similar or different localities in the UK.

Why study localities?

Studying their own locality helps children to know, understand and appreciate the place they live in. There are powerful reasons for studying local area geography. These draw on children's everyday geographies and arise because it is accessible for fieldwork. Not least, it is a requirement for geographical studies from the Foundation Stage through Key Stages 1 and 2.

Among the reasons for studying the local area are the following.

- Investigating the local area draws on children's curiosity, interest, experience and knowledge of their place, enabling them to share the awareness and understanding they bring from their different but overlapping parts of the area.
- Its study develops children's knowledge, understanding and appreciation of their home area. It challenges misinformation and misconceptions they may have.

- It encourages them to develop a sense of their place in the world, where they are related to other places, and their interconnectedness regionally and globally.
- The local environment provides an excellent 'laboratory' to study geographical ideas and skills and to develop children's:
  - geographical knowledge of features and activities, travel and transport, and local facilities and services;
  - geographical understanding, for instance of what goes on where and why it happens, sense of place, awareness of geographical patterns and processes, and of local interdependence with the wider world;
  - environmental change, impact and values/attitudes, related to care for the environment, environmental management, damage and improvement, and feelings for and concerns about the area;
  - geographical enquiry and skills, including fieldwork and mapwork;
  - geographical language, place and environmental vocabulary.
- Local area study builds on links to the local community, an important aspect of place and sustainability education, and offers opportunities to:
  - draw in and draw on local people;
  - use local facilities;
  - connect with local amenity groups;
  - look at local situations, needs and issues.
- Much of the local area is potentially readily accessible to the school. Studying it cries out for fieldwork activities.
- Using the local area can build on and develop geographical studies undertaken initially in the school grounds.

Studying the local area is much more than identifying a range of features and activities, services, changes and connections. For primary children it is about developing their sense of neighbourhood and community, as well as their knowledge and appreciation of the nature of the area. In an increasingly mobile society with ever-greater virtual connections locally, nationally and internationally, there is an important role for geography in helping create more cohesive, resilient and safe communities. Improving community cohesion is a government priority aimed at creating more supportive, positive and enterprising communities where children, young people and adults feel comfortable and welcomed, where diverse identities and backgrounds are appreciated and valued, and where there is a sense for all of belonging (DCSF, 2007, pp136–7). Schools have been given a central role. This links effectively with the development of sustainable schools in sustainable communities, where there is concern to improve the quality of school and local area environments and to value local involvement and a sense of place alongside global awareness and citizenship (DfES, 2006a, 2006b; DCSF, 2007). Both connect strongly with the Every Child Matters agenda, emphasising improved personal and social well-being alongside enabling children's voices to be listened to (DfES, 2003a).

The government's agenda for schools provides strong justifications to develop in children their sense of local environmental well-being (Catling, 2007; DfES, 2006a, 2006b) through geographical studies of the local area. These link directly into a sense of neighbourhood and community, including:

- awareness of one's own community;
- building a sense of belonging and identity locally;
- encouraging concern and respect for 'the local';
- fostering a sense of care for the community;
- becoming engaged with community groups;
- observing and participating in sustainable practices;

- encouraging and empowering children's 'voice' and involvement;
- recognising local interdependence.

Not only does the focus on local geography encourage children to investigate and deepen their understanding of their own area as it is, but it enables them to explore its possible and their preferred futures, developing their sense of responsibility and potential for involvement and participation.

> **PRACTICAL TASK** PRACTICAL TASK **PRACTICAL TASK** PRACTICAL TASK **PRACTICAL TASK**
>
> Think or look back to the points made about children's personal geographies in Chapter 3. Make a list of reasons for studying local geography which draws on children's experience of their neighbourhoods and communities.

What is a locality?

The school's local area and neighbourhood

The local area is the area around the school, the area where the majority of the children live who go to the school. For schools with a very wide catchment area this might be limited to an area that stretches a kilometre or so in each direction. The 'size' of the local area needs to be differentiated thoughtfully for children at different ages and stages of their Early Years and primary education. The local area might be viewed as a series of concentric circles.

- *Foundation Stage*: the school grounds, the streets round about, and a nearby park or play area – the immediate neighbourhood;
- *Key Stage 1*: the school grounds and the close neighbourhood or nearby area around the school – its vicinity;
- *Key Stage 2*: the school grounds and the wider, extended neighbourhood of the school, possibly the school catchment area from within which children travel to get to school. This should be reassessed if many children live far away, but it is a useful rule of thumb.

Progression in studying the local area can start with the school's immediate surroundings and then developing into a wider area as children become more familiar with their local area. It is important to remember that the local environment should be revisited continually through different geographical 'focal lenses' as the children develop and deepen their experience and knowledge of their surroundings and consider increasingly complex aspects and issues.

When comparing localities, it is important to study an area of an equivalent size. The most successful locality studies are of small, contained areas where real and meaningful comparisons to the children's lives can be made, not of large towns, cities or regions. In this sense a locality has close connections with the local community. It needs to be remembered that a locality is not simply a physical entity; its human, community and neighbourhood dimensions are central.

IN THE CLASSROOM

Children in a Year 1 class used photographs of local buildings and street scenes, taken by their teacher, to discuss the variety of features and shops they saw on their way between school and home and when out with their families. They commented on places that they knew – homes where their friends lived, and shops they used – and on some local problems they encountered, such as litter and crossing the roads. They drew their favourite places to visit and were helped to write about why they liked these places. They talked about where or what they did not like and what could be done to improve it or make it more pleasant. They were encouraged to suggest what they might like changed to make their locality more interesting for them.

Localities studied elsewhere in the United Kingdom

Studying another locality in the United Kingdom is an element of the primary geography curriculum, particularly for Key Stage 2. It involves the study of a place of about the same size as the local area of the school focused on its neighbourhood and community. It provides the opportunity for children to examine some or many of the same aspects of their own locality, as well as contrasting aspects (Walker, 2004). Children might study an area that is unfamiliar to them using a variety of secondary sources, but there might be opportunities through a school's residential visit to undertake extended fieldwork.

Complementing the reasons for study of the school locality, the purposes of investigating another locality in the UK include:

- that very many children already have experience of other UK localities, even if limited to day visits, so that it builds on and extends their sense of 'elsewhere' and knowledge of other places;
- their awareness of other places in the UK, through relatives, friends and the media, which may be very similar to or different from their own – a rural locality in contrast to their own lives in an urban environment, or *vice versa*;
- providing opportunities to identify and examine similarities and contrasts with their home locality;
- that there may be the possibility of making a visit to the locality if nearby or, if it is further afield, on a school journey.

IN THE CLASSROOM

A Year 5 class used a variety of secondary sources in their study of the small town of Hawes in the Yorkshire Dales in northern England. Their teacher had collected these resources during visits to the Dales. He provided a display of some of the resources for the children to look at, read and handle. They included photographs, postcards, maps, town trails, bus timetables, tourist guides and leaflets and much else. Videos and websites were also viewed. Following this introduction, the children discussed and recorded their ideas about the sort of place that Hawes is and identified what they wanted to investigate further. They had a variety of questions to pursue, which they selected from and organised as the basis for an enquiry, working in groups. The main focus of their studies was who lives and works in Hawes, the sort of place it is, why it is popular with tourists, what types of services it provides for tourists and local people, whether life there is the same all year round, what some local people might think of the visitors who pass through, and how and why the Wensleydale cheese factory attracts

---

so many visitors. Their studies took place over a term. At the end of term the groups made presentations on their particular topic. Asked to say what they had learnt from their studies, children referred to the variety of jobs, the small size of the town, the importance of tourism to the countryside, that they could probably buy many things there that they could in their local supermarket, the busy traffic on market days, and how attractive a place it seemed to be. They wanted to visit the area.

REFLECTIVE TASK

What do you consider to be the most important learning that children should take from geographical studies of a locality? What are your reasons for this?

What might be studied locally?

There is much that can be studied in any local area. Very often the focus is on the physical features of the area and what it is possible to do there. These are important aspects of a local area and its community to investigate and are among those listed in Figure 10.1.

Nature of places
- Local features and micro-places: e.g. street furniture, buildings, fields, streets
- People's lives and use of the local area, e.g. where they shop and why
- Local activities and events
- Leisure activities, play areas/parks
- Land/building use: types and varieties of use
- Service/goods provision: shops/businesses
- Work: jobs people do, employment
- Access: ease of getting into places and about
- Travel: journeys, transport
- The patterns of streets and layout of locality
- Local weather impact and microclimate
- Security surveillance; local camera monitoring of people, activities and places
- Relationship between features and activities

Character of places
- Focus of area: e.g. suburb, business/industrial park, farmland, shopping centre
- The type of settlement and its community
- The diversity within and cohesion of the community
- What localities are like, feel like, look like

Sense of places
- Views and feelings about people, places and their environments
- Appreciation of places: likes and dislikes about features, activities and places
- Concerns and what is valued about places
- A sense of belonging and identity with the locality; what it means

Management and improvement of places
- Responsibility for local services, e.g. rubbish collection; how these are carried out
- Identifying local issues, e.g. traffic and parking, housing development
- How damage to and pollution of locality are tackled
- Care for the local environment

- What people might want places to be like

Changing places

- How localities have become the way they are
- How and why localities are changing
- Changes in land use, features and activities
- Who makes decisions leading to change and why
- Conflicts over change
- The impact of changes on people, places and environments
- How localities may change and become in the future

Place locations and connections

- Where features and activities occur in the local area
- Links to other places locally, regionally and globally: transport, goods/services, virtually
- Localities in the wider geographical context, local to global: from locality to country to continent to world
- Ways in which places are interdependent, benefits and limitations

Comparing places

- How localities compare with other localities
- How and why localities are similar to and different from other places in the same country and elsewhere in the world
- The valuing commonality and diversity within and between places

Figure 10.1 Aspects of localities to study across Early Years and primary geography

While the list in Figure 10.1 provides a useful checklist of the various possibilities locally, it needs to be translated into an effective local study. Figure 10.2 outlines one way to structure a local area topic.

1. What do we know about our locality?
   - What is our area like?
   - What is special about it?
2. What are the main activities in the area?
   - What facilities and services are there?
   - What do people do for work and leisure?
3. How is the land used across the area?
   - What is the land used for if we look in each direction from school?
   - What can we find out about the land use around our homes?
4. Who lives in our locality?
   - What do they do and like to do locally?
   - What are their connections with other places?
5. How do we think and feel about our place?
   - What is important to people about our locality?
   - What sort of character does our locality have?
6. What is changing in our place?
   - What can we see that shows how our area has developed?
   - What is changing here now?
   - What is the impact of changes?
7. How do we look after our local area?
   - In what ways have people affected out locality?
   - What changes would we like to see in the future and why?

8. What can we tell someone else about 'our place'?
   - What would we show someone about our locality?
   - What do I appreciate now about my area that I did not before?

Figure 10.2 An example of core questions structuring a local geography topic

IN THE CLASSROOM

Undertaking a local study using a similar structure to that in Figure 10.2, a Year 3 class concluded their project by making local brochures that they planned for families who would be new to the locality. As a part of their investigation they asked at home what their families would like to know about the local area if they were new to it. Small groups produced their brochures and these were displayed and shown to three new sets of parents by the head teacher when they visited the school shortly after the project was completed.

There is a value in being more focused in local area studies, particularly if the children at times provide such foci from their interests, experience and knowledge. Rather than undertaking shop or land-use surveys of an area, which can be informative and useful in knowing and understanding what types of shops are available or the range of uses local land has, it can be more stimulating and effective to focus on a particular concern or problem, maintaining the problem-oriented enquiry approach outlined in Chapter 9. For example, the local shopping parade and wider area might be studied for its accessibility for everyone, including those who use wheelchairs, parents with single or double baby buggies, the elderly or infirm, and the partially sighted and hard of hearing. The emphasis might be on how challenging it is to get around the area, what signage helps or hinders, how easy or difficult it is to get into shops, and what can be done to improve matters (Catling, 2005d). See the Unit of Work plan on pages 146–148 in Table 12.3. Inviting the children to suggest and select foci for local studies both identifies their interests and concerns and motivates their engagement in investigations. Figure 10.3 outlines ten possible topics to stimulate your ideas.

What a waste! From local waste bins to refuse collection and disposal.
Is there a parking problem? What is parking like locally and what can be done about local concerns?
There's an empty shop. Who would like the shop used for which service/business, and why?
Who created the local play area? How were decisions made about the local play facilities? And what do children really want there?
Who uses public transport? Exploring the use of bus services (or the lack of them) locally and the impact and value to different users.
Introducing the local area. Produce a leaflet about the locality for new parents and children. What is put in and what is left out?
The best and worst of places. What is most and least attractive about the local area? Children's and adults' perspectives.
What's available? People's perspectives on what is available and what is not – and where you have to go to get it.
Keeping an eye and ear open. Look at the sites of surveillance cameras in the local area and mobile phone use.
Elsewhere here. Identify and explain all those visible local connections to other places.

Figure 10.3 Ten geographical topics to investigate locally

Place, environmental impact and sustainability – topics for local investigation

Localities are rich resources for engaging and creative enquiries. Being dynamic and constantly evolving, they provide good examples of real-life issues and give children the opportunity to ask questions about what is happening and develop potential solutions. Much information about the local area and what concerns people can be gathered through the internet and local newspapers, radio and television. Schools and children can access such information readily.

Local sources, which include the knowledge and perspectives children bring from home and their own experience, provide the potential for a variety of topics and issues to select from. Many local issues focus on changes to the environment and the impact and sustainability of these changes. The following are examples of local problems to examine. You will be able to identify related types of issues from your own area.

- The changing provision of local facilities and services, such as the closure of a local post office and its potential impact on the local population.
- Different people's use of and requirements for services locally, such as leisure facilities, and provision for specific groups of people such as the young and the elderly.
- Development projects which spark local people's opinions about change and improvements in the area, including the potentially conflicting views of different groups of people.
- Examining local heritage to introduce children to their local cultural past, what it means to people, how it has affected the development of the locality, and what its future might be.
- Valuing the local area and developing a sense of place, considering which areas they have feelings for and about, justifying views alongside examining other groups of people's values and attitudes.
- Transport impact, the sufficiency of provision, and possible conflicting views on such issues as parking and plans for road widening or pedestrianisation.

IN THE CLASSROOM

An enquiry undertaken by a Year 6 class was provoked by a headline in the local newspaper.

COMMUNITY MARKET TO CLOSE
AS SHOPPERS FLOCK
TO NEW SUPERSTORE

Using the report in the paper and on the internet, the children built up an idea of what was happening. Their teacher recorded a local TV regional news bulletin from which the children learnt about the views of local people. They planned and organised with their teacher, who provided the photographs for their own risk assessment, a fieldtrip to undertake their own survey of the market and of both the stallholders' and shoppers' views. They considered what the changes proposed would mean locally, the impact on other businesses such as the market suppliers, and other impacts such as traffic increases. They invited in the local councillor to explain the superstore side of the proposal. They debated their own perspectives, drawing on their family views, and took a vote on whether they agreed with the development. What clearly motivated the class was the reality of this local issue.

Citizenship and local environmental participation

Such a problem or issue-based locality study as the one above has clear links with citizenship education. This is particularly strong in many of the issue-based topics investigated in primary geography. It is vital that the connections are made. In investigating a locality, the children engage in investigating matters of concern and importance in their community. This provides opportunities to express and develop their values and attitudes about their place and think about their role as community members. It supports effectively the ethos of citizenship education and the aim of involving children as community participants. Developing such understanding at a local level is highlighted in two QCA citizenship scheme of work units on 'Taking part – Developing skills of communication and participation' and 'Local democracy for young citizens' (DfEE/QCA, 2002). The National Curriculum supports the role that locality studies play in citizenship learning by enabling children to learn about playing *an active role as citizens and developing good relationships and respecting the differences between people* (DfEE/QCA, 1999c). This understanding is initiated in the Foundation Stage 'Knowledge and understanding of the world' focus on communities and respect for each other (DCSF, 2008b, 2008c).

Such enquiries into important issues in local environments initiate and deepen understanding of the processes at play in our society. Children can begin to explore the issues around local sustainability, what might happen to it in the future, and develop a sense of the possible part they can play in determining whether that future is their preferred one. Investigations may also bring to light initiatives such as the transition town and plastic-bag-free towns movements (see websites), empowering children, as future adults, to believe that they may be able to do something positive for change.

PRACTICAL TASK PRACTICAL TASK **PRACTICAL TASK** PRACTICAL TASK **PRACTICAL TASK**

Buy a local newspaper, watch the regional TV news or visit local area websites. Find out about a local issue that is attracting news. It may concern a housing development, the dumping of rubbish or another pollution issue, a traffic problem or road safety matter. Consider how you would encourage a class to identify the main problem to investigate. How you would help them to plan and undertake this, and how might you conclude the project?

Cross-curricular links

Studies in the local area or of another locality, particularly through fieldwork, provide opportunities to make cross-subject links. The strongest links for geography are often with history (Catling, 2006c; Martin, 2004), but good links can be made with literacy, mathematics and science. Table 10.1 indicates some connections that can be made.

Table 10.1 Possible links between geography and other curriculum subjects

Curriculum area	Links to local area study
History	To understand what the local area is like now, investigate the past and how it has changed. Give children opportunities to look at old maps, photographs and newspaper articles about the area, and talk with people from the local community about how it has changed.

Literacy	Writing newspaper articles about a local issue, persuasive letters to the local council about possible changes, and empathetic accounts about living in a different place use and support literacy skills. Oracy skills are developed through listening and speaking in discussions and debates about issues. Reading development is supported when using primary and secondary written sources of information to find out more about the local and other areas.
Mathematics	Collecting data about the local area, analysing and presenting it and using it as evidence to consider the future potential of a local area supports mathematical learning. Using databases, graphing and other ICT software can help analyse, present and interpret data.
Science	Investigating natural habitats in the local area, environmental factors which determine attributes locally, the quality of water supply and why certain building materials are used in that area can support studies of the variety and vitality of a locality.

Resources for locality studies

Useful and effective resources enhance or inhibit successful investigations into the local area or localities further afield. Table 10.2 provides advice on some of the appropriate and informative resources that support a local study. Relate these to the variety of artefacts that can support locality studies (Figure 7.4) and the list of maps and photographs in the section 'Different types of maps' in Chapter 7. The list in Table 10.2 is not exhaustive, and there will be other resources you can add to it.

Table 10.2 Resources to use in a locality study

Resource	Use
Digital cameras (for younger children, DigiBlue and TuffCam)	Essential resources in any investigation for recording a wide range of features, landscapes, activities, etc. Many cameras also have a video facility, which can be invaluable, e.g. for sound.
Hand-held recording devices	Becoming increasingly popular for science work, but are very useful and beneficial for geographical investigations. A wide range of data and information, including GPS, can be recorded, downloaded to interactive whiteboards and used immediately for analysis.
Secondary information sources – leaflets, pamphlets, etc., about localities – internet access – local books and magazines, recent local newspapers, TV news, websites outlining current and topical issues	Provide vital background information for a locality study and can allow children a wider and deeper understanding of their environment.

People from the local community	Provide local and personal information about their use and views on the locality and how it has changed over time and the impact of this.
Local service and facility providers, such as police, fire service	Can explain how the locality works and is run and can answer children's questions on related concerns.
Artefacts and related resources (see secondary information sources above)	Artefacts from the past or particular resources produced and/or used in the locality can bring the study to life and make it much more relevant to the children. Include the ephemera of daily life, such as bus tickets, till receipts and food wrappers.
Videos/DVDs of scenes of the local area and of events of particular note	These can offer the children a strong visual impression of the locality, as well as information and insight. Tourist videos can be examined as marketing materials.
Maps, different types and scales according to children's age – picture maps can be particularly effective	Children develop their map skills, locating places, identifying what is there, beginning to read a landscape, and seeing a context and how places link with others.
Photographs of the locality and wider region	Allow children to visualise the look of an area and aspects of it, and relate to maps.

IN THE CLASSROOM

To initiate a locality study linking geography and history, Year 2 children were given copies of two photographs of the same play area, one taken in the 1980s and another recently. They identified similarities and differences between the site shown, discussed their use of the play area and speculated what children would have done in the 1980s. Two parents who had regularly played there in the 1980s shared their memories, and the children discovered that there was much in common across childhoods. They visited the play area to see it used during the school day. They considered what different people thought about the play area. In class they each played the role of someone from a different age group, including grandparents, parents, teenagers and toddlers. In small groups they planned what they wanted to have there, and shared their ideas, noticing common features and different proposals. Using a group approach to 'hot seating', the children questioned each other's groups about their plans. The council planning office was contacted and plans were shared with a local planner who visited the class.

IN THE CLASSROOM

An urban primary school in an area of major regeneration became involved in putting their ideas for redevelopment to the architects and planners. This arose because a number of the children's homes were to be demolished and the families relocated. The head teacher and staff felt that it was important that the children understood and appreciated what was being done. Early in their studies children in different classes looked at the area in a number of different ways. Some took photographs to show features they liked and wanted to remember and others of sites they wanted replaced. Other children made sound and 'scent/smell' maps of the area, to recall a different sense of the locality. Older children imagined how the area had looked 5,000 years ago and 100 years ago and how it might look in 100 years time, annotating their sketches of views from a high point locally. Others wrote about their feelings for the area and, following fieldwork during which they had listed words to record their feelings and views, wrote *haiku* poems which drew on their words. These activities and others enabled the children to decide and propose what they wanted to see emerge during the redesign and rebuilding of the area. In particular, children across the age ranges argued for retaining as much greenery as possible, for child-friendly side streets, safe crossing points, accessible play areas, colour in the environment (not drab building exteriors), and accessible routes to key facilities. They presented their ideas to the architects and planners, who were both surprised and elated by the children's engagement and ideas, which they felt were both realistic and useful. They acknowledged the children 'knew what they were talking about'.

REFLECTIVE TASK

Consider the two classroom examples above. How do they demonstrate teaching that draws on children's geographies?

A SUMMARY OF **KEY POINTS**

This chapter has:

> considered the meaning of locality studies and their importance in drawing on children's geographies and in engaging their interest;

> identified ways in which locality studies can encourage effective links between geography, citizenship and children's involvement in their local community and environment;

> indicated a number of ways to involve children in local investigations, using fieldwork, based on problem-oriented enquiries through several examples of locality topics;

> identified the variety of resources to use in locality studies;

> noted some cross-curricular possibilities.

MOVING *ON* > > > > > > MOVING *ON* > > > > > > MOVING *ON*

Think about a place you know well, perhaps your home area or another place in the UK you have visited often. Your own experience of a place can be a powerful stimulant for children's learning about places, because you can talk from first hand experience and show items you have from the place. What are the things that have made an impression on you about this place? Make a list of the types of resources that you could collect from this locality to use with children. What might be the focus for your locality study? How might you use your resources to help children develop their understanding of what is there, the lives of people, how it feels to be there, and a sense of place?

FURTHER READING FURTHER READING **FURTHER READING** FURTHER READING

There is much advice available on using the local environment for geographical studies. The following offer some further development points.

Catling, S (2006c) Geography and history: Exploring the local connection. *Primary History*, 42, Spring, 14–16.

Macintosh, M (n.d.) *GTIP Think piece: Human geography primary*. GA website
    www.geography.org.uk/projects/gtip/thinkpieces/humangeography/
Martin, F (2006c) *Teaching geography in primary schools: Learning how to live in the world*.
    Cambridge: Chris Kington.
Scoffham, S (ed) (2004) *Primary geography handbook*. Sheffield: Geographical Association.

There is much useful advice and many examples of local area and other UK locality projects and classroom activities published in *Primary Geographer*.

Useful websites

Learning outside the classroom
    www.lotc.org.uk/
Local 21 Agenda
    www.la21.org.uk/
Plastic bag free towns
    www.plasticbagfree.com/
Sustainable schools
    www.teachernet.gov.uk/sustainableschools/
Transition towns
    www.transitiontowns.org/

11
Exploring global dimensions and non-UK localities

Chapter objectives

By the end of this chapter you should:

- appreciate the importance of children learning about the wider world through geography;
- have developed some understanding of the global dimension, global citizenship and distant locality studies in geography;
- know of approaches to teaching and learning about the wider world;
- be aware of some of the challenges faced when teaching about the wider world.

This chapter addresses the following Professional Standards for QTS:

Q1, Q14, Q15, Q25, Q30.

Introduction

Children are fascinated by the world around them. This extends beyond their own direct experiences. They hear about other parts of the world through their family and friends, via the media, and possibly as travellers and tourists. Children like to know more to satisfy their curiosity. This chapter considers the importance of studying the wider world, its places and environments, developing their awareness of the global dimension and as global citizens. Children's perceptions of other places may be partially informed, even stereotypical. It is vital to redress the imbalanced and misconceived ideas they may have.

Why teach about other places?

Reasons for studying places and the wider world include enabling children to develop a sense of what it is like to be or live somewhere outside their own country. These aspects of geography develop their knowledge and understanding as well as encourage them to explore their feelings and values and develop their sense of empathy with others. Primary geography includes the study of localities in other parts of the world. Through locality studies children learn about the interconnectedness of the world in which they live, and by better understanding how others live, appreciate the impact that we have on each other globally (Macintosh, n.d.). Children in the UK live in one of the wealthiest nations of the world. There is a requirement and encouragement to study a locality in a less prosperous part of the world, perhaps in a less economically developed country, in order that children develop a sense of the diversity of people's contexts and lives (DfEE/QCA, 1999c; DfES, 2004b).

There are other good reasons for children to study 'distant' localities and the wider world, as Figure 11.1 sets out. Distant places provide an invaluable context for learning about the world and should be used to engage children in exploring the intricate links between places and people the world over.

- Children hold images of places and peoples from an early age. It is important to recognise and develop their images of other places and people positively.
- Children's curiosity about distant places can be used to help them ask more effective questions and consider carefully the information they find out about places and the world around them.
- It provides a context to explore geographical ideas – similarity and difference, spatial pattern, change and its impact and sustainability – and to use and develop their enquiry approaches and skills, e.g. map reading and language.
- It extends children's knowledge and understanding about the variety of places, environments and cultures around the world.
- It offers contexts to foster awareness of the common needs of life – e.g. homes and clothing, food and water, and work and leisure – and to consider the differences in the resources and opportunities people have available to them and to consider why this might be. This helps children develop a sense of what life is like elsewhere for other people, enabling comparisons with our own lives.
- There are opportunities to examine and clarify children's existing awareness and understanding of places, developed via a variety of sources, including television, films, websites, games, stories and family links.
- Through the study of people and places in contrasting parts of the world, it is possible to address children's ignorance, partiality and bias which frequently are the basis for their misunderstandings, stereotypes and prejudices about people and places in other parts of the world.
- Children's spatial awareness is developed towards a global scale through exploring particular places and their regional, national and global settings.
- It enables children to recognise their interdependence with the rest of the world, appreciating that this is a 'two-way' process, that our actions impact on others, as do theirs on us, not always obviously or directly.
- It builds a global sense extending children's local, national and international perspectives, as informed thinkers about and actors in the world around them.
- This helps children to be better informed and supports their understanding of the lives of others, why places are as they are, and what they might aspire to and become in the future.
- It encourages children to appreciate and value the diversity of people, places, environments and cultures around the world, and fosters tolerance towards others, building positive attitudes to other people both in the UK and around the world.

Source: Adapted from Catling, 1995

Figure 11.1 Reasons for studying distant places

We noted in Chapter 3 aspects of children's understandings about places beyond their direct experience. Scoffham (2007) argues that the study of 'distant' places and learning outside our own experience is challenging.

The requirement to study distant places is perhaps one of the most problematic areas of the primary school curriculum. It raises questions about stereotypes and prejudices, it taps into our historical perceptions and it challenges us [as teachers] to clarify our own attitudes and values.

(Scoffham, 2007, p5)

REFLECTIVE TASK
REFLECTIVE TASK

REFLECTIVE TASK

Why does Scoffham state above that teachers need to clarify their 'own values and attitudes' in relation to studies of other places and the wider world?

The global dimension

The study of specific distant places is an aspect of the global dimension in the geography curriculum. The global dimension is increasingly associated with a wide range of topical and significant areas of study, linked to sustainability education and global citizenship. Young (2004) perceives the global dimension to be:

> *in essence about social justice and living sustainably: how we choose to behave towards each other and towards Earth itself.*

(Young, 2004, p217)

The global dimension is an essential part of the whole-school curriculum and of the ethos of the school (QCA, 2007b). It has particular significance and meaning within geography, since it is fundamentally about the wider world and global perspectives. The global dimension in primary geography not only focuses on learning about different places in the world and how people live in them but also explores the bigger issues to do with moral, social, cultural and spiritual concerns affecting people, places and the environment. It encourages children's interest in living more sustainably and in adopting greater responsibility for their own actions through critical thinking and reflection, and it challenges their preconceived, partial and possibly biased views (Young, 2004).

Eight key ideas form the essence of the global dimension (DfES/DfID, 2005). These resonate strongly with the key concepts of global citizenship and education for sustainable development (see below and Chapter 5). The key ideas of these three areas are set out alongside each other in Table 11.1.

Young presents several vital reasons for incorporating a global dimension into the primary geography curriculum, seeing it as vital in any meaningful geography. She argues that it is essential because:

- we live in an interdependent world and we have responsibilities towards each other;
- of the need to address the discrimination present in our society;
- we need to counter misinformation and stereotyped views about each other;
- there are so many inequalities in the world, which are caused by the way the world works;
- it is imperative that we live more sustainably;
- we can affect what happens in the future;
- it encourages many schools to develop a link with another school;
- teaching approaches which incorporate the global dimension are of interest to pupils and can promote learning.

(Young, 2004, pp218–221)

The whole-school approach advocated for teaching the global dimension is illustrated in Figure 11.2 on page 129.

Table 11.1 The key ideas of the global dimension, sustainable development education and global citizenship

The global dimension	Sustainable development education	Global citizenship
		Sense of identity and self-esteem
Citizenship	Citizenship and stewardship	
Social justice	Needs and rights of future generations	Commitment to social justice and equity
Human rights		
		Social justice and equity
		Ability to challenge injustice and inequalities
Sustainable development	Sustainable change	Sustainable development
	Quality of life	Concern for the environment and commitment to sustainable development
		Respect for people and things
Diversity	Diversity	Diversity
Values and perceptions		Value and respect for diversity
		Empathy
Interdependence	Interdependence	Globalisation and interdependence
Conflict resolution		Co-operation and conflict resolution
		Peace and conflict
	Uncertainty and precaution	
		Belief that people can make a difference
		Critical thinking
		Ability to argue effectively

Sources: DfES/DfID, 2005; Holland, 1998; Oxfam, 2006a

The global dimension can be taught through:

Whole-school development plans, policies and ethos	Activities integrated into the routines of the school, such as running a mini-enterprise or fundraising event	Visits, assemblies, out-of-hours learning and bringing experts into the school
Separately timetabled thematic days, activity weeks and events often including blocked timetabling	Collaborative curriculum projects with partner schools in other countries	Subjects, with links across subjects being made through common topics or themes

Any combination of these

Source: QCA, 2007b, p3

Figure 11.2 Teaching the global dimension

REFLECTIVE TASK

Consider the reasons for learning about distant places and the global dimension outlined above. What would be your core four or five reasons for ensuring these studies are part of each child's entitlement?

IN THE CLASSROOM

A Year 4 class studying Castries in St Lucia began by considering words they associated with the island or what they thought it might be like. Their teacher wrote these in red on the interactive whiteboard around the name St Lucia. The children used photographs of places around the island to add further words, written in green. The teacher provided captions for the photographs, which they matched up, and from these they noted further words, in blue. The children asked that some of their first words be crossed out, since they realised that they were inaccurate. What the children noticed was that as they gleaned further information, they learnt more about the island's context; their knowledge increased. Finally, the children watched a DVD about everyday life in St Lucia and afterwards added further words to their 'list'. This formed the basis for a discussion about how and in what ways their perceptions and understanding of St Lucia were changing. It demonstrated that they should not rely on first impressions, and encouraged them to explore their values and attitudes positively in relation to the people and place.

Global citizenship

Tanner (2007, p52) argues that in primary geography:

> *Global citizenship initiatives are...reflecting the reality that pupils must be prepared not only with knowledge, but also with the skills and values necessary to face and respond to the challenges for the twenty-first century.*

Tanner acknowledged that it is crucial to understand how everything in our world is bound together in a web of interconnections against the backdrop of living in a time of unprecedented change and challenge. It is the skills acquired and the values developed which will underpin children's learning to live effectively and responsibly in our changing world. Oxfam (2006a, p2) noted additionally that primary children should have *the opportunity to develop critical thinking about complex global issues in the safe space of the classroom*.

Young children encounter and are aware of controversial issues and need to be able to explore their own ideas and discuss and express their own views, rather than being given a set of prescribed answers to questions where there is no obvious right or wrong side or view (Oxfam, 2006b). This requires participatory and exploratory teaching and learning methods, including discussion, debate, role play, communities of enquiry and open-ended problem-oriented enquiries (see Chapter 6). Such approaches help to develop children as global citizens, with the qualities of someone who:

- is aware of the wider world and has a sense of their own role as a world citizen;
- respects and values diversity;
- has an understanding of how the world works;
- is outraged by social injustice;
- participates in the community at a range of levels from the local to the global;
- is willing to act to make the world a more equitable and sustainable place;
- takes responsibility for their actions.

(Oxfam, 2006a, p2)

From these perspectives it becomes clear that global citizenship is more than learning about the global dimension, which in turn is more than learning about distant places, as Figure 11.3 shows. Global citizenship is about active participation and engagement, developing children's critical thinking skills, autonomy and capacity to take increasing personal responsibility. Oxfam (2006a, p2) outlines a process through which this can be facilitated, which has close links with the enquiry approach in geography. Through it children:

- absorb new information;
- judge its bias and reliability;
- analyse it;
- synthesise it through a process of reflection on their own current views;
- draw their own conclusions;
- make informed decisions;
- take considered action.

> **Distant-place studies**
> Describing, understanding, comparing and contrasting different people and places.
> The *'What is it like?'*
>
> **The global dimension**
> Explaining the interrelationships and connectedness between people and places.
> The *'Why is it like that?'*
>
> **Global citizenship**
> The ability to analyse situations and injustice, to respect and value similarity and difference, and to take responsibility.
> The *'What can I do?'*

Figure 11.3 Distinctions between distant-place studies, the global dimension and global citizenship

Teaching about distant places, the global dimension and global citizenship is challenging but essential. Martin (2007) notes that teachers need to be well informed and to draw on appropriate subject knowledge, as well as remaining positive about the problems that children investigate rather than overburdening them with worries and uncertainties, which they may take to heart when not able to discuss them because of other priorities. Young with Cummins (2002) and Hirst (2006) assert that where the global dimension and global citizenship are incorporated and embedded, children seem to be more motivated and enthused by what they are learning. It may be that this is fostered through inter-school links where the school's consistent engagement has enabled children to make real connections and develop deeper understandings (Disney, 2004; Disney and Mapperley, 2007).

Hicks (2007) advocates tackling global issues with all children and stresses the importance of helping them understand that problems do not just occur 'elsewhere', and are consequently less relevant, but that every issue has some local impact even if its form varies from place to place. He sees local and global issues as two sides of the same coin. Underlying much of the advice on teaching about these aspects (e.g. DfES/DfID, 2005; National Assembly for Wales, 2008; Scottish Executive, 2001) is the view that it is impossible properly to understand our own local environment and community without understanding what is happening in the wider global context, whether it is to do with food, transport, energy, music or culture, as examples. Thus, we must educate children to become global citizens, able to think and act locally and globally. This involves examining global impacts to do, for instance, with natural disasters and environmental pollution, and necessitates helping children to consider possible resolutions (Hicks, 1998). As Freire (1994, p9) argues, *One of the tasks of the progressive educator... is to unveil opportunities for hope, no matter what the obstacles might be.* Such an approach focuses not simply on the present and the issue but looks to the future, encouraging children to consider possible, probable and preferable solutions for their future.

In the Classroom

Ofsted (2008b, p11) inspections of education for sustainability have identified examples of effective practice.

> One school's 'Fair Trade Fortnight' made very effective use of the expertise of a parent who worked for a fairtrade food company. He helped the pupils establish links with a school near one of the company's plantations in India. Through email exchanges and other correspondence, the pupils gained first-hand experience of the equity of fair trade and the ways in which it had improved the quality of life for the Indian children and their families.

PRACTICAL TASK PRACTICAL TASK **PRACTICAL TASK** PRACTICAL TASK **PRACTICAL TASK**

Find out more about the global dimension and global citizenship through the DEA, QCA and Oxfam websites. Choose a topic or project described there. How are the global dimension and global citizenship exemplified through it?

Bringing distant places into the classroom

In today's world, modern technologies give our classrooms continuous and instant access to the outside world. Websites such as Google Earth and LiveLocal bring otherwise distant and far-off places directly to us, providing children with detailed, if pre-selected, images. This access, supported by other primary and secondary sources such as visitors, books, photo packs, artefacts and stories, can help children construct more informed ideas about places. Studying a variety of places during their primary years and using diverse resources enables children to build a knowledge base about different places and issues in the world.

Studies of distant localities should be of similar size places to the local area of the school (see Chapter 10). It is vitally important that studies of places, whether in Europe or further away across the world, are set in context. The range of geographical topics listed in Figure 10.1 forms the basis for selecting topics for distant locality studies.

IN THE CLASSROOM

Early in their study of Chembakolli, a village locality in southern India (ActionAid, 2002), a class of Year 2 children used a globe, atlases and the internet to find out where the village is and about it. Using the travel experience of some children in the class, they looked at flight routes and times to see how they might travel to India and which city airport was the nearest. They worked out what they needed to pack if they went and found out about the food they would eat. Through these activities they became aware of the relative relationship of the UK and India, the idea of time distance for travel, and planning as a tourist for their journey and stay. (See also: ActionAid, 2008, 2009)

Activities to support learning through locality and global study

It is important, when beginning a place- or issue-based study, to elicit and probe children's pre-existing ideas and to consider some of the balances that need to be included. Your overall focus will be in your outline plan. While your distant locality topic will be planned, it is vital to remain flexible and to respond to children's needs when later you become aware of shortcomings, imbalances, misconceptions, stereotypes or prejudices that should be tackled. Table 11.2 provides some examples of activities to investigate and raise children's awareness in a locality global issue study (Garforth et al., 2006). These activities encourage them to ask questions and discuss matters. These can be used at different points within a project and undertaken as class activities or by groups of children.

Table 11.2 Activities to raise levels of local and global awareness

Activity description	Resources	Outcomes of activity
On an outline map of the country where your locality study is located, write the question: *What do you know about [the country]?* Ask children to write down as many facts, feelings, etc., about that country as possible. Repeat in relation to the locality asking children to draw: *What I would see if I went to [the locality]?*	Large outline map of a specific country with the questions or with the activity title written at the top. Felt-tip pens, crayons, colouring pencils.	To find out what the children know or think they know about the country or locality study. To assess the nature and accuracy of information they have and of views they express. To initiate discussion about a country, to consider how we know this 'information' and why we might need to find out more. Repeat the activities during or at the end of their study, and compare the images to assess development of their understanding.
Give two or three photographs per group. Ask children to think about where the photograph was taken, and to name the city (if appropriate), country and/or continent. Once they have decided, go through the photographs together. Ask each group for their response, and to justify their location. At the end, tell them that the photographs in fact all show the same place.	A set of photographs (around 20) of varied views of the same city, country or continent, either from your own collection or from a published photo pack on a distant place. Photographs can be downloaded from Google Images and laminated. Number the photographs so that they can be easily referred to in the lesson.	Children are surprised that all the photographs show the same place. This provokes discussions about the deceptiveness of appearances, and the issues in categorising and generalising about places. There are variations and differences wherever we are. Use this to challenge stereotypes and redress imbalances in what children believe to be true. Highlight and emphasise the similarities between places and people.
Use an assortment of photographs of different perspectives of a locality or a country. Ask children to diamond rank them according to which are the most and least representative of that locality or country.	Assorted images all from the same locality or country that show very different views and activities or places and events. Have some that are not apparently characteristic of the locality or country and others that are very much so.	As above, in addressing preconceptions children can consider where their ideas come from. Discuss the importance of being receptive and open-minded about the diversity of people, places and environments.
Identify a 'characteristic' child who lives in a particular distant locality. Provide a fact sheet about a typical day in her/his life. Ask children to produce a comparable fact sheet about themselves. They might make a poster about their locality.	A poster showing where a particular child lives and a fact sheet showing a typical day in the life of a child, from the distant locality you are studying.	Encourage looking for similarities. Children will find much common ground between the basic activities that we all do across the world. It develops empathy for the commonality of people's lives and encourages greater tolerance and acceptance of people around us locally and globally.
Use the interactive whiteboard or a large sheet of paper. Write *How can I make [this locality/ the world] a better place?* Discuss what 'making it better' means, thinking about improvements and addressing issues. Ask children to write/ illustrate their ideas about how the locality/world can be 'made better'.	The interactive whiteboard, or A1 or A2 size sheets of sugar or flipchart paper, a large board, felt pens.	Provides the opportunity to discuss and express the concerns they want to see addressed, and how they would do so. These can be locality issues for the people there or significant global issues, hazards and events. Children should consider and discuss what is good and not so good in the locality/our world and what the word 'better' means to and for different people.

As in any locality study there are many activities that may be selected from and used. Figure 11.4 provides examples of a range of activities to adapt imaginatively and creatively. It will be a matter for you to decide how to apply them for an age group and when during a locality study you choose to use them. They complement the ideas in Table 11.2.

- Locate and mark the features and views in photographs on a map of the locality.
- From map and photograph information create a model of the locality. As you find out more from other sources add to or correct the layout of the model. Use it to trace journeys, see what happens where and play out daily life and events.
- Find out why particular features are as they are, such as why the buildings are constructed as they are, why a road may not be made up, or where a stream or river has its source and flows through.
- Consider why particular goods are available, who might buy them, and where they might come from.
- Examine where else people go shopping, for leisure activities, or for work.
- Provide the children with a set of factual statements about the locality to read and discuss. Encourage them to group the statements and explain their categories.
- Provide a jumbled-up set of information about the daily life of a person in the community. The children must arrange the information into an appropriate (correct?) sequence and explain their order.
- Select aspects of daily life or a particular event and create an improvised drama to act through what occurs.
- Encourage children to find out about the life of a particular individual in the locality. Hot seat the character, who answers questions about their daily life, work, activities, leisure and so on.
- Create the 'home corner' or a part of your classroom into a room in a home or shop. Use it to role play what happens there.
- Imagine you are going to visit this locality and plan a trip there. Find out about how you get there, how long it takes, and so forth. Create an itinerary of what you would do there, who you would visit, what you might eat, what you would wear, etc. This might be enacted through spending a day travelling out, visiting and returning, with some children as visitors and others as community members.
- Create a 'balance sheet' of impressions of the locality. Identify what is liked and what is less appreciated. Individuals and groups share their views to identify what is common and what less so. They should consider why this is and how what they know influences their views.
- Invite an external visitor or speaker to share their experiences and knowledge with the children and to answer their questions, which children should prepare beforehand. Visitors might be members of the local community who have travelled in the relevant country or people working with charity organisations who know the country or area. Ask them to bring in some personal possessions, typical of the area that they are talking about to help the children envisage being there.
- Create a poster which shows the similarities and differences between life in your own locality and that being studied.
- Encourage children to write a letter in which they evaluate what they have learnt about the locality. They should note what they have in common as well as how their places differ and diverge, which they should be encouraged to celebrate.

Figure 11.4 Some possible teaching activities to use in a distant locality study

> **IN THE CLASSROOM**
>
> At the end of their study of a distant locality, a Year 5 class spent one lesson identifying what they would include in a pack about their own local area. They were limited to 20 photographs and 10 pages of information. They debated in groups and as a class what they would include and leave out, and why. Through this activity they began to appreciate the limitations of the resources they had used and became aware that their understanding was limited and partial. Several children commented about not assuming too much about the place they studied. They realised they had some understanding but that gaps remained in their knowledge.

PRACTICAL TASK PRACTICAL TASK **PRACTICAL TASK** PRACTICAL TASK **PRACTICAL TASK**

You are asked to plan a short topic looking at a global issue. Decide on your issue and identify six of the activities from Table 11.2 and Figure 11.4 to adapt to use in teaching about the issue. Why have you selected those activities?

Some pitfalls to avoid

Studying distant places is not without its dangers. It is vital to maintain the focus on what children have learnt from the information they have. They should be encouraged always to distinguish facts from opinions. The statements they make and conclusions they draw should be evidence-based and they should acknowledge when they lack information and acknowledge a perception which they might attempt to justify. There are other concerns to be aware of.

● When studying a locality, ensure that other parts of the country are encountered, whether urban environments when a rural locality or *vice versa* (Young, 2004; Young with Cummins, 2002). It is vital that children do not talk about pizza and think that it 'is' Italy. They must become aware of various attributes of a country, including its culture and the diversity of lives and places, so that they are aware the locality is not 'the country'. It is important to avoid sweeping generalisations about a country that can exacerbate stereotyping and paint an unbalanced view of life elsewhere.

● We are quick to identify and emphasise differences between ourselves and others. It is vital to focus on similarities, encouraging children to see how their life compares to those of children in a similarly sized locality. Through this focus diversity can be recognised and valued, even where there are very different circumstances.

● Learning through sympathy and charity, e.g. of those living in poverty, can lead to the problem of tokenism and undermine the sense of equality of people wherever they are. If an international week, where different classes study different countries, is planned and run superficially, it can lead to unbalanced views of those countries, reinforcing stereotypes and perpetuating myths. When focused on a variety of localities where children make comparisons to their own lives and experiences, it can prove to be rich, engaging and informative.

● Photographs may raise issues that children are keen to discuss. These may be challenging, with children asking, for example during a study of a locality in rural Africa or India, why the people's clothes look dirty, their houses are small and cramped and they cook outside. Because this may be a very misleading impression gathered from the resources used, it is important that such questions are discussed together as a class and not avoided though they seem uncomfortable. Discussing such misconceptions or misinterpretations helps children develop values and attitudes based on reality and understanding.

IN THE CLASSROOM

A Year 5 class's locality study was based on a village in Peru. While most of their resources were in English, this study linked appropriately with the primary language that the school had chosen, Spanish. During their studies the children used resources which were in written in Spanish that had been brought back by their teacher from a visit. They looked at information about Peru in Spanish on national and tourist websites. In learning Spanish their teacher ensured that they used relevant everyday geographical words and terms related to directions, streets and buildings, food and clothing, and the physical environment. They extended their vocabulary because of their interest in their project. They also began to learn something of Spanish and Peruvian culture and explored some of the history of Peru to understand why and how the Spanish had come to the country. This linked them into the wider context of international tourism as well as considering the idea of remoteness in finding out about Machu Picchu. They examined the idea of conquest and its lasting impact, giving their project a global dimension and involving global citizenship perspectives.

Resources for distant place and issue investigations

There is considerable and growing support, guidance and resource provision for teaching the global dimension and global citizenship. A wide variety of resources can be used for locality studies. Artefacts and the variety of resources noted in Figure 7.4 and Table 10.2 are invaluable aids. A further way into distant localities and some global environmental issues is through stories (see Appendix 1).

Many voluntary and non-governmental organisations (NGOs) have and continue to produce resources to support primary geography distant locality and global dimension studies (Drake, 1996). These organisations include:

- ActionAid;
- CAFOD;
- Christian Aid;
- Friends of the Earth;
- Oxfam;
- Save the Children;
- UNICEF;
- World Wide Fund for Nature (WWF);
- Red Cross;
- Development education centres, including TIDE, RISC, Leeds, Cumbria and others.

Their resources are produced from a particular context and for a reason, whether to support fundraising or to help change attitudes, challenge stereotypes and break down prejudices. Many have been produced by education officers and through curriculum projects involving practising teachers (e.g. TIDE). It is important to understand the context of a locality pack and other materials before using them. When evaluating such resources, check that it is clear that they offer a balanced and inclusive approach and were developed with the co-operation of the community portrayed. This does not mean that they avoid issues or problems; rather, they provide for different points of view and debate. Such materials usually provide activities, including information and worksheets, role play about local concerns, and materials about the issues faced by communities. You should check the date of publication to ensure that you are not using dated resources, which will have been a year or more in preparation, as well as checking the quality of the photographs and maps, the language level or levels, the variety of ways in which information is presented, and the usefulness of the activities suggested.

REFLECTIVE TASK
REFLECTIVE TASK

One concern in studies of distant localities is using materials that are not up to date. What reasons can you identify that support this concern? How would you define an up-to-date resource for distant locality studies? When might you use older resources?

A SUMMARY OF **KEY POINTS**

This chapter has:

> considered what is meant by the global dimension in geography and advocated the importance of facilitating children's learning about the wider world;

> considered global citizenship in geography teaching and learning and how this may raise children's awareness and a greater sense of responsibility and empowerment;

> introduced you to approaches and activities for effective teaching of locality studies and the global dimension in the geography curriculum;

> noted some of the pitfalls to look out for when undertaking locality and global dimension studies.

MOVING *ON* > > > > > > MOVING *ON* > > > > > > MOVING *ON*

Tanner (2007) sets out four reasons for introducing fair trade into schools.

1. It allows children to make a connection between their everyday lives (buying and consuming a product) and the lives of people living and working in distant places.
2. It lends itself well to children's sense of justice and 'fairness', that people who work hard to make our food, clothes and goods should be paid a fair price.
3. It is an issue in which everyone has a role to play and can take part.
4. There are some excellent resources to support learning and teaching about the practice of fair trade in schools (see Dalrymple, n.d.).

Information and resources are available through the Fairtrade Foundation website, and through Comic Relief and Oxfam (see websites at the end of the chapter). Find out more about fair trade and the ways that it might support studies of a distant locality, the global dimension and global citizenship.

FURTHER READING FURTHER READING **FURTHER READING** FURTHER READING
Garforth, H, Hopper, L, Lowe, B and Robinson L (2006) *Growing up global*. Reading: RISC.

Hicks, D and Holden, C (2007) *Teaching the global dimension*. London: Routledge.

Martin, F (2006c) *Teaching geography in primary schools*. Cambridge: Chris Kington.

Scoffham, S (ed) (2004) *Primary geography handbook*. Sheffield: Geographical Association.

Young, M with Cummins, E (2002) *Global citizenship: the handbook for primary teaching*. Cambridge: Chris Kington.

Useful websites

Comic Relief
   www.comicrelief.com/teach-and-learn/

Development Education Association (DEA) case studies
   www.globaldimension.org.uk/docs/dea_global_matters.pdf

Department for International Development (DfID)
   www.globaldimension.org.uk/

Fair Trade Foundation
   www.fairtrade.org.uk/

Global Gateway
   www.globalgateway.org.uk/

Oxfam Education
   www.oxfam.org.uk/education/

QCA *The Global Dimension in Action*
   www.qca.org.uk/libraryAssets/media/Global_Dimensions_print_friendly.pdf

Teachers in Development Education (TIDE)
   www.tidec.org/

12
Planning geography teaching

Chapter objectives

By the end of this chapter you should:

- **understand the need for effective planning in geography teaching to enable successful learning for children;**
- **recognise the need for short-, medium- and long-term planning in geography;**
- **appreciate the role of different types of plans and understand the importance of adapting these to suit your own needs as well as ensuring their suitability for your situation and circumstances;**
- **be aware of the need for progression and differentiation in planning.**

This chapter addresses the following Professional Standards for QTS:

Q1, Q10, Q14, Q15, Q19, Q22, Q25, Q29, Q30.

Introduction

This chapter considers planning in your geography teaching. Planning is essential in order to give you a clear sense of direction, enabling you to make decisions as your teaching of a geography topic develops. Planning takes place at three levels: long-, medium- and short-term planning. Each of these is considered in this chapter, though your interest is mainly on medium- and short-term planning. Each school's geography policy and objectives will be particular to it. Your planning will take account of its children and their circumstances and needs, the school's local environment and connections to the wider world, particular interests the school has in its geography policy and scheme, and what you bring to your geography teaching, whether in a single subject or cross-subject topic. You will have your own ideas and values about geography and the way you wish to develop your teaching. Combining these with the school's and national requirements in the Early Learning Goals and National Curriculum geography is important in your planning process. Medium-term plans may already be in place and take account of these. However, do not plan too tightly and rigidly. As has been said earlier, this can constrain the children's involvement and contribution in enquiry-based teaching and you may miss important opportunities which you can use by thinking flexibly and adaptively. Your evaluations should enable you regularly to reassess and modify appropriately what you have planned. Your plans are working documents to be annotated and adapted.

Long-term planning

The purpose of a school's long-term geography plan, or scheme of work, is to outline the cover, progression and development of geography across the school. It will ensure that from the Foundation Stage children are given the opportunity to meet the appropriate Early Learning Goals, while during Key Stages 1 and 2 the statutory requirements for geography are incorporated. The geography subject leader will regularly review, evaluate and adapt the geography scheme to ensure its clarity, thoroughness, topicality and balance, as well as its resource needs.

The school's geography scheme of work will have a number of features, drawn from the curriculum requirements, the children's experience and the school's context, such as links with other schools in the UK or abroad. The features of a geography scheme will include:

- recognition that children can contribute from their own geographies;
- continuity and progression between year groups and key stages in the use of core concepts and skills, as well as of the school grounds and local environment;
- enquiry-based learning which encourages children to look for issues, and develop problem-solving skills;
- integration of enquiry methods, skills, themes and real places to develop children's experience, understanding, skills and values;
- a representative range of different places to study across the world, taking account of local links related to the school's community and environment;
- planned opportunities for learning outside the classroom, including fieldwork;
- opportunities to investigate and discuss topical matters and issues that arise;
- a wide range of resources, including maps and plans, photographs, artefacts, ICT software and appropriate websites, books, resource packs, and much more;
- appropriate cross-curricular links.

(Carter, 1998; DfEE/QCA, 1999b; Owen and Ryan, 2001; Richardson, 2004b)

Very many schools continue to base their geography schemes of work around the units of work provided in the guidance materials developed by the QCA (Catling et al., 2007; DfEE/QCA, 1998/2000; Ofsted, 2008a). This advice has been more recently complemented by a SuperScheme 'library' of units, bringing many of the QCA units up to date (Geographical Association, 2005–07), which similarly contains a variety of units from which schools might select to update their geography scheme. The strong advice is that schools should adapt any such units if they do not use them as stimuli to create their own units.

It is more usual to set out the school's geography scheme of work as the units or topics to be covered in an overall subject matrix. Table 12.1 provides such an example. In this example the school has selected a number of geography units from the QCA (DfEE/QCA, 1998/2000) geography scheme of work as well as identifying three topics from the Foundation Stage requirements and guidance. The focus, content and sequence of each of the units or topics will be provided in the medium-term plans for each one.

Considering progression

Two key elements that should inform long-term planning are progression and consistency. Consistency occurs through regular geography teaching across each school year and in each year, and progression is enabled as the children are engaged in greater depth and breadth with their studies as well as through tackling issues in greater detail and with more complexity, developing their understanding of their own and other people's values and attitudes about places and issues (Richardson, 2004b). Progression is supported through the following elements (Owen and Ryan, 2001):

- increasing breadth of geographical knowledge;
- increasing depth of geographical understanding;
- extending the scale of the areas studied;

Table 12.1 A whole-school long-term geography plan

	AUTUMN TERM		SPRING TERM		SUMMER TERM	
R	Ourselves Around us	Movement Going places	The environment Local area	Ourselves Around us	Movement Going places	The environment Local area
Yr 1	Around our school: local area Continuous unit: Barnaby Bear explores		How do we make our local area safer? Continuous unit: Barnaby Bear explores		A visit to the seaside (Geography + History) Continuous unit: Barnaby Bear explores	
Yr 2	Tocuaro, Mexico Continuous unit: Our school grounds		An island home Continuous unit: Our school grounds		Our local area (Geography + History) Continuous unit: Our school grounds	
Yr 3	Local parking problems Continuous unit: Story places		Finding out about the world (Geography + History) Continuous unit: Story places		Our weather (Geography + Science) Continuous unit: Story places	
Yr 4	Continuous unit: Story places		Egypt past and present (History + Geography) Continuous unit: Story places		Improving our environment: Getting around our neighbourhood Continuous unit: Story places	
Yr 5	A visit to Greece: Today and yesterday (Geography + History) Continuous unit: What's in the news?		Continuous unit: What's in the news?		Water and rivers in our landscape (Geography, Science + History) Continuous unit: What's in the news?	
Yr 6	Cleaning up the world Continuous unit: Passport to the world		Continuous unit: Passport to the world		School journey: Investigating coasts and localities (Geography, Science + History) Continuous unit: Passport to the world	

- development of more abstract ideas through the core geographical concepts;
- increasing complexity and range of issues studied;
- development of knowledge, values and skills.

In planning a geography scheme of work the geography subject leader might consider how particular opportunities can be taken to develop progression and provide for the initiation, reinforcement and deepening of geographical learning. Ofsted (2008a) has noted that it is not usual for schools to consider their long-term planning of geography in this way. One way this might be achieved is through the use of key learning environments, such as the school grounds and local area. Figure 12.1 outlines a sequence of learning opportunities that might form the basis for using a school's grounds progressively for children from the Foundation Stage to Years 5 and 6 across a geography scheme.

Foundation Stage: *Encountering the geography of the nursery*
- Observe and name features around the nursery area, including the weather
- Make journeys around the nursery and school, using relative directions
- Notice changes to activities and resources and where they are

Years 1 and 2: *Developing geographical awareness on the school site*
- Describe features and relative locations and directions around the grounds and school
- Consider people who work in school: where and what they do, and why
- Observe and make weather records: observation, leading to recording temperatures, windiness, sun/cloud, etc.
- Consider how weather and seasons affect 'me and you', and how school grounds are used in different weathers and different times of year
- Places 'we' like and dislike, why and how we would change them

Years 3 and 4: *Engaging children in geographical studies of the school*
- Examine room and space use in the school building, and land use around the school site
- Notice and map patterns of features and activities
- Look at changes around the school: older and newer features, dating features and building(s), considering changes in use of parts of the school inside and outside, development of the school site, and discuss changes that might improve the school
- Caring for our school: energy watch, litter watch
- Weathering and erosion around the school

Years 5 and 6: *Becoming involved in developing the geography of the school*
- Study water in the school grounds: soaking in, puddles and run-off, evaporation; how to make use of rainwater in school
- Consider the school as a settlement and community: features, people and groupings, services, uses, access and change
- Look at reasons for patterns on the site, how these might change and why, with links to ways to improve the use of the school site
- Ideas for a 'school of the future' on the site: what it is like, what happens there, who works and goes there, and much more
- Plan a school guide for future parents and children

Figure 12.1 Planning for development in geographical studies of the school site

It is vital also to take into account children's developing awareness and learning. Figure 12.2 summarises in broad terms expectations for children's developing understanding of the global dimension. To support progression in their geographical learning the geography subject leader's knowledge and application of appropriate and challenging expectations in children's geographical, social and cultural understanding can inform the way in which a geography scheme of work is planned effectively through a primary school.

Foundation Stage children are offered a variety of experiences that encourage and support them to begin to make connections between different parts of their life experience. They become aware of their relationships to others and of the different communities that they are part of, for example, family and school. They begin to develop awareness of diversity of peoples, places, cultures, languages, and religions. They begin to understand fairness, the need to care for other people and the environment, and to be sensitive to the needs and views of others.

Key Stage 1 children begin to develop a sense of their own worth and the worth of others. They develop a sense of themselves as part of a wider world and gain awareness of a range of cultures and places. They learn that all humanity shares the same basic needs but that there are differences in how and to what extent these needs are met.

Key Stage 2 children develop their understanding beyond their own experience and build up their knowledge of the wider world and of diverse societies and cultures. They learn about the similarities and differences between people and places around the world and about disparities in the world. They develop their sense of social justice and moral responsibility and begin to understand that their own choices can affect global issues, as well as local ones.

Source: DfES/DfID, 2005, p5

Figure 12.2 Expected progression in understanding of the global dimension

PRACTICAL TASK PRACTICAL TASK **PRACTICAL TASK** PRACTICAL TASK **PRACTICAL TASK**

Using the information about children's personal geographies provided in Chapter 3 and the ideas about place studies and local area studies in Chapters 4 and 10, write a summary of expectations for local area study along the lines of that in Figure 12.2.

Medium-term planning

Medium-term planning is the planning of a geography unit of work or topic for your class. It may last just a few weeks, a half-term or a full term, with one to two hours teaching a week. It is focused on a topic and identifies the learning objectives and expectations. Some geography units or topics might be continuous units, which are dipped into and out of during a term or over a year. These might relate to topical events, several being picked up across the year linked through a focus on, for instance, natural hazards or places and communities in the news.

Many primary schools have in place planned and structured geography units of work, related to the geography scheme of work. They may provide a broad outline or set out in some detail the key enquiry questions, the sequence for study, the activities and the resources to use, as the QCA geography units do (DfEE/QCA, 1998/2000). Tables 12.2 and 12.3 provide a fully worked example of a geography unit. The structure follows the pattern used in the QCA geography units. Table 12.2 explains the purpose of the unit, its links with the geography curriculum requirements, the children's learning and expectations of them, vocabulary opportunities, resource needs and cross-curricular links. Table 12.3 sets out the sequence of study using a series of geographical questions to organise and structure progression in the unit.

Table 12.2 The rationale for a geography medium-term plan on mobility and access

UNIT TITLE Getting about – Exploring mobility and access in the locality

AGE GROUP A fully planned unit to adapt as appropriate for the Year 4 class used with

About the unit:

This medium-term unit focuses on movement about the local environment for those who find mobility less straightforward, such as wheelchair users, those with hearing or sight impairments, the infirm, older people, parents/carers with pushchairs. It explores the accessibility of routes and places and identifies good, moderate and poor examples of access, which help or hinder mobility for local people and visitors to the area. It enables children to examine the locality around their school, to consider local needs and concerns, and to propose solutions to difficulties that they find.

The key questions for the issue in this unit are:
● Why is mobility access an issue?
● What are the local issues about mobility access?
● Who is affected and why?
● Where is mobility most and least a problem?
● What do people locally think about this issue?
● What do the children think?
● How can the problems locally be overcome?

This unit offers links with speaking and listening, thinking skills, citizenship, equal opportunities, inclusion and environmental education.

GEOGRAPHY KEY STAGES 1 and 2 PROGRAMME OF STUDY LINKS	
Geographical enquiry and skills ● ask questions ● collect, record, analyse evidence ● examine different views ● use maps ● undertake fieldwork ● draw conclusions and make proposals ● use decision-making skills	**Knowledge and understanding of places** ● school locality ● what places are like ● locations of features ● describing and explaining what the places are like ● proposing how changes may be made
Knowledge and understanding of patterns and processes ● map location patterns ● explain human processes	**Knowledge and understanding of environmental change and sustainable development** ● consider why people may want to improve the local area ● examine how decisions affect people's lives in a locality ● identify ways to improve the local environment ● identify opportunities for children's own involvement

Vocabulary	Resources
In the unit children are likely to use: • access, accessibility, benefits, council, facilities, features, improvements, limitations, mobility, planning, practice, proposals, routes, services, shops, transport, travel They may also use: • other more specific terms associated with the issue linked to disability, features in the local environment, and aspects of equal opportunities and citizenship activity	• range of local maps, including large-scale adapted OS map, street maps • contemporary photographs • council planning department website address • local people and professionals, including residents, shopkeepers, planning access officer, local councillor • examples of interview questions and rating scales • information on any local reports on accessibility issues

PRIOR LEARNING

It is helpful for the children to have:
• studied aspects of their own locality
• used maps and photographs
• developed fieldwork skills
• undertaken geographical enquiries
• been introduced to environmental changes and their impacts

EXPECTATIONS
At the end of the unit,

most children will:	• be able to identify an issue affecting people's lives in their local area and how people may be able to manage and improve it • be able to justify their own views and take account of those of others • be able to use evidence to show the situation found through an enquiry
some children will not have made so much progress and will:	• develop their experience in using photographs and maps and in observing in the local environment • state their own views and the views of others about an issue
some children will have progressed further and will:	• be able to put forward evidenced and reasoned arguments for proposals for change • recognise and describe ways in which people can tackle a local matter of concern linked to equal opportunities and citizenship

FUTURE LEARNING

Children build on their learning in this unit by undertaking a further issue-based enquiry in Year 6 on a topic in which they will largely use information from secondary sources. They might consider other issues affecting people's lives and human rights in other studies with an equal opportunities and citizenship focus, perhaps on education for sustainable development and/or environmental issue linked to a geographical theme, studied at a range of scales.

CURRICULUM CONNECTIONS

Link this work to the non-statutory Guidelines for PSHE/Citizenship, Key Stage 2, particularly: preparing to play an active role as citizens.
Use the opportunity to develop the full range of *Thinking Skills*.
Draw on relevant units in the Scheme of Work for Key Stages 1 and 2: Citizenship.

Table 12.3 The unit of work plan for an enquiry into mobility and access locally

LEARNING INTENTIONS Children learn:	POSSIBLE TEACHING ACTIVITIES Children:	LEARNING OUTCOMES Children:	POINTS TO NOTE
How do people get about in our locality?			
• that people move about locally in various ways • that people visit a range of different facilities locally • to obtain information from photographs and maps	• discuss how, where and why people move about the school • use local photographs to identify and illustrate the variety of forms of travel and transport • use local maps to note the various routes that can be used for different forms of transport to different facilities locally • in groups prepare a poster about travel in the local area	• know that people use different forms of transport • know that there are a variety of different features and places that people travel to and along locally	Graphical skills: encourage the children to look for evidence to support their observations from the photographs and maps
What makes a place accessible for everyone?			
• that people have different travel and access needs • that streets should be accessible to everyone • that local facilities and services should intend to be accessible to everyone • to ask questions • to select appropriate information	• undertake fieldwork in the school building and grounds to identify how easy or difficult it is to move around • use a wheelchair or push/pull a cumbersome case about the school to identify accessible and inaccessible routes and create a map of the school grounds to show the findings • have a presentation from and ask questions of a local council planning access officer about access for everyone in the local area and what should be in place • discuss who has mobility and access needs in the local area and consider why some facilities are accessible while others are not • on a local map identify sites where the children think that accessibility is good and where they think it is poor	• understand that while able-bodied people can access places, it is frequently more difficult for those with mobility problems • know that there are legal requirements for many facilities to be accessible to all	• Fieldwork: use the school grounds to explore questions, needs and issues about access and mobility • Inclusion: encourage the children to consider how all people move about • Speaking and listening: encourage the children to discuss how best to listen and understand the key points made by a speaker; spend time identifying questions to ask • Thinking skills: focus the children on using evidence to justify comments and conclusions

How are people affected by access to places locally?

Learning objectives	Activities	Learning outcomes	Teaching notes
• to collect data in the locality • to use maps at a variety of scales • to identify where people are helped or hindered in accessing local facilities • to undertake an interview	• create a friendly checklist to use to assess the accessibility of various places in the local area • develop a short questionnaire to use to interview people about their experience of and views on the accessibility of places, some or all of the questions in which can be logged on data handling software • plan and carry out fieldwork to investigate accessibility around the locality on routes and for various features, services and facilities • take photographs of examples of good and poor access	• understand the value of investigating the environment to appreciate an issue • refer in an informed manner to local facilities • identify types of questions from which data can be recorded and can ask suitable questions to interrogate the data collected	• Enquiry: involve the children in developing the checklist and interview questions by providing examples of such approaches for different topics • Safety: ensure the off-site visits are organised to meet LEA and school guidelines • ICT: have the children consider which data-handling software to use

What are the mobility access issues in the local area?

Learning objectives	Activities	Learning outcomes	Teaching notes
• to analyse data and identify key information • to make a map to show specific information • that people hold different views about an issue	• make maps to show where access was rated highly and poorly • use a database to record and show the categories and balance of good, moderate and poor access • categorise the information about people's views on access locally • in groups analyse the data to draw conclusions and prepare a report about their findings	• summarise and organise information and present findings • identify good and poor practices in the provision of access for everyone • recognise that people hold different views	• Thinking skills: encourage the children to use evidence to justify their conclusions • ICT: use suitable software (e.g. Local Studies) to support children in relation to their mapping and data handling

Who is involved in trying to improve mobility access?		
• how and why people are trying to improve the local area • who is involved in making decisions that affect the local area	• reconsider the points about access locally made by the planning access officer to evaluate these points against the findings from the fieldwork • invite a local shopkeeper, a local resident who has mobility needs and a local councillor into school to discuss the problems and possibilities of making improvements and how these are decided	• understand who will benefit from improvements • appreciate some of the problems in making improvements • become aware of who makes decisions that affect the local area and of what impact these decisions might have	• Inclusion: take the opportunity to explore the values and attitudes involved in trying to ensure access for all to streets, buildings and other places and services • Citizenship: use the opportunity to help children begin to understand how decisions are made locally
How can access for everyone be improved locally?		
• to identify alternative ways in which improvements can be made • that resources are needed to make improvements • that there may be limits to making changes • to present a case and use persuasive argument	• draw up a balance sheet to show the arguments for and against making local improvements, using the information and evidence they have gathered • identify a number of ways in which improvements could be made locally to improve access for everyone • create a role play public meeting, with children taking the roles of different people in the community, to put the range of arguments for and against improvements • write an illustrated newspaper report of the debate, outlining the issues • write to the local council presenting the case for improvements and giving proposals	• suggest ways in which mobility access can be improved • use role play to debate the issues of improving accessibility • express and justify their own views and proposals	• ESD/Environmental Education: this provides the opportunity for children to see how they can contribute to making improvements to the environment • Literacy: apply reporting, analytic and persuasive oral and writing skills

Points to consider when planning a geography unit

Increasingly primary schools are adapting or preparing their own geography units. You may be provided with only a brief outline of the geography unit you are to teach. You will need to plan it much more fully, perhaps almost to the extent set out in Tables 12.3 and 12.4. In such units children's ideas may not be strongly present, because their involvement is not fully planned for. However, you may have more licence and flexibility to plan your own unit.

There is no necessary sequence for the study of a locality or an environmental or global issue, but there are points of guidance that can help you bring children's contributions more evidently into the study. The following questions provide a guide about how you might go about your medium-term planning. They refer to locality or global dimension topics but can be adapted for any geography unit planning.

- What is the focus of your study and its purpose? Is it focused on the locality as a place or has it more global interests and does it illustrate an environmental issue and explore sustainability – or both? An important initial decision is the purpose and context of the study. You might develop several guide geographical questions for the topic. What do you want the children to understand by the end of the unit?
- What do you and the children know of the locality and its country context or of the issue? An elicitation activity can be a useful starting point to find out what information or general conceptions the children have. Some activities given in Table 11.2 can be used here.
- Where in the world are the locality and its country or the issue located, on the globe, and in relation to your own place? This provides a sense of 'global where-ness', using atlases and globes. To locate a locality or issue, national and larger-scale maps are needed. These may be provided in a photo pack about the locality or a focused issue, if that is the resource being used. Searches through, for example, Google may provide further locational information.
- What do we want to investigate about this place or global issue? This is where the children contribute to the development of the study through generating, selecting, refining and structuring their enquiry questions, perhaps using photographs, a video, their initial ideas or other information to stimulate these. For younger children these might be within a broad structure that you have set out or which is provided through the school's scheme of work for geography. With older children, the children's questions might provide the structure for much of the enquiry. (See Chapter 6.)
- How are we going to find out? What resources are available? What other resources can be found? With a structured study you may well provide all the resources. For a more child-structured enquiry it is useful for the children to use the resources provided but they may need to find out about others and try to obtain them, possibly via the internet or by inviting a visitor in. However, this may not always work and they need to recognise the limitations this imposes.
- How are we going to organise our study? It will be important to decide how to work on the various questions, individually and/or in groups, who with whom, as well as which aspects might be considered as a whole class. This is also the point at which to indicate the range of outcomes that might be worked towards: posters, a report, a role play or drama, and so on.
- What are we learning from the sources we have? What do we know, or know something about, this place or issue? What are we finding difficult or impossible to find out, and so where are our gaps in understanding going to be? Rather than at the end of a study, it is useful to have 'checkpoints' along the way, for children to take stock and perhaps refocus their particular area of study. This might be because more stimulating questions have emerged or because there is a problem with resources. It is helpful to agree that it is worth continuing or to close one line of enquiry and move to another.
- What conclusions can we draw from our study? Towards the end of the study children need to be focused on what the information and ideas they have gathered tell them about the locality or issue and their focus on it. The children's conclusions need to be reasoned and evidence based, but they might also include their own perspectives and speculations.

- What have we learnt about finding out about other places or our issue? What should we apply in future studies? Evaluation helps children realise and learn from what they have done in terms of what they now understand that they did not know initially, how their own views and preconceptions have changed, and what they have learnt about the process of study they can use in a new context.
- How has our study of this locality or issue provided us with a lens to re-look at our own locality and lives? How does it compare? What might we not know about our own place or context? A key value in undertaking a locality and issue-based study is to enable comparison with other places, particularly our own place. Children will have learnt that they can compare but they must recognise there are gaps. Can they identify the similarities and differences between their own and the other locality or context? Through this they might appreciate that they do not know everything about their own area and local lives and issues.

When you have planned your geography unit, you might use the following questions, building on Owen and Ryan (2001, p55), as a checklist to ensure you have covered the main elements.

- Are two or more aspects of geography included, linking place and environmental matters and issues?
- Do your learning objectives draw on the Early Learning Goals or the geography programmes of study, and are they linked to expectations and assessed outcomes?
- Have you involved children to a lesser or greater extent in asking geographical questions and planning the structure, sequence and progression of your enquiry?
- Are there opportunities for outdoor area or fieldwork, linked with indoor or class work?
- Have you planned to introduce new ideas and skills the children will need to use and for development of their understanding and skill use during the unit?
- Have you planned for a variety of approaches to teaching and learning and of activities and resources, for differentiation other than by outcome, and for variety in assessment?
- Are there opportunities to support literacy, numeracy and ICT and links with other subjects or cross-curricular elements?

REFLECTIVE TASK

Find on a suitable website (see, for example, the GA, QCA, Standards sites) a unit plan for a geographical study of a locality or issue. Examine the plan and consider to what extent the advice given above applies. Which aspects are used and which are not? Consider why this might be the case. How would you amend the plan to involve children's questions and ideas more fully?

Cross-curricular connections

In the Foundation Stage where geography is taught within the broader context of knowledge and understanding of the world, it will not be obvious that you are planning specifically for geography. In Key Stages 1 and 2, where geography is increasingly covered within 'topic' or 'thematic' work linking relevant subjects together for the topic, it is essential that the geographical content and skills are explicit in the planning. This ensures that children clearly have the opportunity to develop their geographical knowledge and skills. It has been advocated that making children aware of the nature of the subjects they are using and learning (meta-cognition) enables more effective understanding and subsequent achievement (Knight, 1993). Do not hide geographical learning from them.

Geography is linked inherently to other subjects. Links need to be specific and significant, not tenuous for the sake of a cross-curricular element. Learning about a distant locality can be considerably enhanced by, for example, links to music, art, dance and food technology. Making these links affords a wider understanding of the character of that place and area of the world. Carrying out a local enquiry on an environmental issue can encourage successful links with science. If children undertake an audit of energy use, they can relate it to their personal use and investigate energy sources. They would look at the wider context of energy usage within school and home and consider possible efficiency savings or introducing alternative types of energy. Work on map skills is greatly enhanced through effective development with mathematics of children's familiarity with scale and co-ordinates and grids. This supports progression in both subject areas, providing an engaging context and relevance for geographical and mathematical learning.

Short-term planning

Short-term planning focuses on the geography lessons you teach. It turns the intentions in the medium-term plan into individual activities and lessons, but it can cover a sequence of two or three linked lessons, such as leading into, undertaking and following up fieldwork. This is the day-to-day planning of teaching. Your planning needs to be adequately detailed to identify what is being taught, your learning objectives, the time available, how you will teach, how children are expected to learn and the resources you need. It is evidently dependent on your continuing lesson evaluations and formal or informal assessment of children's learning. Owen and Ryan (2001) identify a number of features to include when making short-term plans, such as:

- clear and specific objectives for teaching and learning and on which to assess the children, with clear criteria;
- key teaching points and questions;
- how the children will be organised, groupings, etc.;
- engaging activities and resources which will be matched to the children's ability and experience and informed by previous assessment;
- differentiation, as appropriate;
- appropriate resources, including ICT, to enable and enhance the learning;
- feedback opportunities;
- clear sequence and progression, including an introduction and conclusion.

In the Foundation Stage your planning will be specific and dynamic, open to adaptation and change according to children's progress and development through regular observations and assessment. This is focused on the specific needs of the children and how these can be most effectively met. Clearly, such planning includes consideration of the resources needed on a daily basis, for example, in setting up a supermarket in the role-play area and the timing, space or room arrangements needed for such an activity. In Key Stages 1 and 2, key questions and related concepts help to focus the lesson plan and ensure that the essential elements of study are covered.

Figure 12.3 presents a lesson plan for one of the lessons from the medium term unit in Table 12.3. It employs key questions, includes a variety of appropriate activities, and is clear about the outcomes expected from the lesson. It is a class-based lesson but it includes a fieldwork activity in the school grounds as part of the lesson. Further planning information is contained in one of the SuperSchemes units (Catling, 2005d), a series which provides many good examples of unit and lesson plans (Geographical Association, 2005–07).

- *What relevant children's experience is being used?*
  - mapping experience
  - use and knowledge of the school's grounds
  - awareness that some people, including children, have mobility problems getting around the environment
- *Which aspect of the topic does the activity contribute to?*
  - study of school/local mobility access
  - consideration of minorities and social justice issues
  - extending mapping skills and use
  - provides focus and experience prior to local area fieldwork
- *What is the focus of the activity?*
  - making a route access map of the school grounds
- *How long is the session?*
  - 75 minutes
- *What do I want the children to learn?*
  - the children will:
    - understand that access is important for everyone
    - on a base map record accurately routes into and around the building and grounds
- *Key geographical questions:*
  - where is access good or a problem in the school building and grounds for someone with mobility difficulties?
    - which places can only certain people go?
    - are all publicly available spaces accessible?
    - why are they accessible or not?
    - what solutions to access problems might be proposed?
- *Which resources are needed?*
  - base plans of the school grounds: copy per child
  - picture map of the school grounds: copy per pair of children
  - clipboards
  - pencils
  - plain paper
  - plan of school grounds on interactive whiteboard to use for class discussions
- *What will the children do?*
  - introduce the session:
    - discuss what is known of the school grounds and what they are used for, e.g. playground, wild area and pond, field, etc.
    - discuss how we move around the school, which routes and entrance ways
    - encourage questions about whether everywhere can be accessed by everyone, including those with various mobility difficulties, and what may help or hinder accessibility (check understanding)
    - show base plan of school grounds; recap on what the plan shows; refer to it as a base plan, one which we can write on: annotate
    - explain the fieldwork activity: to check routes and access around the building and grounds and to record these on base plan

- identify the fieldwork activities the children will do:
    - children in pairs: who works with whom
    - pair to mark on base plan whether they consider the access is good or a problem on routeways or entrances, and to note why
    - each group to check their resources: base plan, clipboard, pencil, and ensure they have them
    - pairs go out as a class but work independently in time limit of 20 minutes, with an adult on hand for help, guidance and monitoring
    - on completion to return to class
- on return to class:
    - discuss access along routeways and at entrances; compare base plans to pool information
    - remind all about use of map key, to show routes, access points and access problems
    - pairs to use second base plan to complete a neat map showing good and poor access points in building and school grounds
    - pairs who finish before end of lesson to make notes on the questions: why do some access points and routes have good access, and why do others have poor access for everyone?
- *How am I ensuring appropriate differentiation?*
    - four pairs to receive teacher/TA support when checking location of parts of school on plans and to ensure annotation correct
    - three of these pairs will use a picture map
- *How did it go?*
    - note how effectively the mapping task was completed
    - consider whether I needed to differentiate more carefully
    - check all the children have a grasp of the idea of access for everyone

Figure 12.3 A Year 4 class-based lesson plan incorporating fieldwork – Investigating accessibility to the school

PRACTICAL TASK PRACTICAL TASK PRACTICAL TASK PRACTICAL TASK PRACTICAL TASK

Select the focus for a geography lesson of your own choosing. You might draw on various of the topics referred to in preceding chapters or on one of the appropriate websites. Select an age group of children in Key Stage 1 or 2 with whom you have worked. Using the guidance above, plan a geography lesson. Alternatively, you might wish to plan geography-oriented activities for the outdoor and indoor areas of the nursery.

Differentiation

A key element in short-term planning is planning for differentiation, to create more focused and personalised learning for children. Owen and Ryan (2001) recommend three key considerations to use when planning. These are:

- different approaches and strategies to engage the differing learners in the class;
- a range and variety of resources which will appeal to the children and engage them with the work through different media;

- a variety of assessment methods to gain a more holistic sense of children's success and to identify where there might be gaps or misunderstandings to tackle.

Halocha (1998) noted the need to appreciate children's prior learning and their level of understanding in order to plan successfully for their further progress. Differentiation can be provided through a variety of further approaches.

- *By differentiated task* – The class is organised into different groups, each with a task to complete. The class, working in groups, is following a local trail, with one group of children using fairly simple directional and feature language while others have more complex challenges and resources using maps, record sheets, a compass, and so on.
- *By outcome* – The class carries out similar tasks with the expectation that different children finish with different results. For example, producing a leaflet on the benefits of recycling can be completed according to the capabilities of the children. This is the most common form of differentiation and can be overused or used without due care or preparation. The expectations for different children must be made clear to them so that tasks are adequately challenging and inclusive.
- *By scaffolding and sequencing* – The class starts with the same set of tasks which become progressively more challenging, with the most able being expected to complete all or the majority of them. For example, this may be a sequence of activities using photographs about an environmental issue where all children start on the same task and during which children work through them at their own speed.
- *By adult support* – Individuals or groups of children are given adult support for particular tasks, perhaps through having a story about an environmental issue read to them or through guidance and help in undertaking fieldwork observations.
- *By recording* – Using a variety of methods to record observations, findings, viewpoints or feelings, not just the written word but through photographs, video, drama, blogs, graphs, and so on, guided by their teacher or self-selected.

In practice the last two approaches may well be used alongside other approaches, so that it is not a matter of supporting children by a single means alone.

A SUMMARY OF **KEY POINTS**

This chapter has:

> **considered long-, medium- and short-term planning of geographical learning and teaching;**

> **provided examples of planning from schemes of work to lessons and indicated criteria to support your planning at these levels;**

> **discussed progression and consistency in children's geographical learning through rigorous and well-thought-out planning;**

> **noted the value in making effective cross-curricular links in planning;**

> **considered approaches to differentiation.**

MOVING *ON* > > > > > > MOVING *ON* > > > > > > MOVING *ON*

At a primary school you know or visit, ask to see the long- and medium-term plans for geography. Consider how geography is organised across the classes and the type of medium term planning that is available to teachers.

FURTHER READING FURTHER READING **FURTHER READING** FURTHER READING

The following books provide useful overviews of and advice about planning geography teaching.

Hoodless, P, Bermingham, S, McCreery, E and Bowen, P (2009) *Teaching Humanities in Primary School*s. Exeter: Learning Matters.

Martin, F (2006c) *Teaching geography in primary schools*. Cambridge: Chris Kington.

Owen, D and Ryan, A (2001) *Teaching geography 3–11*. London: Continuum.

Palmer, J and Birch, J (2004) *Geography in the early years*. London: RoutledgeFalmer.

Pollard, A (2008), *Reflective teaching*. London: Continuum.

Scoffham, S (ed) (2004) *Primary geography handbook*. Sheffield: Geographical Association.

Issues of *Primary Geographer* include discussions of planning at different levels, particularly in relation to medium- and short-term planning. The planning for lessons can often be discerned from the articles on classroom and fieldwork teaching.

Useful websites

Early Years Foundation Stage: Planning and Resourcing
www.standards.dfes.gov.uk/eyfs/site/4/tables/4_5_5_0.htm
Geographical Association SuperSchemes
www.geography.org.uk/eyprimary/superschemes/#top
Geography Teaching Today
www.geographyteachingtoday.org.uk/
Planning for geography
www.standards.dfes.gov.uk/schemes2/geography/principles?view=get
QCA Innovating with Geography
www.qca.org.uk/geography/innovating/key2/planning_matters/index.htm
QCA/DCSF Standards Site and Schemes of Work
www.standards.dfes.gov.uk/schemes3/?view=get

13
Assessing geographical learning

Chapter objectives

By the end of this chapter you should:

- **understand the value and role of assessment for learning in geography;**
- **distinguish between formal and informal assessment and formative and summative assessment;**
- **appreciate the importance of using a variety of approaches to assessment in geography and of linking this to planning;**
- **understand the purposes of questioning, feedback and self and peer assessment, and how they might help children take a greater responsibility for their own learning;**
- **appreciate the role of key stage attainments, targets and level descriptions;**
- **understand the value in monitoring and recording children's geographical learning.**

This chapter addresses the following Professional Standards for QTS:

Q1, Q10, Q11, Q12, Q14, Q15, Q26, Q27, Q28.

Introduction

Assessment is central to teaching and learning. A teacher might formally conclude a geography unit with a task that has been designed to elicit children's understanding of a particular local issue they have been investigating. A child undertaking one of her geography tasks might become concerned that she does not understand some of the vocabulary she has read and seeks help, both informally self-assessing and providing feedback on her developing understanding of a rivers topic to her teacher. In Chapter 12 you encountered reference to assessment in units and lesson plans. This chapter considers the role of assessment and a variety of the ways it can be applied in geographical learning.

What is assessment?

Harlen et al. (1992) noted that the term 'assessment' covers a wide range of activities, including monitoring, assessment tasks and outcomes, recording, reporting, and accountability. Its importance is expressed in the Early Years Foundation Stage guidance:

> To help children progress, practitioners [teachers and other adults] need information about what the children know, understand and can do. Through observing children and by making notes when necessary about what has been achieved, practitioners can make professional judgments about children's achievements and decide on the next steps in learning. They can also exchange information with parents about how children are progressing. This process, often known as 'assessment for learning' is central to raising achievement.
>
> (DCSF, 2008c)

Teacher assessment is the source of feedback from teachers to children, while self-assessment provides feedback from children to teachers. These are used to plan, adapt and modify the direction, nature and focus of activities that children are given to do subsequently (Black and Wiliam, 1998). Assessment occurs informally or formally during lessons, across the weeks of geography teaching, at the end of units and the year's work, and in preparation for transition between key stages. There will be continuous informal assessment, part of day-to-day practice, as well as periodic planned or formal assessment, including formative and summative assessments (Briggs et al., 2008), used to provide understanding about a child's geographical learning, achievements and needs.

Why assess in geography?

Unlike the core subjects, no formal or summative assessment is statutory in geography. This might mean that it appears neglected, so disadvantaging children and hampering their geographical development and understanding. It is, however, essential. Without assessment no teacher understands or appreciates what a child has learnt or where they next need to be supported or challenged. Certainly, as Ofsted have noted (2008a), summative assessment is not well developed and aspects of formative assessment need focus and development. Ofsted (2008a, p5) notes limitations in providing *constructive feedback to pupils about their geographical knowledge, skills and understanding*. To aid learning it is vital that informative and accurate feedback occurs through informal day-to-day assessment as part of good practice in teaching and learning.

Assessment, as Butt (n.d.) has argued, referring specifically to geography, is vital to:

- enhance students' learning;
- measure (or possibly raise) standards;
- check teaching objectives against learning outcomes;
- recognise and plan for students' learning needs;
- place students against different descriptors of achievement;
- discover what students know, understand and can do;
- help plan future learning objectives;
- help students to devise personal targets;
- evaluate teacher effectiveness and performance;
- motivate teachers and students.

To these reasons we might add that assessment is also for children to:

- understand and evaluate their own learning;
- become more fully involved in identifying their own progress, achievements and needs;
- plan their next areas of focus for learning (linked to personal target setting);
- identify how they will recognise they have achieved their targets.

An elicitation activity, as a formative assessment, might form the starting point to initiate a geography topic. When providing their responses children might note, using a traffic-lights system, their confidence in their knowledge and understanding about the topic. The teacher can use the outcomes to revise the initial planning of her geography unit, taking account not only of how she views the children's responses but involving the children's self-evaluation (Weeden and Lambert, 2006). This can help children and teachers focus on the topic and be a stimulus and motivator for geographical learning.

During a geography topic, children might be asked to identify where they consider they are mistaking or misunderstanding the ideas, skills or content they are studying (Weeden, n.d.). Common problems can be highlighted and teaching adjusted, perhaps through some whole-class or group teaching or by providing time for children who understand the work to work together with those in need of support.

IN THE CLASSROOM

To initiate the study of a locality in India, their teacher gave each of five groups in her Year 5 children a large cut-out letter from the word I-N-D-I-A. She asked the groups to write or draw what they knew about India. This was 20-minute activity, which she followed up by asking the children to list questions that they wanted to use in their enquiry. After the lesson she reviewed the children's ideas about India and examined the questions they had listed. From their first activity she became aware of misconceptions, misunderstandings and misinformation which she felt needed to be addressed. She adjusted her plan to engage the children in identifying some core information about India before returning to the questions, which she then wanted the children to reconsider and revise, as well as group and then organise into priorities for their enquiry.

These examples of formative assessment approaches underpin the essence of assessment for learning (AfL). At the heart of AfL lies the principle that all children are able to improve their learning, supported by the following core features (QCA, n.d.a).

- Learning intentions are shared with children.
- Children understand and appreciate the expectations and standards they are aiming for.
- Feedback identifies clearly for children what they need to do to improve.
- Supported by their teacher, children evaluate their performance and progress and develop their self and peer assessment skills.

REFLECTIVE TASK

Why is it important for both teachers and children to be involved in assessment for geographical learning?

Approaches to assessment

A number of approaches can be used in AfL to support and develop children's learning. Four are considered here. Others might include observation and listening, concept mapping, labelling and testing (Briggs et al., 2008).

Sharing learning intentions

The value in sharing the purpose of what children will be learning in a geography unit or lessons is to focus their interest during their studies, for them to be aware of the learning goal and to motivate them. This is not to share the plan of activities for the unit or lesson but to help children understand the progress they are being challenged to achieve. It is about involving the children in their own learning, ensuring that they participate in their own development. To support the children, it is helpful to let them know the success criteria for the work, so that at the end of a geography lesson, for example, they can see whether they have achieved the learning intention set. It can also be helpful for children to be told how the purpose of the lesson relates to the subject they are doing (Clarke, 2001).

IN THE CLASSROOM

The focus of the Year 2 class's geography lesson was on drawing out the children's knowledge and views about their local area. The teacher's intention was to draw from the children what their knowledge and views were about their local area. She saw this as the basis for children sharing their knowledge and views and for widening their awareness of the vicinity of the school.

On the whiteboard she shared the following with the children.

Learning intention: We are going to find out what we know about our neighbourhood, and we are going to say what we think about it.

Success criteria: We listed different features or places we know and have written a sentence saying why we like or do not like them.

She also said to the children that knowing about and sharing our knowledge of features and places in the neighbourhood helped in understanding what places are like, as part of geography.

Effective questioning

At the core of the enquiry process in geography is questioning, not least children's capacity to generate a variety of questions that provide an effective focus for their investigations. Questioning is an equally vital aspect of assessment, whether the informal questions asked of children about the particular work they are engaged in or in the context of a summative assessment activity. Questioning and discussion inform teachers about children's knowledge, understanding, skill use and values. They can expose misconceptions and misunderstandings. Children can use questions of each other to find out information, to see who can help them or in relation to peer assessment.

While questioning can inform us about children's knowledge, it can also be used to probe the thinking underpinning that understanding. Children can be asked to give examples or explain the meaning of particular geographical terms. The wording of questions is important and open questions tend to be far more revealing and informative than closed questions. Closed questions might be those concerned directly with particular information, such as *What is the capital of India?*, but they may also seek knowledge of a particular system, for instance *what are the main elements of the water cycle?* The question, *Is there equal access to clean, safe drinking water in the world?* will lead to a straightforward 'No'. This question might be rephrased as an open question, in the form of, *Why is there not equal access to clean and safe drinking water in the world?* where the given situation is the basis for the question, not the question itself. Such an open question should lead to discussion about a range of possible reasons, some of the issues involved and avenues to explore further.

Questioning offers many opportunities. It is important to be clear about the reasons for questioning. Too often questions are asked of the same sort, only to particular children, in too difficult language, without providing children with time to think, and without using the response to build on (Brown and Wragg, 1993). During a lesson a teacher will use a variety of questions, some of which will seek information and be closed, while others encourage thinking and probe, seeking to engage children in understanding their own developing knowledge and insights. Drawing on guidance from QCA (n.d.b), such open questions might take these forms, which could all be applied to geographical contexts.

● How can we be sure that (local people do not want housing on the wasteland)?
● What is the same and what is different (between our neighbourhood and the area of Swanage that we investigated)?
● Is it ever/always true/false that (people move from the countryside to the city to find work)?
● How do you know (what children would most like to change in the playground)?
● How would you explain (the amount of litter we found on the beach)?
● What does that tell us about (how and where we use energy in school)?
● What is right/wrong with (saying that fair trade is always a good thing)?
● What reasons can you give for (people parking where they should not)?
● Why did you (choose the questions about access to water that you did)?
● How might you (find out what people would like to see replace the empty shop)?
● Why have you proposed that (the pedestrian area needs to be less cluttered for disabled people)?
● Why do you think (it will be better if the shanty town is rebuilt)?

While closed questions usually seek succinct responses and may not be followed up, open questions require children to think before replying and may usefully be discussed by children with others first. Questioning is an important teaching strategy while also providing assessment information. Weeden (n.d.) has suggested that it might be used in the following ways.

● *Discussion partners* – Pairs of children discuss the answer to a question and feed back to the rest of the class.
● *Snowballing* – Groups of children explain their answers to each other and then to other groups.
● *Explaining* – The emphasis for explaining answers is encouraged by asking prompt questions such as *Why?, Tell me more..., Go on.*
● *Phone a friend* – Children nominate someone to help them answer a question.

PRACTICAL TASK PRACTICAL TASK **PRACTICAL TASK** PRACTICAL TASK **PRACTICAL TASK**

It is helpful to have in mind a number of open and probing questions to use during a lesson. Use a geography lesson you have taught or the one outlined in Figure 12.3. Devise a number of open questions that you might use to help probe and encourage children's thinking about the topic.

Providing feedback and marking work

It is essential when giving feedback on children's work to make it relevant, meaningful and directly related to the learning intention and specific assessment criteria. For instance, when assessing a child's ability to locate a point on a map using four-figure grid references, their skill in giving the correct references is the focus. If an intention is met, feedback should praise this; if not, it should show how the child can meet it. Feedback should be used to scaffold children's learning and help them use their knowledge and skills to develop their own conclusions and solutions. This will encourage them to work through problems and situations on their own or with peers and to become more self-reliant and responsible for their own learning and progression. Feedback can be written on the work and, thus, marked, but it is discussion of their assessment with individual children that is more effective and enduring than written feedback. Such dialogue encourages children to be more confident in asking questions to aid their own learning and seeking progress (Owen and Ryan, 2001). The purpose of feedback is to help children identify their strengths and areas to develop by setting future targets. Marking provides a record for the child to refer to. It should be a reward and guide system, providing positive comments on the work and their attainment and stating specific targets and actions for improvement.

When giving feedback about a piece of work in geography, you must ensure that it is subject and topic specific, though you might comment on the quality of the language, graphics or other form of presentation where this is pertinent to effective communication of the geographical information and understanding. The geographical focus is vital for children to identify and recognise clearly their attainment in geography and to give them targets for what to do to progress further (QCA, n.d.c).

IN THE CLASSROOM

Talking to Lucy about her summary of the problems associated with lack of ready access to water for many people, her teacher commented that: *You have explained very clearly several of the causes and impacts of lack of water access. You have given examples of ways to tackle these. Can you think of other situations where people are faced with similar problems in daily life which they have to deal with, and how this affects them? You have used geographical vocabulary well, included the sources you used and presented it attractively.*

Ofsted (2008a, p12) recognise the positive impact of marking but make the point that:

> *Although the marking of pupils' work is important in raising expectations, too often work is not properly marked or the comments on it do not relate enough to the geographical content.* The best marking identifies strengths and what needs to be done next, as well as showing some evidence of the work being marked with the pupil present. *(Emphasis added)*

REFLECTIVE TASK

Look at the extract from a Year 4 child's report on findings from fieldwork related to a local development issue in Figure 13.1. It includes references relevant to geography and science. Consider whether the comments at the bottom are specific enough to highlight the geographical learning. How might the feedback be written to reflect the child's geographical learning?

Self and peer assessment

Self-assessment concerns children understanding the learning intentions and realising what they need to do to achieve them. When it involves children setting their own targets from feedback on their work – and once practised at it – it becomes a highly effective form of assessment (Kelly, 2007). Children carrying out self-assessment become more reflective and realistic about their work, gaining the confidence to admit when they do not understand something and seeking help to address this. They begin to recognise possible gaps and weaknesses and consider effective forms of addressing these. Clarke (2005) suggests a useful three-stage process to support children's development in self-assessment.

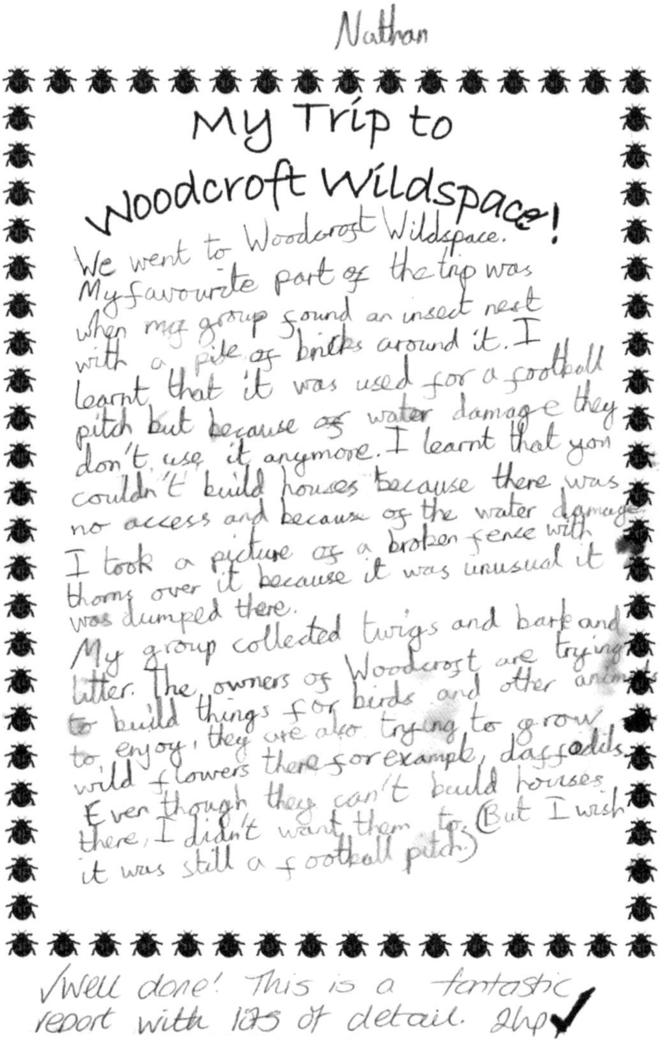

Nathan

My Trip to Woodcroft Wildspace!

We went to Woodcroft Wildspace. My favourite part of the trip was when my group found an insect nest with a pile of bricks around it. I learnt that it was used for a football pitch but because of water damage they don't use it anymore. I learnt that you couldn't build houses because there was no access and because of the water damage I took a picture of a broken fence with thorns over it because it was unusual it was dumped there. My group collected twigs and bark and litter. The owners of Woodcroft are trying to build things for birds and other animals to enjoy, they are also trying to grow wild flowers there for example, daffodils. Even though they can't build houses there, I didn't want them to. (But I wish it was still a football pitch.)

✓Well done! This is a fantastic report with lots of detail. 2hp✓

Source: St Paul's CE Primary School

Figure 13.1 A marked piece of written Year 4 work

Stage 1: students identify their own successes.
Stage 2: students identify an aspect of their work for improvement.
Stage 3: students identify their successes and make an 'on the spot' improvement.

For the youngest children self-assessment is likely to be best fostered where they use a simple symbol, such as smiley or frowning faces, to indicate where they feel they have done well or think they need more help. For older children it can be appropriate to invite them to note what they feel they have learnt (Figure 13.2), to say what they feel they need to focus on and what they want to learn in a topic or from one lesson to the next. Another approach to use, perhaps at the end of a geography unit, is a summative self-assessment approach. The example in Table 13.1 below links self-assessment to the levels of attainment for geography.

Source: John Halocha

Figure 13.2: Children assessing their own work with support of the teacher

Table 13.1 Self-assessment criteria for a locality study in Year 4

Should you go to St Lucia?	Level 2	Level 3	Level 4	Level 5
Describe the physical and human features of St Lucia.	I can recognise some features of St Lucia.	I can describe some physical and human features of St Lucia.	I can show good understanding of the main physical and human features of St Lucia.	I can show good understanding of the main physical and human features of St Lucia and explain some of them.
Analyse evidence and draw conclusions about whether to visit St Lucia.	I can use the evidence I have collected to give some simple reasons for visiting St Lucia.	I can use the evidence I have collected to give several reasons for *or* against visiting St Lucia.	I can use the evidence I have collected to give several reasons for *and* against visiting St Lucia.	I can use the evidence I have collected to give several reasons for and against visiting St Lucia. I can write a conclusion which explains why I believe that people should or should not visit.
Understand sustainable tourism and how it affects people, places and environments.	I can give an example of how tourism can affect the environment of a place in St Lucia.	I can give an example of how people are trying to protect the environment of a place in St Lucia.	I understand ways in which tourism can damage the environment in St Lucia. I can describe some ways of improving the environment.	I understand what sustainable tourism means. I can give several examples of why and how St Lucia is trying to encourage sustainable tourism.

Source: Owens, 2008b

Other ways to support children's self-assessment include adapting the approaches mentioned above, adopting other approaches given on some of the websites listed at the end of this chapter, and using these two approaches.

- Encourage children to look through a piece of their own work and to indicate how specific statements or observations could be improved by annotating it with improvement comments. This can then feed into further work.
- Take photographs of children working and encourage them to annotate them with comments about what they were learning, what they understood at that time and what they have learnt since then. They can then consider how to take their learning on to the next stage.

Peer assessment encourages children to recognise the learning intention and the reason why they are learning through discussion, so clarifying their own understanding as well as assessing the work of their peers. It can be most supportive when children are not sure whose work it is that they are commenting on, but, if this is not possible, it is wise to ensure that they mark different children's work each time, avoiding opportunities to be competitive. Ofsted (2008a) views peer assessment as providing opportunities to engage children in discussion about achievement and learning intentions, involving the children actively. It has been shown to have a positive impact on the children's geographical learning and understanding.

> *In one school, pupils assessed each other's work against clear descriptions of levels and grades. This helped them to understand the quality of their own work better; good diagnostic marking also contributed to this. Pupils recorded their results on a progress chart and indicated with an arrow whether they had improved, remained the same or fallen. They also noted specific targets. All pupils were very clear about the process and how to achieve their geography-focused targets.*

(Ofsted, 2008a, p23)

Linking teaching and assessment

One way to ensure assessment opportunities during the teaching of a geography unit is to plan activities into your teaching that provide insight into children's understanding as well as being stimulating learning tasks. A number of the activities mentioned earlier in this book can be used in this way. Table 13.2 provides further examples of activities that serve both learning and assessment roles.

Table 13.2: Examples of geographical activities enabling teaching and assessment

Geographical focus	Teaching and assessment context
Sort 4–8 photographs into sets to show likes and dislikes related to a locality or environmental matter.	To be able to give and explain criteria for their decisions about what they see.
Make a postcard to show what a particular place or site is like.	To use information to create an appropriate image or view or a place studied or self-chosen.
Write a story which is based on a map, either provided or self-made, of a place where the action occurs.	To be able to use a mapped environment, demonstrating the use of map skills and understanding of activities.
Create a map or mapped trail to show the way around the classroom, school or neighbourhood.	To select features and use mapping skills (at various levels) to communicate a route effectively.

Select maps, atlases and globes to use in different contexts, such as visiting a new town, keeping in your lounge and showing visitors round the school.	To be able to identify, select and justify the appropriate resource for a range of activities and people's needs.
Write and illustrate a report on a topical item in the news about an event to show how it has a geographical dimension.	To identify and explain the aspects of geography that appear in or underpin an event.
Find out information about a particular country or on physical features such as mountains.	To use a variety of sources and resources to gather and select relevant information, sort it, and demonstrate factual knowledge of the topic.
Prepare a personal or class glossary of geographical terms built up during a unit, e.g. lake, canal, watermill, in a rivers topic.	To show understanding and ability to explain accurately key geographical words and phrases.
Use role play to explore the issues concerning development in a particular locality by taking on a character's role and arguing a case in a 'public debate'.	To develop and demonstrate knowledge and understanding of a local issue, to be able to take account of different arguments and to argue persuasively.
Make a short radio or video programme about a particular environmental issue.	To organise and communicate to an audience what has been learnt, including information, explanation and a personal viewpoint.

Ofsted (2008a, p13) have noted that there is limited support to help teachers provide good assessment opportunities for themselves and children. The result is that:

> *In assessing pupils' geographical understanding, there is a general tendency in primary schools to focus on geographical vocabulary and skills such as map work, particularly because the outcomes are easier to identify. Geographical under-standing is harder to measure and assessment therefore remains underdeveloped. As a result, the analysis of achievement and attainment does not always present a sufficiently accurate picture of what pupils have learnt.*

There are several considerations that can help overcome this and support planning for assessment (Owen and Ryan, 2001, p145) to ensure it is meaningful and engaging. We need to be clear about:

- which aspects of geography are to be assessed – knowledge, understanding or skills;
- our criteria for assessing the geography we are focusing on;
- suitable activities and questions that allow children to show what they know and understand or can do;
- providing attainable learning intentions and tasks, appropriate for the children, so that they have opportunities to show what they can do and to succeed;
- how we will monitor and record the evidence of children's learning;
- some sense of the types of responses expected from the children, to be able to match their outputs against;
- ways in which the assessment outcomes are to be recorded and used.

BEELFECLIAE 1A2K
REFLECTIVE TASK

Go through the previous chapters, particularly Chapters 6 to 12, and identify eight to ten activities that could provide both teaching and assessment opportunities. Note the activities and which aspect of learning they might support, as in Table 13.2.

Using the geography attainment levels

Both the Foundation Stage 'Knowledge and understanding of the world' and primary geography for Key Stages 1 and 2 have expectations against which to judge children's attainment at the end of the relevant key stages (DCSF, 2008b; DfEE/QCA, 1999a; QCA, n.d.c). The following elements have a geographical dimension in relation to 'Knowledge and understanding of the world'. The child:

- shows curiosity and interest by exploring surroundings;
- identifies simple features and significant personal events;
- identifies obvious similarities and differences when exploring and observing;
- investigates places . . . using all the senses as appropriate, identifies some features and talks about those features they like and dislike;
- asks questions about why things happen . . . looks closely at similarities, differences, patterns and change;
- finds out about . . . present events in own life and in those of family members and other people they know, begins to know about own culture and beliefs and those of other people;
- communicates simple planning for investigations and constructs and makes simple records and evaluations of her/his work; identifies and names key features and properties, sometimes linking different experiences, observations and events; begins to explore what it means to belong to a variety of groups and communities.

In Key Stages 1 and 2, the geography attainment target provides level descriptions that include the four main aspects of the statutory content. Table 13.3 provides an outline which relates the content of the level statements to each of the four areas. Levels 1–3 apply to Key Stage 1, with level 2 as the expectation for the end of Year 2, and levels 2–5 apply to Key Stage 2, with level 4 as the expectation for the end of Year 6.

The attainment targets and level descriptions were devised for end of key stage assessment, but they may now be used to provide the basis for summative assessment at the end of a geography unit, as Table 13.1 illustrates. In using the geography attainment target you are looking for a 'best fit' description for the child's work. This involves making a judgment about how the child's achievements relate best to one of the attainment target levels (DfEE/QCA, 1999a). It may be that in a particular geography unit only certain aspects of the attainment target level are evident, so the 'best fit' should relate to these. Over the year and key stage a fuller picture will emerge, giving a more rounded sense of which level best reflects a child's overall learning and achievements in geography.

Recording and reporting geographical learning

There should be a record of children's work and achievement in geography. Such a record should show children's progress in geography as they move through the Foundation Stage

Table 13.3 The level descriptions and four main aspects of statutory content

Assessing progress in geography

Name of pupil: **Year:**

Level	Enquiry and skills	Places	Space: Patterns and processes	Environmental impact and sustainability	Comment
1	Pupils use resources that are given to them, and their own observations, to ask and respond to questions about places and environments.	…show their knowledge, skills and understanding in studies at a local scale.	…recognise and make observations about physical and human features of localities.	…express their views on features of the environment of a locality.	
2	Pupils carry out simple tasks and select information using resources as above. They use this information and their own observation to help them ask and respond to questions about places and environments. They begin to use appropriate geographical vocabulary.	…show their knowledge, skills and understanding in studies at a local scale. They show an awareness of places beyond their own locality.	…describe physical and human features of places, and recognise and make observations about those features that give places their character.	…express views on the environment of a locality and recognise how people affect the environment.	
3	Pupils use skills and sources of evidence to respond to a range of geographical questions, and develop the use of appropriate vocabulary to communicate their findings.	…show their knowledge, skills and understanding in studies at a local scale. They are aware that different places may have both similar and different characteristics. They offer reasons for some of their observations and for their views and judgements about places.	…describe and compare the physical and human features of different localities and offer explanations for the locations of some of those features.	…offer reasons for some of their observations and for their views and judgements about environments. They recognise how people seek to improve and sustain environments.	
4	Drawing on their knowledge and understanding, pupils suggest suitable geographical questions, and use a range of geographical skills from KS 2 PoS to help them investigate places and environments. They use primary and secondary sources of evidence in their investigations and communicate their findings using appropriate vocabulary.	…show their knowledge, skills and understanding in studies of a range of places and environments at more than one scale and in different parts of the world.	…begin to recognise and describe geographical patterns and to appreciate the importance of wider geographical location in understanding places. They recognise and describe physical and human processes. They begin to understand how these can change the features of places, and how these changes affect the lives and activities of people living there.	…understand how people can both improve and damage the environment. They explain their own views and the views that other people hold about an environmental change.	
5	Drawing on their knowledge and understanding, they select and use appropriate skills and ways of presenting information from the KS2 PoS to help them investigate places and environments. They select information and sources of evidence, suggest plausible conclusions to their investigations and present their findings both graphically and in writing.	…show their knowledge, skills and understanding in studies of a range of places and environments at more than one scale and in different parts of the world. They recognise some of the links and relationships that make places dependent on each other.	…describe and begin to explain geographical patterns and physical and human processes. They describe how these processes can lead to similarities and differences in the environments of different places and in the lives of people who live there.	…suggest explanations for the ways in which human activities cause changes to the environment and the different views people hold about them. They recognise how people try to manage environments sustainably. They explain their own views and begin to suggest further relevant geographical questions and issues.	

Source: Slightly modified from Woodhouse (2003), adapted from DfEE/QCA (1999a)

and Key Stages 1 and 2. It should contain both brief written comments, which might refer to particular learning, interests and/or misconceptions, and the achievements related to the geography attainment target. These might be provided at the end of each geography unit or at the end of the year.

Records of learning provide information to be passed to the next teacher and across key stages, for example at transfer from primary to secondary school. They also enable reporting to parents. Reports should focus on the positive outcomes of children's geographical learning and should indicate areas for development, perhaps to be picked up in later geography units. This might refer to the particular aspects of geography shown in Table 13.3, where achievements are highlighted. Areas for development might be identified by learning targets that have been agreed by the child and teacher. An additional record might be the child's self-evaluation of her/his geographical learning, completed at the end of each unit or the year.

PRACTICAL TASK PRACTICAL TASK **PRACTICAL TASK** PRACTICAL TASK **PRACTICAL TASK**

When you next visit a school, ask about the records that are kept for geography. What is the school policy? Who keeps them? When and how are they used?

A SUMMARY OF **KEY POINTS**

This chapter has:

> explained the purpose, role and types of assessment in geography;

> outlined practices associated with assessment for learning and detailed a number of different methods for implementing it;

> stressed the importance of including assessment opportunities in planning for children's geographical learning and indicated ways in which this might be done;

> explained the role of self and peer assessment and recommended ways to implement and develop them;

> noted the key geographical aspects of 'Knowledge and understanding of the world' and of the primary geography requirements;

> noted that children's geographical learning and achievements should be recorded and be available to report to parents.

MOVING *ON* > > > **> > >** MOVING *ON* > > > **> > >** MOVING *ON*

When you next plan a geography lesson or unit, consider carefully your core learning intentions and expectations so that you are able to state clearly criteria against which to assess the children's learning. Be able to phrase these so that the children can understand and use them for self-assessment.

FURTHER READING FURTHER READING **FURTHER READING** FURTHER READING

The following publications provide further insight into assessment practices in Early Years and primary geography.

Hoodless, P, Bermingham, S, McCreery, E and Bowen, P (2009) *Teaching Humanities in Primary Schools*. Exeter: Learning Matters.

Martin, F (2006c) *Teaching geography in primary schools*. Cambridge: Chris Kington.

Ofsted (2008a) *Geography in schools: Changing practice.*
www.ofsted.gov.uk/Ofsted-home/News/Press-and-media/2008/January/Geography-in-schools-changing-practice/(language)/eng-GB

Owen, D and Ryan, A (2001) *Teaching geography 3–11*. London: Continuum.

Scoffham, S (ed) (2004) *Primary geography handbook*. Sheffield: Geographical Association.

Woodhouse, S (2003) *Assessing progress*. www.qca.org.uk/geography/innovating/examples/assessing_progress.pdf

Useful websites

Assessment for Learning
www.assessment4learning.co.uk/?gclid=CPHnlv-p3ZYCFShUEAodbU8-3A

QCA Assessment in geography
www.curriculum.qca.org.uk/key-stages-1-and-2/assessment/assessmentofsubjects/assessment
ingeography/index.aspx?return=/search/index.aspx%3FfldSiteSearch%3DGiving+pupils+
opportunities+to+demonstrate+attainment%26btnGoSearch.x%3D27%26b

QCA Innovating with geography
www.qca.org.uk/geography/innovating/

QCA National Curriculum in Action
www.curriculum.qca.org.uk/key-stages-1-and-2/assessment/nc-in-action/index.aspx

Staffordshire Learning Net Geography website
www.sln.org.uk/geography/afl.htm

14

Conclusion: developing learning in geographical education

Chapter objectives

By the end of this chapter you should:

- **be aware of the value in developing children's geographical understanding;**
- **have been introduced to geographical outcomes by the end of Year 6;**
- **have encountered one approach to sequencing geography across primary schooling;**
- **be aware of the possibilities for research in primary geography;**
- **be able to identify several ways in which you can investigate children's geographical learning in your classroom.**

This chapter addresses the following Professional Standards for QTS:

Q1, Q7, Q8, Q10, Q14.

Introduction

This final chapter begins by reiterating the importance of children's developing geographical understanding. It then sets out expectations for the outcomes of primary geography education and outlines one sequence for geography through the primary school. As a primary teacher you are expected to review and develop your practice. One approach to this is to consider how you might undertake some research in your classroom to learn more about your geography teaching and the geographical understanding and learning of the children you teach. We end with some concluding remarks.

Developing children's geography

The emphasis in this book has been that the basis for geography in the primary curriculum must be children's everyday geographies. Here we summarise the basis for teaching geography through five elements in geographical learning (Catling, 2001a).

Exploring geographically

Children's desire to explore the world is intense. As outlined in Chapter 3, their experience initially is episodic in their home and local world, and through their family, friends and peer group, stories and the media with the wider world. From this experience they construct an informed though partial awareness of places, the wider environment and environmental concerns. Their understanding gains increasing coherence as they mature. Children bring to their Foundation Stage setting and into school an excitement about their experiences, which must be drawn upon to extend knowledge and understanding of the world. They bring growing skills in observing and noticing, in enacting what they have seen about them through play, in their making sense of their images and perceptions, and through their evolving appreciation and understanding of the world. This experience supports children's geographical learning in the Foundation Stage and Key Stage 1 and 2 curricula, enabling them to become increasingly better informed and more insightful about their local and the wider world. Essential in this development is that children from the earliest age and throughout their primary schooling explore and investigate the school grounds, the local area and the wider world through first-hand and indirect experience.

Engraving geographical learning

Children's exploration – their active learning about the world, about people, places and environmental matters – engraves their awareness, understanding and appreciation of their world into their self-identity and affects their sense of themselves. Children's learning and self-esteem can be constrained by the limitations of their experience and by the inconsistency, partiality and stereotyping that they encounter as they learn – a situation that cannot go unchallenged. A teacher's responsibility is to ensure that children not only become well informed about the world around them but also reflect critically on their understanding. In developing children's place and environmental knowledge and understanding and by tackling misunderstandings and prejudices about their own and the wider world, geography very clearly matters.

Embedding geographical perspectives and understanding

Teaching geography involves embedding for children awareness and, gradually, a range of skills, understandings and values, to develop their capacity for critical reflection on their perceptions, knowledge and ideas about places and environmental matters. Essential to this development is children's involvement in geographical enquiry, built around questions, interests and problems, encompassing description, analysis, evaluation and clarification of their own viewpoints. The process of embedding learning necessarily involves challenging children to explain what they have found and to justify their conclusions, to have considered the different perspectives in problems and debates, particularly where controversy and preferences are involved. Developing competence in undertaking enquiries fosters an ingrained inquisitiveness alongside a healthy criticality, where the limits of their geographical awareness, understanding and speculation are recognised and personal perspectives are developed with due thought. Vital in this embedding of geographical learning for younger children is constant and consistent use of geographical concepts and vocabulary in their studies. This enables children to investigate further and communicate their understanding of how and why places and environments have developed as they are. It helps them begin to realise and appreciate what might happen next, consider alternative possible, preferable and probable futures, and consider how such decisions might be made and their impact on a sustainable future. Through these experiences children examine values and attitudes, their own as well as those of others.

Enabling the use of geographical skills

Children's growing competence in using a variety of geographical skills lies at the heart of enabling them to undertake useful and informative enquiries about places and environmental matters. Literacy, oracy and numeracy skills provide access to much core information and data about the world, particularly beyond personal experience. Children need to be introduced to and develop capability in using graphicacy skills, a wide range of maps, pictures, artefacts and equipment to investigate the real environment and secondary sources about the world. For young children fieldwork is an essential source and inspiration for geographical learning. Based in children's fascination in exploring outside and absorbing primary and secondary sources about the world, geography's skills in observation and investigation and values in responding to places, landscapes, and people's lives, provide access to the reality at its core. Younger children begin to understand and appreciate geography's core concepts and develop their own values and attitudes through being enabled by using its skills and resources.

Engaging in geographical commitment

Emerging through their developing experience, understanding, capability and values, children construct a 'geographical citizenship'. Such a citizenship enables children to learn to take responsibility personally and alongside others locally and in and for the global community. Through engaging in their learning about the world, its places, peoples and environments and in becoming increasingly aware of their personal perceptions, knowledge, images, values and ideas about how they would like the world to be, children develop and clarify their personal ethic about their world. It is the children of the present who will carry the responsibility for the future of the world as their generation matures. They recognise this. Fundamentally, then, primary teachers must ensure that younger children begin to understand and take on board the values inherent in environmental sustainability, to do with the equitable distribution and use of resources and social justice across the world. Engagement with the local and global community necessarily requires that through their geographical education younger children develop their analytic perspectives and become clearer about their personal values for their community and the wider world. This is contentious (Standish, 2009), since it involves fostering in younger children the values of care for and improvement of the world, its people, places and environments. Such geographical engagement moves beyond explanation to involvement; it requires commitment alongside study and it shifts from evaluation to action (Hart, 1997; Palmer and Birch, 2004).

Taking geography forward

The primary curriculum has been under formal review recently. Two major reviews have considered among other things the basis for constructing and focusing the primary curriculum. While *The Independent Review of the Primary Curriculum* (DCSF, 2009) has described a potential curriculum of six Areas of Learning, the *Primary Review* (Alexander, 2009; Alexander and Flutter, 2009) has identified eight domains around which schools might construct their curriculum. The *Independent Review* report has included in its areas of learning 'Historical, geographical and social understanding'. The *Primary Review* has referred to 'Place and Time' within its list of domains and includes geographical ideas and understanding. Geography remains explicit in the new curriculum thinking.

Primary geography outcomes

While geography has a long tradition of description, analysis and explanation, it is not a neutral discipline and its role in the primary curriculum cannot be other than value based, while scrutinising those values through the careful and balanced study of places, people, environments and related concerns (Martin, 2006e). This approach provides a basis for geographical understanding developed through consistent geographical learning from the Foundation Stage across Key Stages 1 and 2. Such consistency provides benefits (Leeder, 2006). Figure 14.1 presents a set of possible outcomes by the end of primary schooling for geographical education, drawn from the aspects of geography explored in this book. If such outcomes for geographical learning were even partially achieved there would be a good basis for progress for children to their secondary schools.

By 11 years old, children should:
- know about places, environments and people in different parts of the world;
- know of and give reasons for some natural, physical and social characteristics of communities, places and environments, and explain some of the commonalities shared and diversity between them;
- be able to locate important places in the news and in relation to their own experience and interests on maps from the world to local scales;
- have some awareness and understanding of the links that connect places and people and create interdependence locally, nationally and globally;
- show some understanding of the role of location and of the distributions and patterns formed by natural, physical, economic and social features;
- be able to describe and explain how some natural, physical, economic and social processes and activities can cause changes to places, environments and people's lives;
- be able to express their sense of wonder at some of what they see of the world and their concern over other aspects of the world that they encounter;
- describe and explain how people, including themselves, may have planned or unintended impacts on places and the environment, near and far, and that people may hold different views about ways places and environments do and might change;
- begin to recognise, appreciate and express some of the concerns associated with resource distribution, the quality of life and environmental and social justice, at local and global scales;
- be able to act on their understanding of how to live increasingly sustainably and explain why this is important for their own future and that of others;
- consider and develop informed views about places and the environment and why and how they might commit to taking actions to influence the present and future;
- raise interests, questions, problems and issues to investigate using enquiry, draw on a variety of skills and resources, and communicate their findings and viewpoints;
- make use of modern technologies, including the web, mobile phones and GPS, to find out about, make sense and use of and communicate about their world, near and far;
- be able to use maps to find their way around, know the relationship between globes and atlases and how to use these to locate and find out about places, and create maps of their own at a range of scales.

Figure 14.1 Key geographical outcomes for younger children by the end of Year 6

At the end of Year 6 children might complete a self-evaluation of their competence and confidence in geographical understanding to take with them for their secondary school geography teacher. This might form part of a portfolio of their work with their teacher's and their own earlier geography unit evaluations. Such a self-evaluation might be a piece of directed or free writing or use a proforma such as that in Table 14.1.

Table 14.1 An example of a Year 6 geography self-evaluation form

Statement of my geographical understanding I am confident that I can:	My level of competence		
	High	Medium	Low
1 show you where the UK and other important countries and features are on a globe and map of the world			
2 talk about the main features, activities and events in my locality and community, explain why they are important, and draw you a map of the area			
3 tell you about one or two other localities, explain what it is like to live there and why, and compare them to my own area			
4 use examples to describe some natural and human processes and how they can change features and places			
5 explain why it is important to know where places are, using examples from the news			
6 say how changes in places and environments have helpful or damaging impacts on people's lives			
7 give examples of one or more geographical patterns in the environment			
8 give examples of ways that people damage and improve the environment and why this happens			
9 prepare some useful geographical questions and say why they are useful			
10 explain how to undertake a geographical enquiry, and say which skills will help me investigate a problem or an issue and how to share what I find out with other people			
11 say clearly what I think about a particular event or issue, give reasons for my point of view and what actions I think should be taken, and recognise that other people may have other views and why they might hold them			
12 give examples of geographical words and terms and use them correctly			
13 select and use a suitable map to find my way around an area and choose appropriate maps and atlases to find out about other places			
14 say how useful photographs, pictures and drawings are in informing us about places and environments, and explain why they might be of limited help when used without other information			
15 use the web and other sources to find out information about places, environments and issues, and be able to check their accuracy and usefulness			
In my geographical learning I have really enjoyed:			

Use the outcomes of geographical learning listed in Figure 14.1 and see how they are expressed in Table 14.1. How confident do you feel about the statements in Table 14.1?

A sequence for learning in primary geography

One way to express the development of the geography curriculum to achieve these outcomes across the Foundation Stage and Key Stages 1 and 2 is to consider the focus for learning. This might be thought of in terms of two-year age phases, rather than year by year. This approach is applied in the *Independent Review of the Primary Curriculum: Final Report* (DCSF, 2009). In this way it is possible to indicate progression broadly in the development of children's geographical learning (Catling, 2004a, 2005a). Figure 14.2 offers an example of the development of such a geography curriculum.

Through their geography curriculum children should:

In the Early Years Foundation Stage: encountering geography
- observe and find out about features in the nursery/school and local streets;
- build up their vocabulary about the everyday world about them, of features, events, directions and space;
- talk about what they like and dislike about their environment and other places and consider how to care for places;
- talk about the lives of other people in other places using photographs and descriptions;
- play with environmental toys and listen to stories about people in places.

In Years 1 and 2 in primary school: geographical awareness
- investigate features and activities, changes that have taken place, and people's lives in their local area;
- examine places elsewhere, what they are like, ways people live and activities that happen there, and make some reasoned comparisons;
- use questions, fieldwork, photographs, maps and other resources, and extend their vocabulary, to investigate, describe and comment on places near and far;
- through stories and play explore lives and activities in places and environments;
- find out about a local issue, be aware of other views and express their own, and participate in activities about improvements locally;
- recognise roles that people can and do play in affecting, caring for and sustaining environments.

In Years 3 and 4 in primary school: geographical engagement
- contribute to planning geographical enquiries and how they can be carried out, including through fieldwork, and begin to evaluate how informative they have been;
- begin to use more geographically appropriate vocabulary to describe and express findings and views about places and the environment;
- know where significant places and environments are that they hear about;
- examine the location of features and patterns that particular features make, using maps as an aid to investigation and communicating their findings;
- consider how some changes they have identified in places and environments are caused and have an impact, and offer views on the effect of these changes;

- look at variations in people's lives in different places and their impact on these places and other people, exploring more than one place in detail, and make comparisons;
- begin to recognise and appreciate the connections between and the interdependence of people and places;
- consider how people interact with their environment, can improve it, what 'improve' might mean for whom, and how to act sustainably.

In Years 5 and 6 in primary school: geographical involvement

- plan, undertake and share geographical enquiries using a variety of resources, including fieldwork, maps, photographs, numerical and literary sources;
- use, accurately, geographical terms and skills to describe, explain, communicate and evaluate their investigations;
- know where significant places are, and be able to use appropriate globes, atlases and maps to find places new to them;
- describe ways in which human and natural processes create and shape places and aspects of the environment, such as rivers or towns, and affect locations and spatial patterns;
- examine and begin to explain the importance of the interdependence of places and people;
- compare what places are like and how they are changing, giving reasons for their comparisons and the changes they note;
- examine how places and environments can be cared for sustainably, what this means, and why it is vital for the present and the future;
- consider how decisions affect places and environmental issues, and begin to appreciate why different people's views have different impacts on decisions and events;
- identify and justify actions in which they can be involved in improving and sustaining environments.

Source: Adapted from Catling (2004a, p83), taking account of the Independent Primary Review (DCSF, 2009).

Figure 14.2 Possible core elements for the Foundation Stage and primary geography curriculum

REFLECTIVE TASK

What for you are the most important aspects of geography to include in the geography curriculum for primary children? How do your ideas reflect children's everyday geographies? What is your justification for your choice? What has influenced your views and selection?

Researching geographical learning and teaching

Developing understanding of children's geographical learning in your class is not always a matter of marking the children's work or observing an activity they are doing. It requires more careful investigation with a purpose. The move to developing your research skills is important because it is concerned with improving your practice in the classroom (and outside) for the benefit of children's learning. You might examine children's learning in a particular sequence of geography lessons over a short period. You may over a longer period, perhaps a year, investigate how children's understanding has developed through two or three geography topics.

Research related to primary geography is mixed. There is much research into children's geographies, their experience in their environments, their spatial awareness, and to a lesser extent their sense of the wider world. Other than in learning about maps (Wiegand, 2006), the research into children's geographical learning in school – and into teaching geography in primary classrooms – is sparse and small-scale (Catling, 1999a, 1999b, 2000, 2005b; Catling and Martin, 2004a). Few publications have focused on primary geography research (Bowles, 2000, 2004d; Catling and Martin, 2004b; Schmeinck, 2006).

There are three elements in primary geography that are central and critical foci for research: children's geographical learning, approaches to teaching geography, and the geography curriculum. Figure 14.3 illustrates the need and opportunities that exist to investigate and develop our understanding of primary school and classroom practice and of younger children's learning in geography (Catling and Martin, 2004a; Martin and Catling, 2004). This list provides a variety of possible areas to investigate in your own teaching.

---

1. **Children learning in geography**
   - Ways in which children's personal geographies affect their learning in and of geography
   - How children's environmental experience and perceptions can be built on and enhanced in their geographical learning
   - The understanding that children have of specific geographical concepts and vocabulary, such as village/town, transport/travel, holiday/leisure, land use/development, etc.
   - The nature of children's geographical misconceptions and misunderstandings
   - Ways in which children undertake and respond to geographical investigations and enquiries, perhaps compared to their ways of working in science
   - Ways in which children read and understand 'geographical' photographs
   - How children's geographical learning has an impact on the ways they understand and appreciate the 'world' around them.

2. **Approaches to teaching geography**
   - Teachers' expectations of children in geography
   - How teachers approach and plan geographical enquiries and investigations
   - The role of questioning in geography lessons to promote higher-order thinking skills
   - The uses of ICT to promote geographical analysis, evaluation and the communication of the findings of topics
   - How teachers identify and address children's misconceptions in geography teaching and devise strategies to tackle these
   - Ways in which teachers plan and teach for differentiated needs in geography
   - The effect of different strategies used in teaching geography on children's learning, e.g. fieldwork, role play, modelling, mapping, etc.
   - Ways in which resources are used effectively in geography teaching, e.g. stories, the school grounds, photo packs, maps, etc.
   - How teachers assess children's geographical understanding during topics.

---

3. The geography curriculum
- Teachers' understanding of geographical concepts and skills which they (will) teach
- Teachers' attitudes to and valuing of geography and children's geographical learning
- What teachers select to teach and how they plan to teach in geography
- Ways in which teachers' geographical understanding affects their teaching
- Schools' approaches to planning for geography throughout a school and of progression in geographical experience and learning
- How and with what impact teachers intervene to support and extend children's geographical learning
- How and why teachers select and use resources in their geography teaching.

Figure 14.3 Some areas in need of classroom research in primary geography

Approaching classroom research

During your course you investigate and evaluate aspects of your own teaching and its impact on children's learning. You do this using reflective approaches (Pollard, 2008). Another way is to undertake research for a special assignment or dissertation, in which you investigate systematically and rigorously an aspect of children's learning or your own teaching over several lessons or a geography topic.

Much advice is available about research approaches to investigate children's learning and the nature and impact of your teaching. This includes advice about research philosophies and methods (e.g. Cohen et al., 2007; Denscombe, 2007; Lowe, 2007; Opie, 2004, Thomas, 2009), insights into particular research topics, and reasons for using specific methods and the benefits and limitations of such research (e.g. Christensen and James, 2000; Fraser et al., 2004; Green and Hogan, 2005; Lewis et al., 2004). Some advice focuses on researching alongside children (e.g. McLeod, 2008). Kellett (2005) argues for involving children as researchers. However, there is comparatively limited support in geographical education (Bowles, 2000, 2004d; Catling and Martin, 2004a; Williams, 1996). Some research has been published in the journals *International Research in Geographical and Environmental Education* (IRGEE) Environmental Education Research. Occasional research summaries appear in *Primary Geographer*, and research reports may be published in the range of education research journals you will find in your library.

You must consult the literature on research philosophies and methods when initiating and developing your research project. You may need to use more than one method to gather your data, to trust it. There are various research foci and approaches you might use. The examples below illustrate some of these. Table 14.2 outlines several methods you might consider, but these need appropriate and thoughtful use, not simplistic application.

RESEARCH SUMMARY RESEARCH SUMMARY **RESEARCH SUMMARY** RESEARCH SUMMARY

Owens (2004b) researched 4–7 year olds' environmental values and the connection with vocabulary use and development to express their values. One technique used was concept drawings, which involved children drawing and talking about things that were special to them in the school grounds. It required annotating the children's drawings as they talked. Field notes were made of the reasons children gave for their valuing of features. It was found that:

- children valued features that they make more than one use of;
- their first-hand experience using features enhanced their vocabulary acquisition;
- there was a strong link to playtime activities;
- involvement in outdoor learning activities could have long-lasting effects;
- the use of rules about care for the environment had a positive impact.

She describes the value and effect of free activity play, the role of rule learning and the impact of teacher–learner engagement on the development and application of children's environmental values.

Children's feelings about geography

Children may be aware that they have been studying geography topics. Certainly older primary children have ideas and views (see Chapter 3). You might investigate what children understand geography to be about, whether they like their studies or what they think the main aspects of their learning in geography have been. You might ask the children to write about their ideas and views, or to prepare a poster or other visual image of 'geography'. Analyse their writing and images to identify common and minority ideas, understandings and themes that run through their 'statements'. Which aspects of their geographical learning appear consistently or less often? You might interview a sample of children about what they wrote or drew, asking them for reasons or more detail. You might consider how this relates to your teaching of geography and to the geography curriculum of the school.

How you plan your geography teaching

Keep a journal whenever you plan your geography teaching, noting, for example, what you have chosen to include, why you have started where you have, why you have sequenced a lesson in a particular order, how you came to use specific resources, what the constraints or opportunities in your planning have been, how you have taken account of the children's questions, experience and learning, and so forth. Maintain this record throughout your teaching, noting how you develop, amend or utterly change your initial plan, always noting the reasons why to explain what happens so that you can analyse how you went about your planning and understand what has been helpful and what might have inhibited you. By reviewing your planning you learn about the planning process for future topics.

Exploring children's geographical learning

Focusing on a particular aspect of children's geographical learning helps you become clearer about how their learning might be influenced by your teaching. In a topic select a particular geographical concept or skill, such as land use or understanding the use of symbols on maps. Ensure that you plan your teaching of your focus explicitly and provide a variety of opportunities for children to use the ideas or skill. Plan activities through which the children show you their understanding or capability. You might start a topic by eliciting their initial understanding, check how this is developing through the topic using specific tasks, and use a summative assessment of their learning. You would compare the children's responses from the different timings to see how their understanding has evolved. You might keep field notes during your research on learning events that you consider might have influenced the nature of the children's understanding at that point. From your notes, the children's evolving understanding and your overall reflections on your teaching and their engagement, consider what the main influences might have been on their geographical learning.

Table 14.2 Five research methods to use in geographical education research

Method	Brief description	Geography research examples
Field notes	A descriptive, contemporaneous account of what happened, was observed and was heard. Brief, note form, from summary to direct quotations. Can include reflections made at the time. Essential that a clear focus, possibly with criteria, is used to direct your observations. Can include the incidental and unexpected.	Describes the sequence of teaching events during a geography lesson; identifies who did or said what in various tasks; notes the engagement of children, impact of the tasks; notes responses to the resources used, ways in which children adapted/developed tasks and learning.
Interviews	A face-to-face interview can be structured or semi-structured, using closed or open (or a mixture of) questions with children to explore their understanding, ideas, views, feelings, etc. Careful planning must be given to the questions.	To find out what children have thought about the geography topic they have studied, devise a number of semi-structured open questions to gather their views about the way they studied the topic, what was helpful/unhelpful, what they consider they learnt, etc.
Episode analysis	Focus on a 'typical' episode in a lesson, such as a dialogue between two or three children during a group task. Record and transcribe the discussion. Analyse the nature of the discourse involved.	Record a discussion between a group of children (perhaps led/stimulated by yourself) about a geography concept or topic, e.g. river flow, traffic issues locally. Examine the nature of the understanding shown and the thinking skills involved.
Problem-solving activity	Set up a problem for a group to tackle, perhaps one with no specific solution but various possibilities. Observe who leads, who needs support, how they understand the problem, ways they tackle the problem, how they agree on the outcome(s).	Group of five or six children is given a set of resources about an environmental issue and asked to develop a presentation for the rest of the class to help them understand what the specific issues are and possible solutions might be. Observe the ways members of the group work and their thinking about the topic they have been given.
Assessment task	Develop an assessment activity for the children to undertake during or at the end of a topic, requiring them to work at different levels: description, explanation, evaluation, synthesis. Be clear about the focus: what the children know, can do, understand, value.	Provide individual children with information and two or three photographs about a particular place or theme, e.g. benefits and concerns associated with water. Set them questions or tasks requiring them to describe the place/theme, explain key points, offer their own views, etc.

Source: Catling (1999a, 2000); see also Greene and Hogan, 2005; Kellett, 2005; Cohen et al., 2007; Denscombe, 2007; Thomas, 2009

RESEARCH SUMMARY RESEARCH SUMMARY **RESEARCH SUMMARY** RESEARCH SUMMARY

Thurston (2006) investigated the effects of collaborative group work on the attainment of Year 4 children in their geography topics. Curriculum materials were designed for topics on water and (linked with science) Earth in space. An experimental approach was used in which small groups investigated the topics, with listening, discussion and communication central. Pre- and post-attainment tests were used with the children, who followed a structured programme which involved a child-oriented enquiry approach. Observation of the children's discourses employed video and discussion transcripts. The discourse was analysed and evaluated and used to help explain attainment outcomes and developments. Evidence emerged of increased attainment in geographical learning resulting from the discourse interactions of the children in small groups where the tasks required in-group activity rather than individual contributions.

REFLECTIVE TASK

Select one of the examples of research from the references, read the paper, book or chapter and follow it up by finding out about the research method used. Consider why the researcher used that particular method and reflect on whether you might use that method in a study of your own.

Concluding remarks

Geographical awareness and understanding are fundamental to all our lives. We use geographical ideas and skills regularly. Our everyday geographies are underpinned by an experiential and internalised sense of the world. While primary geography has a lengthy history, it remains a contested and contentious area of the curriculum. There continues to be debate about the quality of its teaching, the time available in younger children's education for it, how and how effectively children learn geography, and exactly what its curriculum should be. These concerns will not go away.

Children's changing lives, still strongly influenced by their families and peers, are increasingly supplemented and extended by a range of technologies which are changing our connections with people and places around the world. These include mobile phones, now owned by an ever-increasing majority of Key Stage 2 children; their access to the world which the web, email-type systems and social networks provide; and the forms of representation of places, lives and events through television, computer games and advertising that they see and engage in. It is essential that younger children develop a critical awareness of their involvement in their real, cyber and imaginary environments – the 'stuff' of their everyday geographies. These are not the only geographies affecting children. The topical issues of today – climate change, poverty–development issues, access to key resources such as water and food, war, transport, urban development, conservation and care for the environment – will continue to be real concerns for the future. Children know of these and enquire after them at increasingly younger ages. None of this will stand still, which makes it more rather than less important that geography's role and responsibility in the primary curriculum is recognised, revitalised and enhanced.

In this book we have aimed to provide you with a background understanding of geography, particularly focusing through place and environmental impact and sustainability. We have emphasised the nature of children's geographical experience and the ways in which the various geographies of others impact on children. We have explored a number of ways in and through which primary geography is and can be taught to be insightful, to challenge, to foster understanding and provide skills, to be sensitive, to motivate and to engage. Geographical studies examine the challenges but also focus on the positive, enjoyable and valuable in our lives, communities, places, environments and the wider world. Geography looks, too, at ways in which the 'future world' matters and can be improved and children's responsible and active involvement in this. We hope that we may have provoked and stimulated some interest on your part in geography, its essential value and its teaching and learning.

A SUMMARY OF **KEY POINTS**

This chapter has:

> reflected on the importance of geography in children's development;

> identified a set of geographical outcomes for primary children;

> offered a basis for constructing the primary geography curriculum, with a suggested sequence of focus from the Foundation Stage to Years 5 and 6;

> noted some of the needs in research in primary geography;

> provided you with some examples and approaches to research in primary geography.

MOVING *ON* > > > > > > MOVING *ON* > > > > > > MOVING *ON*

In this book you have read about children's geographical background, the nature of geography, its focus for primary children, key aspects of and approaches to teaching geography, its planning and assessment, and points about research in primary geography. From the range of material covered in this book, which area(s) have most interested you? Consider how you might follow these up by reading and reflecting on a selection of the references.

FURTHER READING FURTHER READING **FURTHER READING** FURTHER READING

Inevitably there is much that you might read. The following are offered as important texts in primary geography to use.

Catling, S and Martin, F (eds) (2004b) *Researching primary geography*. London: Register of Research in Primary Geography.

Cooper, H (ed) (2004a) *Exploring time and place through play*. London: David Fulton.

Cooper, H, Rowley, C, Asquith, S (eds) (2006) *Geography 3–11: A guide for teachers*. London: David Fulton.

Martin, F (2006c) *Teaching geography in primary schools*. Cambridge: Chris Kington.

Roberts, M (2003) *Learning through enquiry*. Sheffield: Geographical Association.

Scoffham, S (ed) (2004) *Primary geography handbook*. Sheffield: Geographical Association.

Journals

International Research in Geographical and Environmental Education, Taylor & Francis

Primary Geographer, Geographical Association

Environmental Education Research, Taylor & Francis

Useful websites

Geographical Association
  www.geography.org.uk
Geography Teaching Today
  www.geographyteachingtoday.org.uk
National Geographic
  www.nationalgeographic.com
QCA geography subject home page
  www.qca.org.uk/geography
Royal Geographical Society (with IBG)
  www.rgs.org

Appendix 1
Some examples of geographical picture storybooks

Places

Angelou, M (1994) *My painted house, my friendly chicken, and me*. London: Bodley Head.
Binch, C (1994) *Gregory Cool*. London: Frances Lincoln.
Birch, B and Chidley, A (1995) *The village in the forest by the sea*. London: Bodley Head.
Hedderwick, M (1984) *Katie Morag delivers the mail*. London: Bodley Head.
Hedderwick, M (1999) *The Katie Morag collection*. London: Bodley Head.
McLerran, A and Cooney, B (1991) *Roxaboxen*. New York: Harpertrophy.
Oakley, G (2000) *The church mice take a break*. London: Hodder Children's Books.
Patton Walsh, J (1992) *Babylon*. London: Red Fox.
Provensen, A and Provensen, M (1993) *Shaker Lane*. London: Walker Books.
Wheatley, N and Rawlins, D (1988) *My place*. North Blackburn: Dollins Dove.

The global dimension

de Beer, H (1987) *The little polar bear*. New York: North-South Books.
Heide, F and Gilliland, J (1997) *The day of Ahmed's secret*. London: Puffin Books.
Kloll, V and Carpenter, N (1994) *Masai and I*. London: Puffin Books.
Readman, J and Roberts, L (2002) *The world came to my place today*. London: Eden Project Books.
Readman, J and Honor Roberts, L (2006) *George saves the world by lunchtime*. London: Random House Children's Books.
Rose, D L and Saflund, B (1990) *The people who hugged the trees*. New York: Roberts Rinehart.
Sheldon, D and Hurt-Newton, T (1994) *Love, your bear Pete*. London: Walker Books.
Smith, D and Armstrong, S (2003) *If the world were a village*. London: A. & C. Black.
Sutton, E (1978) *My cat likes to live in boxes*. London: Puffin Books.
Williams, K and Stock, C (1991) *Galimoto*. New York: Mulberry Books.

Environmental and sustainability themes

Anholt, L (1997) *The forgotten forest*. London: Frances Lincoln.
Baker, J (1992) *Window*. London: Red Fox.
Baker, J (2004) *Belonging*. London: Walker Books.
Blathwayt, B (1992) *The little house by the sea*. London: Red Fox.
Brown, R (1991) *The world that Jack built*. London: Red Fox.
Foreman, M (1972) *Dinosaurs and all that rubbish*. London: Puffin Penguin.
Grindley, S and Foreman, M (1995) *Peter's place*. London: Andersen Press.
Hedderwick, M (1993) *Katie Morag and the new pier*. London: Bodley Head.

Keeping, C (1989) *Adam and Paradise Island*. Oxford: Oxford University Press.
Morimoto, J (1990), *Kenju's forest*, London: HarperCollins.

For ideas about how various books might be used with children of all ages, consult the book reviews written for and presented by the Geographical Association.
www.geography.org.uk/eyprimary/geographysubjectleaders/inspireme/bookreviews/#top

Appendix 2
Examples of ICT in virtual fieldwork, mapwork and communication

Mywalks

An excellent way to connect children with their local environment: *...the concept of Mywalks is a simple yet effective idea to engage all ages with their surroundings* (Owens, 2008a, p25). Walks in the local area can become a real adventure with children stopping at various places to take photographs and record on a digital recorder or video, what they see, feel and discover. Download the photographs and annotate them orally or with text from the evidence recorded. The concept comes originally from Mywalks Northumbria and has invaluable learning and experiential possibilities.
http://nuweb.northumbria.ac.uk/mywalks

Worldmapper

A highly visual and immediate web-based project which *...presents a large number of world maps, each depicting how the world would look if each country was drawn not according to the area taken up by its land, but by some other variable* (Pritchard, 2008, 30). Some maps depict the Western world hugely distorted in size using a wealth variable, while others distort other global regions considerably using a variable such as child labour. The maps raise many important and relevant issues. Links between geography and citizenship can be made. The website contains useful areas for ideas about using the maps in the classroom, including with older primary children.
www.worldmapper.org/index.html

Google Earth

The site provides detailed images of different places across the world and allows children to take 3-D virtual tours to otherwise inaccessible spots. The technology continues to develop and becomes more sophisticated, offering more insights to our environment and its processes. Children can create maps and plans of their local and other areas, tagging places on the map with photographs and information. Google Earth can be used to help children learn to use satellite navigation and global positioning systems (GPS) to create their own hyperlinks on a virtual tour they create using images. By using the facility 'virtual tour' and choosing a place you want to visit, children can be encouraged to explore and investigate the images and features. Video footage can be particularly effective in recreating scenes and bringing them to life. *YouTube* offers footage of many different environments. Other resources are available at websites such as the Times Educational Supplement and Geography Teaching Today.
www.earth.google.co.uk

Google Street View

This facility provides photographic views through an increasing number of UK cities, towns and villages. The street views are taken by car-mounted cameras. It was launched in March 2009, amid some controversy since the photographs capture whatever was happening in the street at the time. These still photographs may not be entirely up to date for an area you might access. If it is a place you can visit, you may be able to investigate changes that have taken place and look at the impact of change.
http://maps.google.co.uk/

Blogs

An increasingly popular and accessible way of sharing knowledge, information, ideas and skills, blogs can provide a very effective and interactive way to enhance children's learning through their interest and enthusiasm. An excellent example, initiated and maintained by Wendy North of the Geographical Association, shows how blogs can be used. It can be seen at the primary geography 'blogspot', a dynamic website offering many examples of innovative and excellent practice. Children can be encouraged to contribute to school or class geography blogs, developing ICT with geographical skills.
http://primarygeogblog.blogspot.com/

Appendix 3
Website sources

Education information sites

Department for Children, Schools and Families (DCSF)
    www.dcsf.gov.uk
Every Child Matters
    www.everychildmatters.gov.uk
National Curriculum in Action
    www.ncaction.org.uk/index.htm
Primary Strategies
    www.standards.dcsf.gov.uk
Qualifications and Curriculum Authority (QCA)
    www.qca.org.uk
QCA National Curriculum, Subjects
    www.curriculum.qca.org.uk/key-stages-1-and-2/subjects/index.aspx
QCA/DCSF Standards Site and Schemes of Work
    www.standards.dfes.gov.uk/schemes3/?view=get

Early Years

DCSF Early Years Foundation Stage
    www.standards.dfes.gov.uk/eyfs/site/index.htm
Early Years Foundation Stage: Planning and Resourcing
    www.standards.dfes.gov.uk/eyfs/site/4/tables/4_5_5_0.htm
Early Years Teaching Ideas
    www.teachingideas.co.uk/earlyyears/contents.htm
Playing with sand, water, etc.
    www.communityplaythings.com/c/resources
Practice Guidance for the Early Years Foundation Stage
    www.teachernet.gov.uk/publications

Education interest sites

The good childhood enquiry
    www.goodchildhood.org.uk
National Children's Bureau
    www.ncb.org.uk
The Primary Review:
    www.primaryreview.org.uk/
The Independent Review of the Primary Curriculum:
    www.dcsf.gov.uk/primarycurriculumreview
    www.teachernet.gov.uk/publications
    www.qca.org.uk/qca_22276.aspx

For geography

Geographical Association
  www.geography.org.uk
Geographical Association Early Years and Primary geography
  www.geography.org.uk/eyprimary
Geographical Association SuperSchemes
  www.geography.org.uk/eyprimary/superschemes/#top
Geography Teaching Today
  www.geographyteachingtoday.org.uk
Innovating with Geography
  www.qca.org.uk/geography/innovating
NC Programmes of Study Geography with maps for KS2
  www.nc.uk.net
  www.standards.dfes.gov.uk/geography
National Geographic
  www.nationalgeographic.com
Ofsted geography reports and school reports
  www.ofsted.gov.uk/geography
  www.ofsted.gov.uk/Ofsted-home/News/Press-and-media/2008/January/Geography-in-schools-changing-practice/(language)/eng-GB
Planning for geography
  www.standards.dfes.gov.uk/schemes1/geography/principles?view=get
  www.standards.dfes.gov.uk/schemes2/geography/principles?view=get
Royal Geographical Society (with IBG)
  www.rgs.org
QCA geography subject home page
  www.qca.org.uk/geography

Enquiry and philosophy

Open Spaces for Dialogue and Enquiry
  www.osdemethodology.org.uk
Philosophy for Children
  www.sapere.net/
TeacherNet Philosophy
  www.teachernet.gov.uk/teachingandlearning/subjects/

Out-of-classroom learning and experience

Field Studies Council
  www.field-studies-council.org/
Health and Safety of Pupils on Educational Visits
  www.publications.teachernet.gov.uk/eOrderingDownload/HSPV2.pdf
Learning Outside the Classroom
  www.lotc.org.uk
Learning Outside the Classroom Manifesto Newsletters
  www.extranet.ijack.com/lotc/indexfeb.html

Learning outside the Classroom Manifesto
www.teachernet.gov.uk/teachingandlearning/resourcematerials/outsideclassroom/
Learning through Landscapes
www.ltl.org.uk
Let's walk to school
www.walktoschool.org.uk
Mywalks@Northumbria
nuweb.northumbria.ac.uk/mywalks
Ofsted Report: Learning outside the classroom
www.ofsted.gov.uk/publications/
Play England
www.playengland.org.uk
Real World Learning
www.field-studies-council.org/campaigns/rwl/index.aspx
Safe Kids Walking
www.safekidswalking.org.uk
Teaching Outside the Classroom
www.teachingoutsidetheclassroom.com/
The Magdalen Project
www.themagdalenproject.org.uk/

Photograph and map sites

Cassini maps
www.cassinimaps.co.uk/
GA photo gallery
www.geographyphotos.com/
Google Earth
www.earth.google.com
Live Local
http://maps.live.com/
Multimap
www.multimap.com
Ordnance Survey maps
www.ordnancesurvey.co.uk/oswebsite/getamap/
Quikmaps
http://quikmaps.com/
Soft Teach Education (Local Studies)
www.soft-teach.co.uk/
Valuing Places CPD Units – Think Maps
http://www.geography.org.uk/projects/valuingplaces/cpdunits/thinkmaps/#924
Worldmapper
www.worldmapper.org/index.html

Sustainability and environment sites

Best Foot Forward
www.bestfootforward.com/
Campaign for School Gardening
www.rhs.org.uk/SCHOOLGARDENING/default.aspa

Celebrate World Environment Day
 www.unep.org/wed/2008/english/
Eco-Schools
 www.eco-schools.org.uk/about/
Forest Schools
 www.forestschools.com/index.php
Growing Schools
 www.teachernet.gov.uk/growingschools
Local 21 Agenda
 www.la21.org.uk/
Ofsted Report: Schools and sustainability
 www.ofsted.gov.uk/publications/070173
Plastic bag free towns
 www.plasticbagfree.com/
Sustainable Development Commission
 www.sd-commission.org.uk
Sustainable Learning
 www.sustainablelearning.info/
Sustainable Schools
 www.teachernet.gov.uk/sustainableschools/index.cfm
Sustainable Schools Downloadable posters and other information
 www.teachernet.gov.uk/sustainableschools/framework/framework_detail.cfm
Sustainable Schools completing Ofsted SEF advice
 www.teachernet.gov.uk/sustainableschools/tools/tools_detail.cfm?id=2
Transition towns
 www.transitiontowns.org/
WWF One Planet Campaign
 www.wwf.org.uk/oneplanet/ophome.asp

Global dimension

ActionAid
 www.actionaid.org.uk/100006/schools.html
CAFOD
 www.cafod.org.uk/
Christian Aid
 www.learn.christianaid.org.uk/
Comic Relief
 www.comicrelief.com/teach-and-learn/
Development Education Association (DEA)
 www.dea.org.uk/
DEA case studies
 www.globaldimension.org.uk/docs/dea_global_matters.pdf
Department for International Development (DfID)
 www.globaldimension.org.uk/
Fair Trade Foundation
 www.fairtrade.org.uk/
Friends of the Earth
 www.foe.co.uk/

Global Gateway
    www.globalgateway.org.uk/
International Schools Award
    www.globalgateway.org.uk/Default.aspx?page=4174
Oxfam Education
    www.oxfam.org.uk/education/
Oxfam advice on Handling Sensitive and Controversial Issues
    www.oxfam.org.uk/education/teachersupport/cpd/controversial/
Oxfam and successful school partnerships
    www.oxfam.org.uk/education/teachersupport/cpd/partnerships/files/oxfam_gc_guide_
    building_successful_school_partnerships.pdf
QCA The Global Dimension in Action
    www.qca.org.uk/libraryAssets/media/Global_Dimensions_print_friendly.pdf
Red Cross
    www.redcross.org.uk/education_section.asp?id=64442
Reading International Solidarity Centre
    www.risc.org.uk/
Save the Children Fund
    www.savethechildren.org.uk/en/1136.htm
Teachers in Development Education (TIDE)
    www.tidec.org/
UKOLWA
    www.ukowla.org.uk/main/toolkit.asp
UNICEF
    www.unicef.org.uk/resources/index.asp
WWF One Planet Schools
    www.wwf.org.uk/oneplanetschools

Citizenship

DCSF: Standards Site: Citizenship
    www.standards.dfes.gov.uk/schemes2/ks1-2citizenship/?view=get
National Curriculum Citizenship
    www.teachernet.gov.uk/citizenship
    www.citized.info

Sources

Becta
    www.becta.org.uk/
Staffordshire Learning Net
    www.sln.org.uk/geography/
Teachers TV
    www.teachers.tv/
Times Educational Supplement
    www.tes.co.uk/

ActionAid (2002) *Chembakolli*. Bristol: ActionAid.

ActionAid (2008) *From Bangalore to Chembakolli: A journey through south India*. Bristol: ActionAid.

ActionAid (2009) *Chembakolli: Life and change in an Indian village*. Bristol: ActionAid.

Adams, E and Ingham, S (1998) *Changing places*. London: The Children's Society.

Aitken, S (2001) *Geographies of young people*. London: Routledge.

Alexander, R (2009) *Towards a new primary curriculum: A report from the Cambridge Primary Review. Part 2: The Future*. Cambridge: University of Cambridge Faculty of Education. www.primaryreview.org.uk

Alexander, R and Flutter, J (2009) *Towards a new primary curriculum: A report from the Cambridge Primary Review. Part 1: The past and present*. Cambridge: University of Cambridge Faculty of Education. www.primaryreview.org.uk

Alexander, R and Hargreaves, L (2007) *The Primary Review interim reports: Community soundings*. Cambridge: University of Cambridge: The Primary Review. www.primaryreview.org.uk

Ansell, N (2005) *Children, youth and development*. London: Routledge.

Armitage, R and Armitage, D (1994) *The lighthouse keeper's lunch*. Leamington Spa: Scholastic.

Ashbridge, J (2006) Is geography suitable for the Foundation Stage? in Cooper, H, Rowley, C and Asquith, S (eds) *Geography 3–11: A guide for teachers*. London: David Fulton, pp.115–127.

Ataöv, A and Haider, J (2006) From participation to empowerment: Critical reflections on a participatory action research project with street children in Turkey. *Children, Youth and Environments*, 16 (2), pp127–152.

Baker, J (1991) *Window*. London: McRae Books.

Baker, J (2004) *Belonging*. London: Walker Books.

Balchin, W and Coleman, A (1965) Graphicacy: Should be the fourth ace in the pack, reprinted in Bale, J, Graves, N and Walford, R (eds) (1973) *Perspectives in geographical education*. Edinburgh: Oliver & Boyd, pp78–86.

Barber, D, Cooper, L and Meeson, G (2007) *Learning and teaching with interactive whiteboards*. Exeter: Learning Matters.

Barrett, M (2007) *Children's knowledge, beliefs and feelings about nations and national groups*. Hove: Psychology Press.

Barrett, M, Lyons, E and Bourchier-Sutton, A (2006) Children's knowledge of countries, in Spencer, C and Blades, M (eds) *Children and their environments*. Cambridge: Cambridge University Press, pp57–75.

Bell, D (2005) The value and importance of geography. *Primary Geographer*, 56, pp4–5.

Bell, S (2006) Scale in children's experience with the environment, in Spencer, C and Blades, M (eds) *Children and their environments*. Cambridge: Cambridge University Press, pp13–25.

Bellamy, C (2003) *The state of the world's children 2003: Children's participation*. New York: UNICEF.

Bellamy, C (2004) *The state of the world's children 2005: Childhood under threat*. New York: UNICEF.

Beunderman, J, Hannon, C and Bradwell, P (2007) *Seen and heard: Reclaiming the public realm with children and young people*. London: Demos.

Bilton, H (2005) *Learning outdoors: Improving the quality of children's play outdoors*. London: David Fulton.

Binch, C (1994) *Gregory Cool*. London: Frances Lincoln.

Black, P and Wiliam, D (1998) *Inside the black box*. Slough: NFER-Nelson.

Blatchford, P (1998) *Social life in school*. London: Falmer Press.

Bonnett, A (2008) *What is geography?* London: Sage.

Bowles, R (ed) (2000) *Occasional Paper No.1: Raising achievement in geography*. London: Register of Research in Primary Geography.

Bowles, R (2004a) Children's understanding of locality, in Catling, S and Martin, F (eds) *Researching primary geography*. London: Register of Research in Primary Geography, pp29–42.

Bowles, R (2004b) Comparing children's and adults' understanding of locality in Catling, S and Martin, F (eds) *Researching primary geography*. London: Register of Research in Primary Geography, pp211–224.

Bowles, R (2004c) Weather and climate in Scoffham, S (ed) *Primary geography handbook*. Sheffield: Geographical Association, pp230–245.

Bowles, R (ed) (2004d) *Occasional Paper No. 4: Space and place*. London: Register of Research in Primary Geography.

Bowles, R (n.d.) *GTIP orientation piece – Using ICT (Primary)*. www.geography.org.uk/projects/gtip/orientationpieces/usingict1/#top

Bradshaw, J and Mayhew, E (eds) (2003) *The well-being of children in the UK*. London: Save the Children.

Bridge, C (2004) Mapwork skills in Scoffham, S (ed) *The primary geography handbook*. Sheffield: Geographical Association.

Bridge, C (n.d.) *Project: Primary geography handbook extension project – Maps and stories (8–11)*. Geographical Association website.

Briggs, M, Woodfield, A, Martin, C and Swatton, P (2008) *Assessment for learning and teaching*. Exeter: Learning Matters.

Brocklehurst, H (2006) *Who's afraid of children*. Guildford: Ashgate.

Brown, G and Wragg, E (1993) *Questioning*. London: Routledge.

Brown, K and Kasser, T (2005) *Are psychological and ecological well-being compatible?* (Unpublished paper).

Bruce, T (2001) *Learning through play: Babies, toddlers and the Foundation Stage*. London: Hodder Arnold.

Bruce, T (2005) *Early childhood education*. London: Hodder Arnold.

Butt, G (n.d.) *GTIP Orientation piece – Assessment*. www.geography.org.uk/projects/gtip/orientationpieces/assessment/#top

Cadwell, L (1997) *Bringing Reggio Emilia home*. New York: Teachers College Press.

Carter, R (1998) *Handbook of primary geography*. Sheffield: Geographical Association.

Catling, S (1995) Wider horizons: The children's charter. *Primary Geographer*, 20, pp4–6.

Catling, S (1999a) Issues for Research in UK Primary Geography. *Research in Geographical and Environmental Education*, 8 (1), pp60–65.

Catling, S (1999b) Developing research in primary geography. *Primary Geographer*, 38, pp15–17.

Catling, S (2000) The importance of classroom research in primary geography, in Bowles, R (ed) *Occasional Paper No.1: Raising achievement in geography*. London: Register of Research in Primary Geography, pp29–38.

Catling, S (2001a) Primary geography matters! The geography curriculum: Principles, practice and evaluation, in Houtsonen, L and Tammilehto, M (eds) *Innovative practices in geographical education*. Proceedings of the Helsinki Symposium of the IGU Commission on Geographical Education. Helsinki: Department of Geography, University of Helsinki, pp8–17.

Catling, S (2001b) English primary schoolchildren's definitions of geography. *International Research in Geographical and Environmental Education*, 10 (4), pp363–378.

Catling, S (2002) *Placing places*. Sheffield: Geographical Association.

Catling, S (2003) Curriculum contested: Primary geography and social justice. *Geography*, 88 (3), pp164–210.

Catling, S (2004a) Understanding and developing primary geography, in Scoffham, S (ed) *Primary geography handbook*. Sheffield: Geographical Association, pp75–91.

Catling, S (2004b) On close inspection. *Primary Geographer*, 55, pp34-6.

Catling, S (2004c) An understanding of geography: The perspectives of English primary trainee teachers. *GeoJournal*, 60, pp149–158.

Catling, S (2005a) *Children, place and environment*. Lecture Plus, Geographical Association Annual Conference, University of Derby. www.geography.org.uk/download/Evcatling1.doc

Catling, S (2005b) Seeking younger children's 'voices' in geographical education research. *Research in Geographical and Environmental Education*, 14 (4), pp297–304.

Catling, S (2005c) Children's personal geographies and the English primary school geography curriculum. *Children's Geographies*, 3 (3), pp325–344.

Catling, S (2005d) *Superschemes: Improving the environment: access for all*. Sheffield: Geographical Association.

Catling, S (2006a) Young children's geographical worlds and primary geography, in Schmeinck, D (ed) *Research on learning and teaching in primary geography*. Karlsruhe: Pädagogischen Hochschule Karlsruhe, pp9–35.

Catling, S (2006b) What do 5-year-olds know of the world? Geographical understanding and play in young children's early learning. *Geography*, 91 (1), pp55–74.

Catling, S (2006c) Geography and history: Exploring the local connection. *Primary History*, 42, Spring, pp14–16.

Catling, S (2007) ECM6 = Environmental well-being? *Primary Geographer*, 63, Summer, pp5–8.

Catling, S (2008) Children's geographies and new technologies. *Primary Geographer*, 67, Autumn, pp7–10.

Catling, S (2009a) The happiness of everyday geographies. *Primary Geographer*, 68, Spring, pp12–14.

Catling, S (2009b) 'Thinking of Britain' in children's geographies. *Primary Geographer*, 69, Summer, pp16–19.

Catling, S (2009c) Creativity in primary geography, in Wilson, A (ed) *Creativity in primary education*. Exeter: Learning Matters, pp189–198.

Catling, S (2010) Organising and managing learning outside the classroom, in Arthur, J and Grainger, T (eds) *Learning to teach in the primary school*. London: Routledge.

Catling, S (n.d.), *GTIP Think Piece-Making and using maps*. www.geography.org.uk/projects/gtip/thinkpieces/makingmaps/#top

Catling, S and Martin, F (2004a) The state of research in primary geography, in Catling, S and Martin, F (eds) *Researching primary geography*. London: Register of Research in Primary Geography, pp15–25.

Catling, S and Martin, F (eds) (2004b) *Researching primary geography*. London: Register of Research in Primary Geography.

Catling, S and Taylor, E (2006) Children thinking about geographical significance. *Primary Geographer*, 60, pp35–37.

Catling, S, Bowles, R, Halocha, J, Martin, F and Rawlinson, S (2007) The State of Geography in English Primary Schools. *Geography*, 92 (2), pp118–136.

CBBC (2008) *Web worlds useful for children*. www.news.bbc.co.uk/1/hi/tecnology/ 7415442.stm. Accessed 6 June 6 2008.

Cele, S (2006) *Communicating place: Methods for understanding children's experience of place*. Stockholm: Stockholm University.

Chawla, L (1992) Childhood place attachments, in Altman, I and Low, S (eds) *Human behaviour and environment, Vol. 12: Place Attachment*. London: Plenum, pp63–86.

Chawla, L (ed) (2002) *Growing up in an urbanising world*. London: UNESCO/ Earthscan.

Chawla, L and Malone, K (2003) Neighbourhood quality in children's eyes, in Christensen, P and O'Brien, M (eds) *Children in the city*. London: RoutledgeFalmer, pp118–141.

Christensen, P and James, A (eds) (2000) *Research with children: Perspectives and practices*. London: RoutledgeFalmer.

Christensen, P and O'Brien, M (eds) (2003) *Children in the city*. London: RoutledgeFalmer.

Claire, H and Holden, C (eds) (2007) *The challenge of teaching controversial issues*. Stoke on Trent: Trentham Books.

Clarke, S (2001) *Unlocking formative assessment*. London: Hodder & Stoughton.

Clarke, S (2005) *Formative assessment in the secondary classroom*. London: Hodder & Stoughton.

Cohen, D and MacKeith, S (1991) *The development of imagination*. London: Routledge.

Cohen, L Manion, L and Morrison, K (2007) *Research methods in education*. London: Routledge.

Collins, J and Foley, P (eds) (2008) *Promoting children's well-being: Policy and practice*. Bristol: Policy Press.

Conway, D, Pointon, P and Greenwood, J (2008) 'If the world is round, how come the piece I'm standing on is flat?' Early Years geography, in Whitebread, D and Coltman, P (eds) *Teaching and learning in the early years*. London: Routledge, pp377–398.

Cooper, H (ed) (2004a) *Exploring time and place through play*. London: David Fulton.

Cooper, H (2004b) We're going camping, in Cooper, H (ed) *Exploring time and place through play*. London: David Fulton, pp117–130.

Cooper, H, Rowley, C and Asquith, S (eds) (2006) *Geography 3–11: A guide for teachers*. London: David Fulton, pp115–127.

Council for Learning Outside the Classroom (2008) *Out and about guidance*. www.lotc.org.uk/out-and-about-guidance

Countryside Commission (1997) *Public attitudes to the countryside*. Northampton: Countryside Commission.

Cresswell, T (2004) *Place: A short introduction*. Oxford: Blackwell.

Cullingford, C (1999) *The human experience: The early years*. Guildford: Ashgate.

Cullingford, C (2000) *Prejudice*. London: Kogan Page.

Cullingford, C (2007) *Childhood – The inside story*. Newcastle: Cambridge Scholars Publishing.

Dalrymple, H (n.d) *Fair trade school handbook: a small but useful guide to help you become a fair trade school*. Leeds: Leeds Development Education Centre.

Daly, N (1987) *Not so fast, Songololo*. Hamondsworth: Puffin.

Day, C (2007) *Environment and children*. London: Elsevier/Architectural Press.

DCSF (2007) *The children's plan: Building brighter futures*. London: TSO. www.dfes.gov.uk/publications/childrensplan

DCSF (2008a) *Statutory framework for the Early Years Foundation Stage*. Annesley: DCSF Publication. www.teachernet.gov.uk/publications

DCSF (2008b) *The Early Years Foundation Stage: Setting the Standards for Learning, Development and Care for children from birth to five*. Annesley: DCSF Publications. www.teachernet.gov.uk/publications

DCSF (2008c) *Practice Guidance for the Early Years Foundation Stage: Setting the Standards for Learning, Development and Care for children from birth to five*. Annesley: DCSF Publications. www.teachernet.gov.uk/publications

DCSF (2008d) *The Independent Review of the Primary Curriculum: Interim Report*. www.teachernet.gov.uk/publications

DCSF (2009) *The Independent Review of the Primary Curriculum: Final Report*. www.teachernet.gov.uk/publications

de Blij (2008) *The power of place*. Oxford: Oxford University Press.

Denscombe, M (2007) *The good research guide*. Maidenhead: Open University Press.

DES (1989) *The teaching and learning of history and geography*. London: HMSO.

DES (1990) *Geography for ages 5 to 16*. London: DES.

DES (1991) *Geography in the National Curriculum (England)*. London: DES.

Devine, D. (2003) *Children, power and schooling*. Stoke-on-Trent: Trentham Books.

DfE (1995) *Geography in the National Curriculum (England)*. London: DfE.

DfEE (1998) *Health and safety of pupils on educational visits*. London: DfEE. www.publications.teachernet.gov.uk/eOrderingDownload/HSPV2.pdf

DfEE/QCA (1998/2000) *A scheme of work for Key Stages 1 and 2: Geography*. London: DfEE/QCA. www.standards.dfes.gov.uk/schemes2/ks1-2geography/?view=get

DfEE/QCA (1999a) *The National Curriculum for England: Geography*. London: HMSO. www.curriculum.qca.org.uk/key-stages-1-and-2/subjects/index.aspx

DfEE/QCA (1999b) *The National Curriculum handbook for primary teachers in England*. London: HMSO.

DfEE/QCA (1999c) *The National Curriculum for England: Citizenship*. London: HMSO. www.curriculum.qca.org.uk/key-stages-1-and-2/subjects/index.aspx

DfEE/QCA (2002) *A scheme of work for Key Stages 1 and 2: Citizenship*. London: DfEE/QCA. www.standards.dfes.gov.uk/schemes2/ks1-2citizenship/?view=get

DfES (2003a) *Every Child Matters*. London: DfES.

DfES (2003b) *Excellence and enjoyment: A strategy for primary schools*. London: DfES.

DfES (2004a) *Every Child Matters: Change for children*. London: DfES.

DfES (2004b) *Putting the world in world-class education*. London: DfES.

DfES (2006a) *Sustainable schools for pupils, communities and the environment: Consultation paper*. London: DfES. www.teachernet.gov.uk/sustainableschools

DfES (2006b) *Sustainable schools for pupils, communities and the environment: Government response to the consultation on the sustainable schools strategy*. London: DfES. www.teachernet.gov.uk/sustainableschools

DfES (2006c) *Manifesto for learning outside the classroom*. London: DfES.

DfES/DfID (2005) *Developing the global dimension in the school curriculum*. London: DFID.

Disney, A (2004) Children's developing images and representation of the school link environment, in Catling, S and Martin, F (eds) *Researching primary geography*. London: Research Register in Primary Geography, pp139–147.

Disney, A and Mapperley, J (2007) Sustaining a school link. *Primary Geographer*, 62, pp16–18.

Dixon, J and Day, S (2004) Secret Places: 'You're too big to come in here', in Cooper, H, (ed) *Exploring time and place through play*. London: David Fulton, pp92–108.

Dower, N and Williams, J (2002) *Global citizenship: A critical introduction*. London: Routledge.

Downs, R and Stea, D (1977) *Maps in minds*. New York: Harper & Row.

Drake, M (1996) Resources for global understanding, in Steiner, M (ed) *Developing the global teacher*. Stoke on Trent: Trentham, pp63–70.

Dudek, M (ed) (2005) *Children's spaces*. London: Architectural Press.

Else, P (2009) *The value of play*. London: Continuum.

Filer, J (2008) *Healthy, outside and active: Running an outdoors programme in the early years*. London: David Fulton.

Fog Olwig, K and Gulløv, E (eds) (2004) *Children's places*. London: Routledge.

Fraser, S, Lewis, V, Ding, S, Kellett, M and Robinson, C (eds) (2004) *Doing research with children and young people*. London: Sage.

Freire, P (1994) *A pedagogy of hope*. London: Continuum.

Garforth, H, Hopper, L, Lowe, B, and Robinson, L (2006) *Growing up global*. Reading: RISC.

Garrick, R (2004) *Playing outdoors in the early years*. London: Continuum.

Gauntlett, D and Jackson, L (2008) *Virtual worlds – Users and producers. Case study: Adventure rock*. www.childrenvirtualworlds.org.uk/papers.htm. Accessed 5 June 2008.

Geographical Association (2005–07) *SuperSchemes Geography at Key Stages 1 and 2*. Sheffield: Geographical Association.

Geographical Association (2009) *A different view: A manifesto from the Geographical Association*. Sheffield: Geographical Association. www.geography.org.uk/adifferentview

Gill, T (2007) *No fear: Growing up in a risk averse society*. London: Calouste Gulbenkian Foundation.

Glaser, M (2007) *Virtual worlds for kids enshrined with real world*. www.pbs.org/mediashift/2007/06/your_take_roundupvirtual_world.html. Accessed 5 June 2008.

Glauert, E, Heal, C, and Cook, J (2003) Knowledge and understanding of the world, in Riley, J, (ed) *Learning in the early years: A guide for teachers of children 3–7*. London: Paul Chapman, pp125–155.

Greene, S and Hogan, D (eds) (2005) *Researching children's experience: Approaches and methods*. London: Sage.

Guldberg, H (2009) *Reclaiming childhood: Freedom and play in an age of fear*. London: Routledge.

Gunter, B and Furnham, A (1998) *Children as consumers*. London: Routledge.

Hallett, C and Prout, A (eds) (2003) *Hearing the voices of children*. London: Routledge.

Halocha, J (1998) *Coordinating geography across the primary school*. Lewes: Falmer Press.

Halocha, J (2001) *Pocket guides to the primary curriculum: Geography*. Leamington Spa: Scholastic.

Hare, R, Attenborough, C and Day, T (1996) *Geography in the school grounds*. Bristol: Southgate.

Harlen, W, Gipps, C, Broadfoot, P and Nuttall, D (1992), Assessment and the improvement of education. *The Curriculum Journal*, 3(3), pp215–30.

Harris, J (2001) *Blackberry wine*. London: Black Swan Books.

Hart, R. (1997) *Children's participation*. London: Earthscan.

Haynes, J (2002) *Children as philosophers*. London: Routledge.

Heal, C and Cook, J (1998) Humanities: Developing a sense of place and time in the early years, in Siraj-Blatchford, I (ed) *A curriculum development handbook for early chidlhood educators*. Stoke on Trent: Trentham Books, pp121–136.

Heide, F and Gilliland, J (1997) *The day of Ahmed's secret*. London: Puffin Books.

Henshall, A and Lacey, L (2007) *Word on the street: Children and young people's views on using the street for play and informal recreation*. London: National Children's Bureau.

Hicks, D (1998) Stories of hope: A response to the 'psychology of despair'. *Environmental Education Research*, 4 (2), pp165–176.

Hicks, D (2002) *Lessons for the future*. London: Routledge.

Hicks, D (2007) Responding to the world, in Hicks, D and Holden, C (eds) *Teaching the global dimension*. London: Routledge, pp3–13.

Hicks, D and Holden, C (eds) (2007) *Teaching the global dimension*. London: Routledge.

Hillman, M and Adams, J (1992) Children's freedom and safety. *Children's environments*, 9(2), pp12–33.

Hirst, B (2006) *The impact of global dimension teaching on children's achievement*. Manchester: North West Global Education Network, Manchester Development Education Project.

HMG (1988) *The Education Reform Act*. London: The Stationery Office.

Holden, K (2004) Educating for Europe: The knowledge and understanding of British children. *Education 3–13*, March, pp39–44.

Holland, G (1998) *A report to DfEE/QCA on education for sustainable development in the schools sector from the panel for education for sustainable development*. www.defra.gov.uk/environment/sustainable/educpanel/1998ar/ann4.htm

Holloway, L and Hubbard, P (2001) *People and place: The extraordinary geographies of everyday life*. London: Prentice Hall.

Holloway, S and Valentine, G (2003) *Cyberkids: Children in the information age*. London: RoutledgeFalmer.

Holt, L (2007) Children's sociospatial (re)production of disability within primary school playgrounds. *Environment and Planning D: Society and Space*, 25 (6), pp783–802.

Hoodless, P (2008) *Teaching history in primary schools*. Exeter: Learning Matters.

Hoodless, P, Bermingham, S, McCreery, E and Bowen, P (2009) *Teaching humanities in primary schools*. Exeter: Learning Matters.

Huckle, J (1990) Environmental education: Teaching for a sustainable future, in Dufour, D (ed) *The new social curriculum*. Cambridge: Cambridge University Press.

Huckle, J and Martin, A (2001) *Environments in a changing world*. Harlow: Prentice Hall.

Hutchins, P (1992) *Rosie's walk*. London: Puffin.

Iwaskov, L (2004) Escape this primary trough. *Times Educational Supplement*, November.

Jeffrey, B and Woods, P (2003) *The creative school*. London: RoutledgeFalmer.

Johansson, M (2006) Environmental and parental factors as determinants of mode for children's leisure travel. *Journal of Environmental Psychology*, 26 (2), pp156–169.

Jones, P (2009) *Rethinking childhood: attitudes in contemporary society*. London: Continuum.

Katz, C (2004) *Growing up global*. Minneapolis: University of Minnesota Press.

Katz, C (2005) The terrors of hypervigilance: Security and the compromised spaces of contemporary childhood in Qvortrup, J (ed), *Studies in modern childhood*. Basingstoke: Palgrave Macmillan, pp99–114.

Kellett, M (2005) *How to develop children as researchers*. London: Paul Chapman.

Kelly, P (2007) The joy of involving pupils in their own assessment, in Hayes, D (ed) *Joyful teaching and learning in the primary school*. Exeter: Learning Matters, pp130–135.

Kenway, J and Bullen, E (2001) *Consuming children*. Buckingham: Open University Press.

Kitchen, R and Freundschuh, S (eds) (2000) *Cognitive mapping*. London: Routledge.

Knight, P (1993) *Primary geography, primary history*. London: David Fulton.

Knight, S (2009) *Forest schools and outdoor learning in the early years*. London: Sage.

Kyttä, M (2004) *Children in outdoor contexts*. PhD Dissertation, Department of Architecture, University of Helsinki.

Kyttä, M (2006) Environmental child-friendliness in the light of the Bulerby model, in Spencer, C and Blades, M (eds) *Children and their environments*. Cambridge: Cambridge University Press, pp141–158.

Laird, E (1994) *The inside outing*. London: Diamond Books.

Layard, R and Dunn, J (2009) *A good childhood: Searching for values in a competitive age*. London: Penguin.

Leeder, A (2006) *100 ideas for teaching geography*. London: Continuum.

Lewis, V, Kellett, M, Robinson, C, Fraser, S and Ding, S (eds) (2004) *The reality of research with children and young people*. London: Sage.

Liebel, M (2004) *A will of their own*. London: Zed Books.

Lipman, M (2003) *Thinking in education*. Cambridge: Cambridge University Press.

Lolichen, P (2007) Children in the driver's seat: Children conducting a study of their transport and mobility problems. *Children, Youth and Environments*, 17 (1), pp238–256.

Lowe, M (2007) *Beginning research*. London: Routledge.

Mackett, R, Banister, D, Batty, M, Einon, D, Brown, B, Gong, Y, Kitazawa, K, Marshall, S and Paskins, J (2007) Final report on 'Children's activities, perceptions and behaviour in the local environment (CAPABLE). www.cts.ucl.ac.uk/research/chcaruse/.

Mackintosh, M (2004) Images in geography: Using photographs, sketches and diagrams in Scoffham, S (ed) (2004) *The primary geography handbook*. Sheffield: Geographical Association, pp120–133.

Mackintosh, M (2007) The joy of teaching and learning geography, in Hayes, D (ed) *Joyful teaching and learning in the primary school*. Exeter: Learning Matters.

Macintosh, M (n.d.), *GTIP Think Piece – Human geography primary*. GA website www.geography.org.uk/projects/gtip/thinkpieces/humangeography/

Madge, N (2006) *Children these days*. Bristol: The Policy Press.

Madge, N and Barker, J (2007) *Risk and childhood*. London: RSA. www.theRSA.org

Malone, K (2009) *Every experience matters: An evidence based report on the role of learning outside the classroom for children's whole development from birth to eighteen years*. Farming and Countryside Education. www.face-online.org.uk/index

Martin, F (1995) *Teaching early years geography*. Cambridge: Chris Kington.

Martin, F (2004) Primary historians and geographers learning from each other. *Primary History*, 32, Autumn, pp18–21.

Martin, F (2005) North–south linking as a controversial issue. *Prospero,* 14 (4), pp47–54.

Martin, F (2006a) Everyday geography. *Primary Geographer*, 61, pp4–7.

Martin, F (2006b) Knowledge bases for effective teaching: Beginning teachers' development as teachers of primary geography, in Schmeinck, D (ed) *Research on learning and teaching in primary geography*. Karlsruhe: Padagogische Hochschule Karlsruhe, pp149–184.

Martin, F (2006c) *Teaching geography in primary schools: Learning how to live in the world*. Cambridge: Chris Kington.

Martin, F ((2007) The wider world in the primary school, in Hicks, D and Holden, C (eds) *Teaching the global dimension*. London: Routledge, pp163–175.

Martin, F (2008) Ethnogeography: Towards liberatory geography education *Children's Geographies*, 6 (4), pp437–450.

Martin, F and Catling, S (2004) Future directions and developments for primary geography research, in Catling, S and Martin, F (eds) *Researching primary geography*. London: Register of Research in Primary Geography, pp301–311.

Martin, F and Owens, P (2004) Young children making sense of their place in the world, in Scoffham, S (ed) *Primary geography handbook*. Sheffield: Geographical Association.

Martin, F and Owens, P (2008) *Caring for our world: A practical guide to ESD for ages 4–8*. Sheffield: Geographical Association.

Martin, G (2005) *All possible worlds: A history of geographical ideas*. Oxford: Oxford University Press.

Massey, D (2005) *For space*. London: Sage.

Matthews, H (1992) *Making sense of place*. Hemel Hempstead: Harvester/Wheatsheaf.

Matthews, J and Herbert, D (2008) *Geography: A very short introduction*. Oxford: Oxford University Press.

Mayall, B (2008) *The Primary Review interim reports: Children's lives outside school and their educational impact*. Cambridge: University of Cambridge: The Primary Review.

McKendrick, J, Bradford, M and Fielder, A (2000) Time for a party!: Making sense of the commercialization of leisure space for children, in Holloway, S and Valentine, G (eds) *Children's geographies*. London: Routledge, pp100–116.

McLeod, A (2008) *Listening to children*. London: Jessica Kingsley.

McLerran, A and Cooney, B (1991) *Roxaboxen*. New York: Harpertrophy.

Milner, A (1996) *Geography starts here! Practical approaches with nursery and reception children*. Sheffield: Geographical Association.

Milner, A (1997) *Geography through play: Structured play at Key Stage 1*. Sheffield: Geographical Association.

Min, B and Lee, J (2006) Children's neighbourhood place as a psychological and behavioral domain. *Journal of Environmental Psychology*, 26 (1), pp51–71.

Mitchell, C and Reid-Walsh, J (2002) *Researching children's popular culture*. London: Routledge.

Mitchell, D (ed) (2009) *Living geography: Exciting futures for teachers and students*. London: Chris Kington.

Moran, J (2008) *Queuing for beginners: The story of daily life from breakfast to bedtime*. London: Profile Books.

Morimoto, J (1992) *Kenju's forest*. London: Angus and Robertson.

Morris, G (n.d.) *Teaching materials and resources* (unpublished).

Moss, P and Petrie, P (2002) *From children's services to children's spaces*. London: RoutledgeFalmer.

National Assembly for Wales (2008) *Education for Sustainable Development and Global Citizenship*. Cardiff: ESDGC. www.assemblywales.org/

NCC (National Curriculum Council) (1993) *An introduction to teaching geography at Key Stages 1 and 2*. York: NCC.

NEF (National Economic Foundation) (2005) *Well-being and the environment*. London: NEF.

Newcombe, N and Huttenlocher, J (2000) *Making space: The development of spatial representation and reasoning*. Cambridge: Massachusetts Institute of Technology.

Nieuwenhuys, O (2003) Growing up between places of work and non-places of childhood: The uneasy relationship, in Fog Olwig, K and Gulløv, E (eds) (2004) *Children's places*. London: Routledge, pp99–118.

Noddings, N (2005) *The challenge to care in schools*. New York: Teachers' College Press.

North, W (2008) *Everyday geographies: Planning with 'big ideas' (or key concepts)*, www.primarygeogblog.blogspot.com/2008/01/planning-with-big-ideas.html Accessed 29 January 2008.

O'Brien, M (2003) Regenerating children's neighbourhoods: What do children want?, in Christensen, P and O'Brien, M (eds) *Children in the city*. London: RoutledgeFalmer, pp142–161.

Ofsted (1999) *Primary education 1994–1998: A review of primary schools in England*. London: The Stationery Office.

Ofsted (2004) *Ofsted subject reports 2002/03: Geography in primary schools*. London: Ofsted.

Ofsted (2005) *Ofsted subject reports 2003/04: Geography in primary schools*. London: Ofsted.

Ofsted (2008a) *Geography in schools: Changing practice*. London: Ofsted.

www.ofsted.gov.uk/publications/

Ofsted (2008b) *Schools and sustainability: A climate for change*. London: Ofsted. www.ofsted.gov.uk/publications/

Ofsted (2008c) *Learning outside the classroom*. London: Ofsted. www.ofsted.gov.uk/publications/

Olle, H (2002) *Young Europe*. London: National Children's Bureau.

Opie, C (ed) (2004) *Doing educational research*. London: Sage.

Osler, A and Starkey, H (2005) *Changing citizenship: Democracy and inclusion in education*. Maidenhead: Open University Press.

Owen, D and Ryan, A (2001) *Teaching geography 3–11*. London: Continuum.

Owens, P (2004a) Can you get to grandma's safely?, in de Bóo, M (ed) (2004) *The early years handbook*. Sheffield: The Curriculum Partnership, pp38–43.

Owens, P (2004b) Researching the development of children's environmental values in the early school years, in Catling, S & Martin, F (eds) *Researching primary geography*. London: Register of Research in Primary Geography, pp67–76.

Owens, P (2008a) Mywalks: Walks on the child side. *Primary Geographer*, 67, pp25–28.

Owens, P (2008b) Level Headed Geography: Planning achievement. *Primary Geographer*, 66, pp15–18.

Owens, P and North, W (2008) *Young geographers – A living geography project for primary schools*. Geographical Association. www.geography.org.uk/projects/younggeographers Accessed 24 July 2008.

Oxfam (2006a) *Education for global citizenship: A guide for schools*. Oxford: Oxfam.

Oxfam (2006b) *Teaching controversial issues*. Oxford: Oxfam.

Palmer, J and Birch, J (2004) *Geography in the early years*. London: RoutledgeFalmer.

Palmer, J and Suggate, J (2004) The development of children's understanding of distant places and environmental issues: Report of a UK longitudinal study of the development of ideas between the ages of four and ten years. *Research Papers in Education*, 19 (2), pp205–237.

Palmer, J, Suggate, J and Matthews, J (1996) Environmental cognition: Early ideas and misconceptions at the ages of four and six. *Environmental Education Research* 2, pp301–330.

Paton Walsh, J (1992), *Babylon*. London: Red Fox.

Patten, B (1990) 'The River's Story', in Patten, B (ed) *Thawing frozen frogs*. London: Penguin, pp110–111.

Patten, C (2000) BBC Reith Lectures: *1. Governance*. London: BBC.

Pickford, T (2006) *Learning ICT in the humanities*. London: David Fulton.

Pike, S (2008) *Children and their environments in Ireland*. Ed.D. Thesis. Belfast: Queens University.

Plester, B, Blades, M and Spencer, C (2006) Children's understanding of environmental representations: Aerial photographs and model towns, in Spencer, C and Blades, M (eds) *Children and their environments*. Cambridge: Cambridge University Press, pp 42–56.

Pollard, A (2008) *Reflective teaching*. London: Continuum.

Powell, M (2007) The hidden curriculum of recess. *Children, Youth and Environment*, 17 (4), pp86–106.

Prezza, M (2007) Children's independent mobility: A review of the recent Italian literature. *Children, Youth and Environment*, 17 (4), pp293–318.

Pritchard, J (2008) Worldmapper. *Primary Geographer*, 67, Autumn, pp30–33.

QCA (2003) *Innovating with geography*. www.qca.org.uk/geography/innovating/

QCA (2005) *Seeing steps in children's learning: Foundation Stage*. London: QCA.

QCA (2007a) *Geography: Programme of Study for Key Stage 3 and attainment target.* www.qca.org.uk/curriculum/geography

QCA (2007b) *The global dimension in action.* London: QCA.

QCA (n.d.a) *Assessment for learning guidance.* www.qca.org.uk/qca_4338.aspx

QCA (n.d.b) *Assessment for learning guidance.* www.qca.org.uk/qca_4337.aspx#effective

QCA (n.d.c) *Assessment in geography.*www.curriculum.qca.org.uk/key-stages-1-and-2/ assessment/assessmentofsubjects/assessmentingeography/index.aspx?return=/ search/index.aspx%3FfldSiteSearch%3DGiving+pupils+opportunities+to+ demonstrate+attainment%26btnGoSearch.x%3D27%26btnGoSearch.y%3D11

Readman, J and Roberts, L (2002) *The world came to my place today.* London: Transworld Publishers/Eden Project Books.

Richardson, P (2004a) Fieldwork, in Scoffham, S (ed) *The primary geography handbook.* Sheffield: Geographical Association, pp134–147.

Richardson, P (2004b) Planning the geography curriculum, in Scoffham, S (ed) *The primary geography handbook.* Sheffield: Geographical Association, pp302–311.

Rissotto, A and Giuliani, M (2006) Learning neighbourhood environments: The loss of experience in a modern world in Spencer, C and Blades, M (eds) *Children and their environments.* Cambridge: Cambridge University Press, pp75–90.

Roberts, M (2003) *Learning through enquiry.* Sheffield: Geographical Association.

Robinson, C and Fielding, M (2007) *The Primary Review interim reports: Children and their primary schools: Pupils' voices.* Cambridge: University of Cambridge: The Primary Review.

Rodgers, A and Streluk, A (2002) *Primary ICT handbook: geography.* Cheltenham: Nelson Thornes.

Rosen, M and Oxenbury, H (1989) *We're going on a bear hunt.* London: Walker Books.

Rowley, C (2006) Are there different types of geographical enquiry? in Cooper, H, Rowley, C and Asquith, S (eds) *Geography 3–11: A guide for teachers.* London: David Fulton, pp17–32.

Rowley, C and Lewis, L (2003) *Thinking on the edge.* Morecombe: Living Earth.

Salaman, A and Tutchell, S (2005) *Planning educational visits for the early years.* London: Paul Chapman.

Schmeinck, D (2006) Images of the world or do travel experiences and the presence of the media influence children's perceptions of the world?, in Schmeinck, D (ed) *Research on learning and teaching in primary geography.* Karlsruhe: Pädagogische Hochschule Karlsruhe, pp37–59.

Scoffham, S (ed) (2004) *Primary geography handbook.* Sheffield: Geographical Association.

Scoffham, S (2007) 'Please Miss, why are they so poor?'. *Primary Geographer,* 62, pp5–7.

Scottish Executive (2001) *The global dimension in the curriculum.* Dundee: Learning and Teaching in Scotland.

Shah, H and Marks, N (2004) *A well-being manifesto for a flourishing society.* London: NEF.

Sharp, J, Peacock, G, Johnsey, R, Simon, S and Smith, R (2007) *Primary science: Teaching theory and practice.* Exeter: Learning Matters.

Sharp, J, Potter, J, Allen, J and Loveless, A (2007) *Primary ICT: Knowledge, understanding and practice.* Exeter: Learning Matters.

Simco, N (2003) Developing a geographical perspective within an integrated theme, in Cooper, H and Sixsmith, C (eds) *Teaching across the early years 3–7.* London: Routledge, pp168–180.

Singer, P (2006) *Children at war.* Berkeley: University of California Press.

Smith, F (1995) Children's voices and the construction of children's spaces: The example of playcare centres in the United Kingdom. *Children's Environments*, 12 (3), pp177–190.

Spencer, C and Blades, M (eds) (2006) *Children and their environments*. Cambridge: Cambridge University Press.

Spencer, C, Blades, M and Morsley, K (1989) *The child in the physical environment*. Chichester: Wiley.

Spink, E, Keogh, B and Naylor, S (2008) Knowledge and understanding of the world in Basford, J and Hodson, E (eds) *Teaching Early Years Foundation Stage*. Exeter: Learning Matters, pp85–97.

Standish, A (2009) *Global perspectives in the geography curriculum: reviewing the moral case for geography*. London: Routledge.

Stea, D, Pinon, M, Middlebrook, N, Eckert, V and Blaut, J (2001) Place and space learning: The 'play pen' of young children, in Robertson, M and Gerber, R (eds) *Children's ways of knowing*. Melbourne: Australian Council for Educational Research, pp164–178.

Steinberg, S and Kincheloe, J (eds) (2004) *Kinderculture: The corporate construction of childhood*. Cambridge: Westview Press.

Steuer, N, Thompson, S and Marks, N (2006) *Review of the environmental dimension of children and young people's well-being*. London: Sustainable Development Commission. www.sd-commission.org.uk

Storm, M (1989) The five basic questions for primary geography. *Primary Geographer, 2*, pp4–5.

Tanner, J (2007) Global citizenship, in Hicks, D and Holden, C (eds) *Teaching the global dimension*. London: Routledge, pp150–160.

Tanner, J (2009) Special places: Place attachment and children's happiness. *Primary Geographer*, 68, Spring, pp5–8.

Taylor, E and Catling, S (2006) Geographical significance: A useful concept? *Teaching Geography*, 31 (3), pp122–125.

TDA (2007a) Professional standards for teachers: Qualified Teacher Status. London: TDA www.tda.gov.uk/standards.

TDA (2007b) Professional standards for teachers: Core. London: TDA. www.tda.gov.uk/standards.

Thomas, D and Goudie, A (eds) (2000) *The dictionary of physical geography*. Oxford: Blackwell.

Thomas, G and Thompson, G (2004) *A child's place: Why environment matters to children*. London: Demos.

Thomas, G (2009) *How to do your research project*. London: Sage.

Thornton, L and Brunton, P (2007) *Bringing the Reggio approach to your early years practice*. London: David Fulton.

Thurston, A (2006) Effects of group work on attainment in primary school geography, in Schmeinck, D (ed) *Research on learning and teaching in primary geography*. Karlsruhe: Pädagogischen Hochschule Karlsruhe, pp61–92.

Thwaites, A (2008) *100 ideas for teaching knowledge and understanding of the world*. London: Continuum.

Titman, W (1994) *Special people, special places*. Winchester: Learning through Landscapes.

Tovey, H (2007) *Playing outdoors: Spaces, places, risk and challenge*. Maidenhead: Open University Press.

Tranter, P and Malone, K (2004) Geographies of environmental learning: An exploration of children's use of school grounds. *Children's Geographies*, 2 (1), pp131–155.

UNICEF (2005) *The state of the world's children 2006: Excluded and invisible*. New York: UNICEF.

United Nations (1987) *Report of the World Commission on Environment and Develop-ment,* United Nations Department of Economic and Social Affairs (DESA). www.un.org/documents/ga/res/42/ares42-187.htm

Uttal, D and Tan, L (2000) Cognitive mapping in childhood, in Kitchen, R and Freundschuh, S (eds) *Cognitive mapping: Past, present and future*. London: Routledge, pp147–165.

Valentine, G (2004) *Public space and the culture of childhood*. Guildford: Ashgate.

van Andel, J (1990) Places children like, dislike, and fear. *Children's Environments Quarterly*, 7 (4), pp24–31.

Vleminckx, K and Smeeding, T (eds) (2001) *Child well-being, child poverty and child policy in modern nations*. Bristol: The Policy Press.

Vygotsky, L (1962) *Thought and language.* Cambridge, MA: MIT Press.

Wall, K, Dockrell, J and Peacey, N (2008) *Primary education: The physical environment*. Cambridge: The University of Cambridge. www.primaryreview.org.uk.

Waller, T (2006) 'Don't come too close to my octopus Tree': Recording and evaluating young children's perspectives on outdoor learning. *Children, Youth and Environment*, 16 (2), pp75–104.

Walker, G (2004) Contrasting localities, in Scoffham, S (ed) *Primary geography handbook*. Sheffield: Geographical Association, pp194–203.

Waters, J (2008) *Education, migration, and cultural capital in the Chinese diaspora: Transnational students between Hong Kong and Canada*. New York: Cambria Press.

Webber, S and Dixon, S (eds) (2007) *Growing up online: Young people and digital technologies*. Basingstoke: Palgrave Macmillan.

Webley, P (2005) Children's understanding of economics, in Barrett, M and Buchanan-Barrow, E (eds) *Children's understanding of society*. Hove: Psychology Press, pp43–67.

Webster, A, Beveridge, M and Reed, M (1996) *Managing the literacy curriculum.* London: Routledge.

Weeden, P (n.d.) *GTIP Think Piece – Assessment for learning*, www.geography.org.uk/projects/gtip/thinkpieces/assessmentforlearning/#top

Weeden, P and Lambert, D (2006) *Geography inside the black box: Assessment for learning in the geography classroom*. London: NFER-Nelson.

Weldon, M (2004) The wider world, in Scoffham, S (ed) *Primary geography handbook*. Sheffield: Geographical Association, pp204–215.

West, A (2007) Power relationships and adult resistance to children's participation. *Children, Youth and Environment*, 17 (1), pp123–135.

Weston, B (ed) (2005) *Child labor and human rights: Making children matter*. London: Lynne Riener.

White, J (2008) *Playing and learning outdoors*. London: Routledge.

Whittle, J (2006) Journey sticks and affective mapping. *Primary Geographer*, 59, Spring, pp11–13.

Whitley, D (2008) *The idea of nature in Disney animation*. Guildford: Ashgate.

Wiegand, P (1991) Does travel broaden the mind? *Education* 3 (13), pp54–8.

Wiegand, P (1992) *Places in the primary school*. Lewes: Falmer.

Wiegand, P (1993) *Children and primary geography*. Lewes: Falmer.

Wiegand, P (2006) *Learning and teaching with maps*. London: Routledge.

Wiegand P (n.d.) *GTIP Think Piece – Using maps and atlases*. www.geography.org.uk/projects/gtip/thinkpieces/usingmapsatlases/#top

Williams, M (1996) *Understanding geographical and environmental education: The role of research*. London: Cassell.

Williams, J and Easingwood, N (2007) *Primary ICT and the foundation subjects*. London: Continuum.

Wilson, N (2009) *Tunisia: Pocket guide*. Singapore: Berlitz Publishing/Apa Publications GmbH & Co. Verlag KG, Singapore Branch.

Wood, E and Attfield, J (2005) *Play, learning and the early childhood curriculum*. London: Paul Chapman Publishing.

Wood, D, Bruner, J, and Ross, G (1976) The role of tutoring in problem solving. *Journal of Child Psychology and Psychiatry,* 17 (2), pp89–100.

Woodhouse, S (2003) *Assessing progress*. www.qca.org.uk/geography/innovating/examples/assessing_progress.pdf Accessed 13 November 2008.

Young, M (2004) Contrasting localities, in Scoffham, S (ed) (2004) *The primary geography handbook*. Sheffield: Geographical Association, pp216–227.

Young, M with Cummins, E (2002) *Global citizenship: A handbook for primary teaching*. Cambridge: Chris Kington.